LIFE ON THE WIRE

LIFE ON THE WIRE
THE LIFE AND ART OF
AL PACINO

BY
ANDREW YULE

SPi.
BOOKS

A division of Shapolsky Publishers, Inc.

S.P.I. BOOKS

A division of Shapolsky Publishers, Inc.

Copyright © 1991, 1992 by Andrew Yule

For any additional information, contact:

S.P.I. BOOKS/Shapolsky Publishers, Inc.
136 West 22nd Street
New York, NY 10011
(212) 633-2022
FAX (212) 633-2123

Originally published in 1991 by Donald I. Fine, Inc., New York

ISBN: 1-56171-161-6

10 9 8 7 6 5 4 3 2 1

Printed and bound in the United States of America

*Dedicated to the memory
of Maxwell Barker*

My thanks to interviewees Marty Bregman, Sidney Lumet, Harold Becker, Hugh Hudson, Charlie Laughton, Michael Hadge and Chris Burt, as well as Al Pacino for the access he allowed, not least the special screening of *The Local Stigmatic*, and to the following journalists, some of whom updated their reports at my request: Helen Dudar, New York *Post*; Chris Chase, New York *Times*; Robin Leach, *US* magazine; Clarke Taylor, Los Angeles *Times*; Joyce Purnick, New York *Post*; Glenn Collins, New York *Times*; Leslie Bennets, New York *Times*; Gerald Rabkin, *SoHo Weekly*; Nancy Mills, Los Angeles *Times*; Paul Rosenfield, Los Angeles *Times*; Mel Gussow, New York *Times*; Guy Flatley, Los Angeles *Times*; Peter Rainer, Los Angeles *Herald Examiner*; Frank Lovece, Los Angeles *Times*; Dorothy Manners, Los Angeles *Herald-Examiner*; Laurence Grobel, *Playboy*, *Rolling Stone* and *Entertainment Weekly*; Carol Lawson, New York *Times*; Ross Wetzston, *Village Voice*; George Haddad-Garcia, *US* magazine; Dian Dincin Buchman, *Show* magazine; Ron Rosenbaum, *Village Fair*; Glenn Plaskin, Los Angeles *Herald-Examiner*; Kathleen Carroll, Los Angeles *Times*; Stephen Farber, New York *Times*; Lee Beaupre, *Variety*; Harvey Aronson, *Cosmopolitan*; Brian Case, *20/20* and *Time Out*; Mary Vespa, *People* magazine; Cindy Pearlman, *US* magazine; Mitchell Fink, Los Angeles *Herald-Examiner*; Melina Gerosa, *Entertainment Weekly*; Julian Schnabel, *Interview*; and Chris Peachment, *Time Out*.

Thanks also to Masaaki Sampei, Jake Eberts, Michael Murray, David Wheeler, Jose Luis Rodriguez, Marisa Forzano, Jim Bullett, Alasdair Marshall, Harry Shaw, Penny Allen, Robert Lee Chu, Charles L. Low, Michael Kamen, Irene Lyons, Hattie Forrest, Geni Marino, Shaun Slovo, Meg and Sam, Jenny Botham, Sally Beaune, Art Fellows, Elias Silk, Robert Shine and Maggie Turnbull, all of whom helped the project along in various ways. A special salute to Elia Kazan for his valuable overview of the acting process in *A Life* (Alfred A. Knopf) and to Leonard Probst for his observations in *Off Camera* (Stein & Day).

CONTENTS

Contents

In 1972 aerialist Karl Wallenda, patriarch of the Great Wallendas, stood by helplessly and watched as his son-in-law plummeted to his death, the same fate that had already struck another son-in-law and a nephew. The very next day the old man was back on the high wire, scorning a safety net. Six years later Karl plunged to his own death, blown off his frail wire as he attempted to walk the sky between two high-rise hotels in San Juan, Puerto Rico.

Al Pacino had followed the Wallendas' career since the first tragedies, unable to get them out of his mind. Now, following the death of Wallenda, Sr., his grandson had immediately declared that the rest of the family would continue flying. "Life is always on the wire," he explained; "the rest is just waiting."

To Al Pacino, it was as if his personal creed had just been articulated.

LIFE ON THE WIRE

CHAPTER 1

THE LITTLE DUDE

Alfred James ("Sonny") Pacino discovered a lot about life on his family's tenement roof. It was a place in which to stretch and breathe, a magic carpet six floors high to fly through the night in, a floating oasis where the noise of the traffic down below could be switched off at will. After work, when James Gerard came home, Sonny would ask his grandfather for a nickel, then watch, with wonderment, as he reached deep into the vast recesses of his baggy pants. How he unfailingly fingered a nickel was one of life's great mysteries.

After Gerard had read his newspaper, he would regale Sonny with stories of his arrival in East Harlem in the early 1900s from the old country and the little town of Corleone, near Palermo, Sicily. His mother had died when he was five years old; then, when he was nine, he had quit school and worked on a coal truck. Training in carpentry had come later, a skill that had been honed and polished over the years. Work —any work—was the joy of his life.

Sonny would act out the parts from the latest movie his mother had taken him to see or mimic the comics and an-

1

nouncers on the radio. *"Bene, bene,"* Gerard would say, beaming approvingly as he puffed on his pipe. He was especially fond of his grandson's imitation of James Cagney in *Yankee Doodle Dandy*.

Although his grandfather was far from demonstrative and constantly underplayed his feelings, the kid loved to touch, kiss and cuddle him. In return he instinctively knew that he was loved. In the absence of a father Gerard provided the role model he needed, helping the boy secure a firm grip on reality and honest dealing. The time they spent together in the tenement penthouse—the kid's first stage—is a fragment of memory that remains forever precious.

PACINO WAS BORN on April 25, 1940, in East Harlem, New York. His stonemason father, Salvatore, walked out of the marriage when the boy was two years old, leaving his mother, Rose, to cope single-handedly with the upbringing of her only child. Since there was no one to look after him when she was out working, Sonny was moved to the Bronx, near the zoo, where his maternal grandparents, James and Kate Gerard, lived. For a while he sat at a table all day long, his parents' pictures in front of him, talking to them and having them say things to each other.

Rose Pacino was able to join her son later, further swelling the Gerard household, which numbered at one point, including a variety of aunts and uncles and their children, nine people living in three rooms. Although both his parents were Italian of Sicilian origin and had baptized their son, the Gerards decided against bringing him up in the strict Catholic tradition.

Starting when he was three years old, Rose regularly took her son to the movies. After each show he would come home, dramatically fall to the floor as if he were dead, then leap to his feet and proceed to act out the leading parts he had just seen. Acting was second nature to him; he soon had Al Jolson down pat and learned the entire scene from *The Lost Weekend* where

Ray Milland struggles to remember where his bottle is hidden. He performed this "party piece" when he visited his father's home, as well as his uncle Frank's, and was at a loss to understand their reaction, for to him it was deadly serious. "Why are you laughing?" he asked. "The guy can't find the bottle!" Later they might ask, "Oh, Sonny, sing that song the way you did the other day." Mimicry was picked up from one of his aunts, who was a deaf-mute.

Until he was six years old and attended school, Sonny was seldom allowed out on the street on his own; the back apartment in which the family lived made it impossible for his grandmother to keep her eye on her charge, so she judged it safer that he either stay indoors or be confined to their yard. Although love was clearly equated with protection, her overprotectiveness left him extremely vulnerable. Sonny never learned to fight and knew nothing about running with street gangs.

At first he was a withdrawn, difficult student, unable to integrate with the neighborhood kids, yet determined to do just that. Being dubbed the little dude, because of his grandmother's habit of changing his clothes every time they were even slightly scuffed or stained, did nothing to help; for a while he lived in constant fear of being beaten up. Girls attended to this at first, regarding the undersized kid as easy prey; then boys began to clobber him. His reaction to being hit was to throw up and fall down. Eventually, when it became a matter of survival, he resorted to defensive fighting. And tall tales. He was from Texas, he told them, he had ten dogs at home—anything that would make him more interesting.

Soon he began to rebel against what he saw as the dismal, stifling regimentation he found at school. Unfortunately the transition to class prankster and gang member was made without pausing for a stopover at model pupil. Lounging in the back of library class one day, he kept pushing volumes until the bookends crashed to the floor. When this was repeated once too often, he found himself confined for a while to what the school called its ungraded class, specifically reserved for emotionally disturbed children. Time and again his mother was summoned to remonstrate with her son about his refusal to study.

Playing "guns" with a classmate in the back lots, Sonny ran full tilt into a barbed-wire fence and caught his mouth. "Gotcha, gotcha," his companion yelled as Sonny hung there, screaming in agony, adding a puzzled "Yeah, but you're dead, you're dead, why aintcha fallin'?" When Rose was finally contacted, she fainted clean away as soon as she saw him hanging from his lip. Episodes like this did nothing to improve her increasingly nervous disposition.

A few months later, tightrope walking on some thin wire five feet from the ground, Sonny slipped and fell, landing with his crotch on the wire before sliding to the ground. While his schoolmates laughed hysterically and pointed, he struggled up and painfully staggered twenty paces before collapsing. Then he got up again and managed another thirty agonized paces before slumping to the pavement. Only after he had crawled against a wall, where he lay curled up, moaning piteously, did his pals realize that something was seriously amiss. They carried him back to his apartment, where his mother, grandmother and aunt inspected his private parts as he lay prostrate on his back. "They're looking at me and playing with me" flashed through the indignant youngster's mind—in between the waves of excruciating pain.

As a result of his propensity for telling stories and enacting movie scenes—showing off, basically—he soon became known to everyone at school as the Actor. In his first school play he was the Italian representative in a pageant about polyglot America; he recited "The Rime of the Ancient Mariner" and read the Bible in the auditorium, and in *The King and I* played what he later described as "the Jewish kid"; anyone not Italian was Jewish to Sonny at this stage, although he was surrounded by blacks and Puerto Ricans, as well as Jews, in his tenement.

His dramatic prowess elicited from his eighth-grade drama teacher the opinion that he had "the fire of the great Sicilian actors." When the remark was repeated in a letter to his mother, Rose vowed to encourage her son's nascent talent. She herself had always had an innate sense of the theater and began to accompany Sonny on visits to Broadway plays. The retention of Pacino as a surname was deemed to be out of the question. It ended in a vowel, which everyone knew was unsuitable for an actor. For a while he signed autographs as "Sonny Scott," which he decided was to be his movie star name.

When a later play called for him to be sick onstage, he *became* sick, eliciting comments like "Hey, lookit, Marlon Brando—this guy acts like Marlon Brando."

"Who's Marlon Brando?" he asked. He genuinely didn't know, having missed out on Brando movies up to that point. When *On the Waterfront* later did the trick for him, Sonny sat through the film twice over, riveted by Brando's performance, the likes of which he had never seen before. It was James Dean, however, to whom Sonny related on a personal level, *Rebel Without a Cause* having the most powerful effect on him.

If Pacino had succeeded in another childhood ambition, that of taking up a career in baseball, the move would have flown in the face of every known indicator. He simply was not good enough. Still, he got his greatest kicks when he managed to do well at the sport. If he was lucky enough to make a catch at third base, he would follow it with an ecstatic double somersault, climaxing in a luxuriant sprawl on the field. His coach wryly noted that he was a better actor than a player. Music was another enthusiasm for the young Pacino; he managed to pick up piano playing without the benefit of formal training. A pair of bongo drums was another early pride and joy.

Innocence was a short-lived, perishable commodity on the streets. Pacino was once approached by an unknown kid, who looked to be in shock. "Sonny, some guy just came up and peed in my mouth," he told him, a bewildered expression on his face.

Pacino remembers wondering how the kid knew his name and thinking what a weird thing that was to have happened. "You'd better go home and tell your mother," he advised him.

Pacino's first sexual encounter is lost in the mists of time, although it is variously recalled as taking place when he was nine years old or maybe a little older. When the girl took her blouse off, he put his hands on her breasts. Since she was standing in front of a mattress spring as she giggled, the logical next step was to push her down on it. Several bounces later Pacino thought he had been laid and went straight out and bought a pack of prophylactics, on the basis that a fellow should always be ready. For a while, though, he had no idea what to do with them.

Pacino's running-away-from-home stage was not rooted in any deep-seated unhappiness. It was more to draw attention to himself, to satisfy his thirst for adventure and to be "one of the gang." That his mother and grandparents understood this served to make these excursions a short-lived phenomenon. Pacino loves to romanticize the period—the traveling gangs, the building of rafts, the dodging of quicksand and other exciting, dangerous, rose-tinted adventures. The vitality of the streets had claimed a willing initiate.

His closest friend became Cliffy, a Jewish boy who wished he were a Catholic. He was the toughest kid Pacino had ever met, a hero to his skinny, short friend, someone he saw as a cross between Richard Burton and the newly discovered Marlon Brando. Cliffy specialized in outrageous stunts like hijacking an entire public bus filled with passengers or stealing a garbage truck and parking it outside his tenement. Once he kicked a store window in to get his new buddy a pair of shoes. Caught in the act by a cop, Pacino hung around guiltily until being extricated by his irate grandmother.

Cliffy had read Dostoyevsky by the time he was fourteen and told Pacino how "terrific" it was, impressing him no end. He was precocious in other ways as well, being far ahead sexually; to his friend it was as if he had known some strange and wonderful secret. Pacino was shocked when he found him trying to "feel up" his mother, although Cliffy seemed not at all put out when Rose laughingly discouraged and shrugged him off.

Another buddy was Brucie, who was inadvertently responsible for Pacino's bow on television at the age of twelve. Playing together on a Bronx construction site one day, Brucie slipped on some rocks and was left clinging for dear life to a pipe over the edge of a pit until Pacino hauled him back to safety. When the incident was reported to *Wheel of Fortune*, an early fifties CBS show, Pacino and Brucie were invited to appear. It was an early, brief and tantalizing whiff of celebrity that carried with it twenty-five hundred dollars in cash and a thousand dollars in prizes. It was also the end of what Pacino calls "the best years of my life. After, the pimples came, everything came, all the problems."

During one school vacation Pacino worked on a fruit farm. With the rest of his friends fooling around outside, the owner came into the store where Pacino was conscientiously sorting out red and green tomatoes. On the earthen floor the farmer drew a diagram of the countryside, complete with trees and highways. "There are two paths in life," he explained, "the right one and the wrong one." Puzzled, Pacino looked at the neat piles of tomatoes he had made. Was he doing something wrong? "Stay with *them*," the farmer told him, gesturing toward his friends outside, "and you'll end up like *them*. Jobless and free."

Cliffy, heavily into drugs, was dead from a junk overdose at thirty; another of Pacino's closest friends died from drug abuse when he was only nineteen. This was one area where Pacino chose not to follow his friends' example. Two things stopped him: his mother's influence and observing at close quarters the dire effects hard drugs had on others. Instead, he started smoking cigarettes at nine, chewed tobacco at ten and smoked a pipe at eleven.

Another escape route he eagerly embraced was that of alcohol; at thirteen Pacino would get an adult in the street to buy a bottle for him. Oddly enough, his first taste of drink, a glass of red wine, was swallowed before an audience. With his grandparents, mother and assorted aunts and uncles watching, he first took a sip of the purple, bitter liquid, then coughed and spluttered. Blushing furiously, he downed the rest in a single gulp. To his astonishment and delight, his relatives applauded. "I don't feel a thing," he assured them, a fixed, shy smile hiding the fire he felt inside, if not his blazing cheeks. Then he held out his glass. "Can I have another?"

He was fascinated by the dreamy, soporific effect alcohol produced, the way it lifted him above the crowd. Drinking and smoking—tobacco and, briefly, marijuana—became a daily part of his life, a veritable badge of maturity. Like acting, booze took him out of himself. Hey, he *was* from Texas! He *did* have ten dogs!

Pacino was voted "most likely to succeed" in junior high school because of his acting abilities. Although it was hardly required, the desire to be an actor was further fueled by a traveling troupe production of Chekhov's *The Seagull*, courageously staged in a massive old movie house in the Bronx. Pacino was overwhelmed by the experience, despite, or possibly assisted by, there being only a dozen or so people in the audience.

Two years at Manhattan's High School of Performing Arts— again recommended by his drama teacher and the only school that would accept him since his scholastic level was so low— proved something of a setback. To Pacino nothing could be so boring as the gospel the school preached of Konstantin Stanislavsky's acting principles. The whole principle of "the Method" and so-called serious acting, having to *feel* it, Pacino found crazy. What was going *on*? Where was the *fun*? In one class he was asked to act out what it was like being in his room alone. Since he had never had a room of his own, he had to improvise a lot harder than the other students. When his teacher mentioned how "natural" he had acted in one piece, he went around for the next few days trying to be "natural." His attitude was: "What do I know from Stanislavsky? *He's* Russian. *I'm* from the Bronx."

Again Pacino refused to study. The Spanish class was given in *Spanish*? "You've gotta be kidding," he told the teacher. Instead of applying himself, he wound up helping the school nurse. And embarking on a typing course, which he also failed.

When his mother became too ill to work—years of analysis had done little to alleviate her nervous debility—enormous pressure was applied on Pacino to leave school and find a job. Overnight he found he had lost one of the great supporters of his acting career, for his mother had taken a grimly realistic look at his prospects. "Acting," Rose now explained to her son, opening a gulf between them that was never bridged, "is for rich people."

Despondently Pacino dropped out of school at sixteen at the end of his sophomore year with the intention of supplementing his grandfather's wages to support the household. He vowed that when he had enough money put by, he would enroll in acting classes. In quick succession he found employment as a messenger, a rest room attendant, a shoeshiner, a supermarket checker, a furniture remover, an office boy, a fruit picker and a newsboy.

Burning with restlessness and resentment at the whole process, he left home and moved in with a girl in another part of the Bronx. He would send money home, but that did not mean he had to live there. It was his first, heady whiff of freedom.

In an attempt to mollify his mother, he kept assuring her he would be doing "something big" soon. At one point he told her he was going to train as a draftsman since he felt that sounded suitably impressive. His deeply troubled mother remained unconvinced.

CHAPTER 2

THE WILD SQUARE

THE LONGEST PACINO held down any job was two years as an office boy at *Commentary* magazine, an assignment that put him on the fringe of New York's intellectual world. Around the office he was regarded as capable, good-tempered and cheerful by contributors Norman Podhoretz and Susan Sontag. Shooting craps with Podhoretz and Sontag, and getting drunk on scotch at parties thrown by the group, were attractive fringe benefits for the junior. "Al was an excellent office boy," Podhoretz later recalled. "Obviously he's one of those people who, whatever he does, he does well."

Pacino had to convince himself he was merely biding his time until he could afford acting classes. An initial skirmish with Lee Strasberg's Actors Studio ended in his rejection after Pacino had made it through the preliminary audition. Not to be denied, he moved from the Bronx to Greenwich Village on his own and at nineteen joined one of Herbert Berghof's classes. There he met acting coach Charlie Laughton, ten years his senior, who introduced him to writers, directors, poets and the rest of the circle that surrounds actors. At last Pacino had found a teacher who made no attempt to con him. Why, he even *talked* to him!

A fine actor, with a striking mop of raven black hair, fine, classically sculpted features and deep resonant speech, Laughton had never pursued a career outside teaching, preferring to feed his wife, the actress Penny Allen, and his daughter on a regular basis. One thespian in the family was considered enough. He practically adopted Pacino into his family circle, treating him as a friend and drinking buddy as well as a promising student. He detected a spark in Pacino, together with a certain grace, that excited him. In one scene at Berghof's Pacino played a Bronx type in confrontation with the law. Something about the way he flung back at the cop, the way he called the shots as he saw them, deeply impressed his teacher.

What soon emerged was that Pacino had just played the scene for real. Having heard that casting sessions were being held in Boston for a gangster play, he and a young friend had driven there, hopes high. After they were stopped by police for speeding, a search of their car unearthed their props, including a fake gun they were carrying. Pacino and his buddy were detained overnight, their fingerprints and mug shots recorded for posterity, before a phone call cleared the matter up the next morning. No charges were ever filed.

One day, on leaving his apartment with Laughton, Pacino ran down the flight of stairs to the mailbox, jumped the last few steps, spun around and looked back to where Laughton was standing. "Al," Laughton quietly pronounced, "you're going to be a big star." What made this single, dramatic announcement all the more remarkable was not the matter-of-fact manner in which it was delivered, simply that it was not in the man's nature to talk that way.

Although Pacino knew this, Laughton's words served only to confirm the knowledge. If determination meant anything, *he would be a star*. Shy as he was, Pacino had cannily added up his assets and liabilities. At five feet seven inches he was short, a minor handicap in his eyes. He was uneducated; but he could learn, and under Laughton's guidance he had become a voracious reader. He was extremely good-looking, with dark, flashing eyes that he knew drove girls crazy. High cheekbones served to divert attention from his too-large nose. And he had a diamond-in-the-rough, brooding intensity. Lack of money might delay the process, but meantime, he would be learning his craft—and in the end he knew he would make it.

THE UNEXPECTED DEATH of Rose Pacino at forty-three came as a traumatic shock to the whole family—but most of all to her estranged twenty-two-year-old son. Pacino was unable to avoid an overwhelming sense of responsibility and desolation. "I went to pieces," he admits.

"He had such personal problems himself," says Laughton, "no money, no job, no place to live, that the true impact of his mother's sickness never got through the morass of his own problems. That's why he felt so badly about her death."

One year later, after a lifetime without a single day's illness, his grandfather's death came as another devastating blow. Pacino felt as if his safety net had been removed. Never a sound sleeper at the best of times, he began to suffer from insomnia. For a while the bereavements even threatened to affect him mentally.

Pacino had earlier avoided army service, being classified 1Y on the basis of his helping support his mother. Knowing that he had to report back within a year, he became anxious about being drafted. Sharing a bottle with Laughton on the roof of his old apartment building in the Bronx, six stories above the sidewalk, Pacino listened with concern as his coach detailed his tax problems. Laughton owed something like sixty dollars in back taxes, which seemed like a fortune at the time, and he was being hounded by the IRS. "Relax, Charlie, it'll work out." Pacino attempted to placate him. When the pupil went on to talk of his imminent draft, it was Laughton's turn to pour oil. "Don't worry about it, Al, they don't *want* you," he assured his friend.

When Pacino went on to fail the army's medical examination, being classified 4F, the rejection, contrarily, managed to make him even more depressed. Soon afterward, in the middle of his weekly delivery of *Show Business*, a newspaper Pacino distributed on Thursdays at Broadway and Forty-eighth Street, he suddenly found he was having trouble seeing, then completely passed out. A doctor who took his pulse pronounced his heart sound but recommended that he register as an outpatient at Bellevue Hospital. This Pacino flatly refused to do, accepting a course of tranquilizers instead.

After he had visited a buddy in a mental institution, Pacino's emotions matched his tattered Salvation Army clothes. As he walked through the hallway, his torn coat trailing on the floor, he was stopped by a sympathetic woman in white. Invited to talk, he did so freely. Perhaps too freely. After half an hour the nurse looked at him earnestly. "There's no hope for you," she told him. "You have to be committed." That did it for Pacino. He realized that he had to pull himself together, because nobody else would.

Pacino remembers developing a keen sense of his own mortality around this period. He had a fantasy of his corpse being carried around in a box, surrounded by dozens of black-clad mourners. "We shouldn't have treated him so badly," one of them cries, dabbing at her eyes with a handkerchief.

With Charlie Laughton in tow, Pacino hung in through his many jobs, picking up the scraps of acting work available in between. He tried his hand at children's theater, satirical revues, even as a stand-up comedian, polishing a sketch he had adapted back in his Bronx days from a Sid Caesar "Man with a Python" joke. Then there was the mental institution sketch he used as a revue opener. The inmate sitting in the institution is telling his friend about how he doesn't belong there. "I've gone through channels," he explains, "tried contact after contact, and I'm still here. I've talked to this doctor and that doctor. This environment isn't helping me, you know." Finally his friend has had enough. "I'm gonna get you out of here," he declares. "I swear it, if it's the last thing I do." As the friend points his finger for emphasis, the inmate lunges forward—snap!—and bites it.

One way and another, comedy paid the bills. Not only that, but Pacino *thought* of himself as a comedian for a while. Off-Off-Broadway venues, such as Elaine Stewart's Cafe La Mama, Greenwich Village coffeehouses, warehouses and even storefronts, provided a stage for these fledgling efforts. "The wild square," Laughton teasingly dubbed his friend, recognizing the cautious "little dude" traditionalist inside Pacino's bohemian thrift shop exterior of pea jacket, baggy pants and balaclava.

Pacino worked for a spell as an usher at the East Side's Cinema V and had fun parrying questions from the patrons: "What time does the show start?" "Is it any good?" He found they believed anything he told them and bet another usher he could get them to line up on the other side of the street from the movie house. He won the bet but was fired when the manager questioned the empty sidewalk outside, then spotted the line formed in front of Bloomingdale's across the street.

At another movie house Pacino suddenly caught sight of himself, resplendent in his new usher's uniform, in a three-sided mirror. Never having spontaneously glimpsed his profile, he was captivated. Who was *this*? He was just about to pivot to an equally enticing view of the back of his head when the manager unexpectedly emerged from his office. "*Pacino*," he yelled, "what the *hell* are you looking at?"

When he was found posing for a second time, the manager threw him out without even pausing to break his stride. "What happened?" friends later asked. "I was fired," he replied. When they asked why, Pacino giggled.

"For looking at myself too much," he told them.

A move into ushering in live theater proved equally unsuccessful. At Carnegie Hall Pacino found the music wonderful but formed the unfortunate habit of showing patrons to the wrong seats. There were also periods when he would disappear into the men's room with a book, lost in dreamland, the customers left to their own devices.

A job moving furniture came next. He was standing in as a favor to Charlie, who worked with a removal company part-time in between teaching. Just when his fellow workers would be getting a little antsy, a taxi would scream to a halt, delivering Pacino—ready to lug pianos up and down stairs for $2.50 an hour. For a while Pacino thought that moving furniture would be his economic salvation. So did Charlie, who was seeking a solution to his tax problems. The two of them briefly contemplated opening their own business, CHAL Movers—an amalgam of CHarlie and AL. When the venture was soon judged impractical—neither of them could drive—it was back to the Automat for a piece of pie, a cup of coffee and the people-watching that inspired them both.

"With no money to go to the theater we'd sit in cafeterias for hours on end, watching the comedies and high dramas taking place," Laughton recalls. "Al got some of his most interesting characters from watching people in the subway and streets of New York. One time, in Bickford's all-night cafeteria on Lexington Avenue, we saw these two guys, obviously very good friends, sitting opposite each other, picking away daintily at their food. When one of them got up to go to the bathroom, we watched the other finish his own plate, look furtively around, then start picking away at his friend's plate. By the time the other guy came back from the john, Al and I were absolutely convulsed in laughter, tears rolling down our cheeks."

FOR A WHILE Pacino shared a single room with Martin Sheen, a fellow struggling actor. Together they hung around Julian Beck's Living Theater as stagehands, hoping to land parts. Since they had founded the venture back in 1951 in their New York apartment, Beck and his wife, Judith Malina, had painstakingly built up one of the most innovative troupes on the international scene, producing the acclaimed *Paradise Now* and *The Brig*. While constantly breaking new ground, their repertoire ranged over the full spectrum from classical precision to experimental theater, from conventional classics to

Brecht and neo-realism. Pacino and Sheen watched a rehearsal of Jack Gelber's *The Connection* one night. "Don't you want to be up there?" Sheen agitatedly asked him. "Don't you want to be on the stage doing that?"

"Hey," Pacino replied, "I'm playing at setting up the stage here!"

"I'll play this part one day," Sheen vowed, the strength of his conviction allowing no room for doubt. *The Connection* went on to provide his first-ever leading role.

In those days, when having money was synonymous with the ability to eat lunch, Pacino habitually slept until four in the afternoon to avoid facing hunger pangs. To save his friend from starvation, Sheen offered Pacino the job of understudying him in a way-off-Broadway venture he was in, *The Wicked Cooks*.

The longest employed spell Pacino enjoyed in his twenties amounted to eleven months spent as a building superintendent. The pay was fourteen dollars a week, with a rent-free apartment thrown in—his first real home since the Bronx. Pacino stuck an eight-by-ten glossy of himself on his apartment door with Band-Aids, wrote "Super" underneath, then waited for the women in the building, their curiosity aroused, to call and check him out.

It worked well enough, but there were a couple of holdouts Pacino was determined to snare, one of them a girl so beautiful he could hardly believe she was real. He decided to blow the fuse for her lights, figuring that when she came downstairs for a replacement, nature would take its course. One problem was that although he had been the super for six months, he still didn't know where the fuse box was. After locating it and blowing the lights, he ran through the building and out into the yard to make sure he had darkened the correct apartment. Delighted with his success, he decided not to wait for her visit. By the time he arrived at her door, he was already exhausted and overanxious. "I can fix your lights," he babbled to the startled girl, "and do you want to see the Village?" It wasn't until the door was slammed in his face that he realized he had come on a little too strong.

For the final holdout he decided to play it cool. It was back to the basement, where he blew what he thought was his romantic prospect's fuse. Then he raced back to his apartment where he confidently awaited her arrival. Unfortunately, when a knock finally came, he found a hulking bodybuilder standing outside his room. He had blown the wrong apartment fuse.

Back on the streets one night, out of a job, even Pacino's favorite street smell of roasted chestnuts failed to quell the hunger inside. In desperation he accepted an offer from an older woman who had been stalking him for weeks. The deal involved a place to stay, food—and sex. Since it was made clear that she wanted him for his body and nothing more, he was turned off by the impersonal nature of the affair. The next morning, feeling like a male prostitute, he excused himself to buy cigarettes, saying he'd return in a few minutes. As soon as the fresh air hit him, he realized he could hardly bear to face himself, let alone the woman. He fled.

On another occasion he stumbled into an alley in Manhattan and fell across the body of an aspiring actor friend who had overdosed on heroin and was already cold and dead. After a few frantic moments Pacino called the police from a pay phone and took off. He felt sick, unable to stand around and watch as the police and ambulance attendants treated his friend like a piece of meat.

Pacino concedes he may have been drunk or even a little high the night he hunkered down in a storefront. He remembers having fifteen dollars in his pocket before passing out, yet waking up without a cent. He knew Charlie Laughton was with his family at the beach in Far Rockaway, and to get there, he had to bum the thirty-cent fare from a friend.

Laughton caught sight of his protégé trudging across the beach, a haggard figure in trailing black, picking his way through the brightly colored beach umbrellas. After listening to his tale of woe, he dug into his wallet and gave him five of the ten dollars he found there. Pacino thanked him, then made his way straight through the crowd, on to the train and back to the city. He had known that Charlie would take care of him. "He always remembers that little act of generosity," says Laughton today, chuckling, "which amuses me, because of his numerous acts of generosity with me."

There were other days when Pacino would come along as one of the family to Far Rockaway. "He was such a kidder," says Laughton fondly. "There he'd be, pale and skinny in his black trunks, wearing his snorkel and playing his bongo drums on the sands like a kid. We called him Al Pacino, the World's First Underwater Bongo Player—otherwise known as the Wild Square!"

CHAPTER 3

SEX IN PERSPECTIVE

Pacino's Off-Broadway debut, his first time performing for paying customers, grew out of a class Charlie Laughton conducted on William Saroyan's *Hello, Out There*. Pleased at how well the readings had gone, Laughton phoned Joe Cino at the Cafe Cino and invited him to come over. When he did, Cino agreed to stage the play—thrice nightly.

As Pacino spoke his first line, the audience broke up—not because they were laughing at him, but because the line itself was funny. Unfortunately this fact had escaped Pacino's attention. Stumbling outside into an alley, he burst out crying. Laughton followed and spun him around, jolting him back to his senses. "Al, you've got to play it twice more tonight," he told him, "then twelve more times after that." It dawned on Pacino that he knew nothing about Saroyan or the play and that he'd better learn fast.

Basement shows furthered his education, as did Laughton's tale of the actor who once broke his leg in the middle of a physically demanding part. To the actor's surprise, he found that with the limitations of a plaster cast his performance actually *improved.* "Actors think they have to psych themselves up with energy," Laughton explained, "but everyone has more than enough natural energy in them to cope with any part. What they need to do is climb *down* a little."

Pacino discovered this truth for himself while performing in Tennessee Williams's *Camino Real* a few years later. Shortly after making his entrance, hyped up to the eyebrows, a fellow actor gave him what was supposed to be a stage smack across the face and left two caps on Pacino's teeth perilously dangling. Forced to subdue his performance, Pacino felt the energy draining away, until he remembered Laughton's parable and began to concentrate on containment. To his surprise, his portrayal gained in intensity.

When Laughton went on to stage Strindberg's *The Creditors,* directing the play in a warehouse on West Broadway after the original director had quit, there were performances when only eight customers showed up. "Al was surrounded by classical actors, and he got scared," says Laughton. "He came to me and said he couldn't do it. So we read it through, and I got him to read it naturally, in his own speech, and we discussed the meaning of each passage. By the time the company reached the end of rehearsals he was bigger and better than any of them because he had perceived what was going on. That was the first *real* glimpse I had of his talent. 'It's the *role* that matters' was the gospel I preached. I remember one member of the cast describing Al's performance in the play as momentous, and Al's stunned, disbelieving expression when he heard it."

While Pacino's own street speech was less than perfect, Laughton compared his rendition of Strindberg with Frank Sinatra's handling of a ballad. The role gave Pacino an inkling of just how much he had going for him and demonstrated how acting might yield the chance to use his gifts. Laughton had shown him that acting was poetry, an art that employs the voice, the body and the spirit. For the first time, Pacino felt like an artist.

"I didn't know anything about the Strindberg world," he

admitted. "I felt I had the license to speak and that I was Everyman and timeless and universal. I felt the great sense of saying, 'I can *talk*, I can *speak*, I've got *something to say.*' It freed me up, made me feel good. I knew that I would do nothing else and that it didn't matter anymore whether I became successful or got a job. I had enough to sustain me."

Further inspiration came as Pacino watched his old buddy Martin Sheen playing the salesman-cum-wife killer Hickey in a scene from Eugene O'Neill's *The Iceman Cometh*. "I think I could do that," he whispered to Laughton, scarcely daring to believe it himself, yet strangely sure. In the absence of a theater to house his performance, he played Hickey on the streets, adopting a favorite alley off Sixth Avenue where he addressed startled passersby, as well as several dozen pigeons. The experience taught him that acting, whether onstage for an audience or on the street for birds and bums, had to be *personal*. He shaped and honed Hickey until it was *his* Hickey, not Marty Sheen's or Jason Robards, Jr.,'s or anyone else's. Just his.

Pacino even turned his hand to directing in 1965, during one of the hottest summers recorded in New York. The stint provided not only professional diversification but what Pacino later fondly remembered as the best time he ever had in his adult life. Friendships were forged with fellow strugglers like actress Sally Kirkland, and in the case of "wild child" Susan Tyrrell, something much closer.

The freewheeling parties that followed the show every night and continued to dawn were more than a match for the heat on the street. It was here that the casual intimacies of the theater, the daily hugging, squeezing and kissing that seemed as natural as breathing, were given the opportunity to expand and ignite into urgent, explosive pairings. "Al was like an animal," is how Tyrrell recalls the Pacino she knew. "Like a stallion with his reins pulled too tight. He needs to have his freedom more than most performers. But when Al is free, he *flies*."

"I love work," Pacino told anyone who would listen, "because it keeps sex in perspective." It was just as well, friends noted, that something did the trick.

Pacino discovered during the season that his enthusiasm could not simply be bought but had to be earned. This represented a major breakthrough, as well as a release from some of the pressures of striving for success. If the work presented a challenge, pennies were sufficient—for the time being at least.

Around this time Pacino began to be compared with another actor just starting to make his mark. They both were short and dark and exuded the same kind of nervous dynamism onstage. Rather than perpetuate the comparison, Pacino turned down the chance of a paying job understudying Dustin Hoffman in Murray Schisgal's *Jimmy Sunshine*.

In 1966 Pacino received his first public recognition in the form of an Obie nomination for the Off-Broadway play *Why Is a Crooked Letter*. The competition for the award was formidable: George C. Scott and none other than Dustin Hoffman himself for his role in Ronald Ribman's *The Journey of the Fifth Horse*. Was there no escape from Hoffman? None, the answer came soon enough, as Pacino's rival scooped up the award.

Pacino went on to audition for a workshop production at the Eugene O'Neill Memorial Theater in Waterford, Connecticut, of *The Indian Wants the Bronx*, by a new playright, Israel Horovitz. His impression that he was up for the milder of the two lead roles was shattered when he was picked to play Murph, a sadistic, drug-crazed psychotic. Cast opposite him in the role of the Indian was a fellow Italian-American, John Cazale, with whom a rapport quickly developed. Soul mates were found in other struggling actors, most notably a quiet, withdrawn youngster named Robert De Niro.

That same year Pacino was finally accepted by the Actors Studio. So was Dustin Hoffman, who had earlier suffered four rejections. Pacino was so overawed by the "profanity in the cathedral" atmosphere he found, that it took him six months before he could mobilize himself. It didn't help that he kept hearing about what a *terrific* actor Hoffman was.

During these months, when Pacino hesitated on the brink of the studio—it had accepted him, but it also scared him— Pacino reached his lowest ebb. He was in the middle of delivering circulars one day when he suddenly felt he could take it no longer. With his last coin he dialed Laughton.

"Charlie, I've had it," he told him. "I'm gonna commit myself to Bellevue."

"Wait right there," said Laughton, thoroughly alarmed. "Hold everything. Where *are* you? We'll grab a cup of coffee and talk."

"It's no use, Charlie. No more. I can't do it. Either I act or I die. . . ."

Laughton could feel his friend slipping away. He took a deep breath. "Al, things aren't so bad. Look, you belong to the Actors Studio. You're an *actor*. That's all that counts. *Accept* that." Laughton managed to talk his friend out of his despondency over the promised cup of coffee, as well as several belts of alcohol.

Steeling himself for his introduction at the studio proper, Pacino finally chose to perform two monologues, one as Hickey, one as Hamlet. Lee Strasberg's curiosity was mildly piqued at this interesting diversity of choice. "Al Pacino?" he murmured, looking at his card. "Hickey *and* Hamlet? O'Neill *and* Shakespeare? Where are you *from*?"

The main function the studio performed for Pacino was to give him confidence to be around people who did what he did. If much of the sixties could be regarded as his lost years, they were surely over. The practical help Pacino received from Strasberg ranged from a lifesaving fifty dollars the maestro authorized from the James Dean Memorial Fund—enabling him to make the payments on the humble Greenwich Village apartment he rented—to the strong bond that was forged with Strasberg himself. Pacino responded to the maestro on an emotional level, Strasberg influencing him and helping him work in an informal way as well as in the workaday classes.

"Al really didn't attend the studio that often," Laughton remembers. "He was much influenced by Lee, but their relationship was very personal. He would wait for him in the lobby sometimes so they could go to lunch together, or they would listen to classical music, which they both loved, in Lee's apartment."

Through the auspices of the studio Pacino felt emboldened to stop looking for odd jobs and stick to acting. In December 1966 he appeared with James Earl Jones in a New Theatre Workshop production of John Wolfson's *The Peace Creeps*.

Within a year of joining the studio, Dustin Hoffman's career was launched with Mike Nichols's *The Graduate*. Soon afterward Pacino found himself accosted one night outside a Broadway theater. "Aren't you Dustin Hoffman?" a lady demanded. When Pacino shook his head, she yelled, "Come on, you *are* Dustin Hoffman, aren't you?" When she began pulling on his shirt, Pacino felt like socking her. "Maybe," he later reflected, "someone's pulling *his* shirt now and saying, 'You're Al Pacino!' "

Completely broke and now sleeping on the floor of Laughton's lower East Side apartment on Grand Street, Pacino heard from his mentor's wife, Penny, who was performing with David Wheeler's Theater Company of Boston. She called with the news that she had arranged an audition for him.

Borrowing fifteen dollars for the bus fare, he set off with a paper bag filled with his "belongings," basically a change of clothing and his beloved bongo drums. After an evening meal of rice and another night spent sleeping on a friend's floor, he arrived at the theater and was handed a script of Bertolt Brecht's *Caucasian Chalk Circle*. Although impressed with his reading, Wheeler explained he could offer him only a minor role. Pacino decided to stick to his belief that he would never learn by watching others act and turned the part down, disregarding the theatrical maxim "Go where the work is" and substituting his personal credo, "Go where you can do what you want to do."

As Pacino prepared to leave, Wheeler assured him there would be other plays during the season, opportunities for other roles, and there was a steady fifty dollars a week that would at least enable him to eat regularly. "Yeah," Pacino replied, all emaciated 125 pounds of him, "but I gotta get back. I got something in New York." So saying, he bummed another fifteen dollars for return bus fare.

Laughton recalls his swift return. "Al, what happened?" he asked incredulously.

"David only offered me a small role," Pacino replied with a shrug. "I told him I don't do small roles."

The trip was to prove far from a waste of time, however, as Wheeler contacted him again. This time, in the fall of 1967, Pacino signed up with the company and played major roles in Clifford Odets's *Awake and Sing!* and Jean-Claude Van Itallie's *America, Hurrah*—for $125 a week, not $50. During the run of *America, Hurrah*, staged at the Charles Playhouse, a small theatrical venue just off Boston Common, Pacino met an intriguing actress. Jill Clayburgh was a tousle-haired brunette with the most bewitching blue-green eyes he had ever seen.

Hers was a classic case of a life saved by acting, for much of her childhood had been spent in aimlessness and misery. Born to a wealthy New York family in 1944, she was a deeply troubled child whose despairing parents sent her to a psychiatrist at the age of nine. Her stay at the all-female Sarah Lawrence College in the early sixties was an unhappy one, marked by a violence and willfulness that assumed self-destructive proportions. It was in 1963 that a friend suggested she take up acting and enroll in the junior company of the Charles Playhouse.

To her astonishment, the profession, even at its outer fringes, had the most beneficial effect, enabling her to act out many of the unresolved psychodramas in her own nature. She was still unhappy and deeply insecure but at least was experiencing the release of some of her pain. Together with young Bobby De Niro, she starred in what was little more than a student movie, *The Wedding Party*, which marked Brian De Palma's directorial debut. Shot in 1964, it was edited in 1966 and finally released in 1969.

"I never spent a more lonely year in my life than the one in Boston before I met Al. I never had a boyfriend before," Clayburgh later admitted. Friends watched, amazed, as she and Pacino seemed to click from the very start. When they moved into a hundred-dollar-a-month fifth-floor apartment in downtown New York, many saw it as a union of the walking wounded. When Clayburgh became known in their circle as Al Pacino's girlfriend, she was almost grateful for the relative facelessness and anonymity the title bestowed.

Pacino continued to drink heavily, whether in the company of Laughton or Clayburgh, and rationalized every bender as it began. If he received good news, he drank to celebrate. If it was bad news, a consoling drink helped. If there was no news, booze itself became the event. No amount of liquor, however, was enough to silence his inner demons, perpetually screaming "Guilty!" over his alienation from his mother and his absence at her death. If only he hadn't left home. Having done so, if only he'd applied himself and studied as a draftsman. If only he'd lifted his selfish gaze from his own navel once in a while and given a thought to his mother's deteriorating mental condition.

How could he ever hope to silence the accusation of guilt? Maybe, just maybe, success in his chosen profession would help.

CHAPTER 4

SEIZING THE POWER

PACINO'S FIRST MOVIE outing was a bit part in a Patty Duke vehicle, *Me, Natalie*. Filmed in New York under the direction of Fred (*A Thousand Clowns*) Coe, the picture was undertaken both as a lark and to earn a few precious dollars.

Friends assured Pacino that he would find the transition to movie acting less of a problem than for many stage actors since his style was less declaratory and more naturalistic than others. Even so, *Me, Natalie* hardly represented much of a stretch, although the hilarious couple of lines he had to deliver in his walk-on as a junkie gigolo probably represent some kind of industry first: "Do you put out?" he brazenly inquires of his dancing partner. After an indignant response, he hisses, *"Listen*, somebody like *you* ought to be asking *me!"*

Pacino reported for work on *Me, Natalie* at seven in the morning and spent the entire day shooting his one scene, dancing what seemed like miles in the course of the day. On his way home that night he thought, "Hey, I've made my first movie!"

The Indian Wants the Bronx was a one-act drama staged as the second and more substantial half of a double bill. Preceding it on the program at New York's Astor Place Theater on January 17, 1968, was another Horovitz play, *It's Called the Sugar Plum*, which featured an appearance by Jill Clayburgh. *Sugar Plum* was dismissed by *Variety* as "an implausible, thin black comedy," the paper's praise reserved for Horovitz's tale of two young hoodlums terrorizing an aged Indian, a study in urban savagery *Variety* hailed as "convincing and frightening." "Particularly effective," it noted, was Pacino's "uncommonly naturalistic, unstagey performance."

"Al seized the power" is how Charlie Laughton describes Pacino's triumph in the play. "What I saw was his whole life come out on that stage. When we talked later, he was aglow. That was the beginning of his life, and he knew it."

Following a run of 204 performances, the role won him an Obie for Best Actor in an Off-Broadway production, the award Dustin Hoffman had snatched from under his nose two years earlier. There was a Best Supporting Actor nod for John Cazale and Best New Play accolade for Israel Horovitz. "I think Al Pacino is the best actor in New York City," said Horovitz. With the troupe invited to appear at the Spoleto People's Theater Festival in Italy, Pacino packed his bags and said his good-byes. "Charlie," he said, "I have the feeling I'll be doing this from now on."

Initially Pacino had looked at *The Indian Wants the Bronx* as he had many other projects, expecting neither the transfer uptown nor the critical acclaim. Gradually, very gradually, that had changed. "I began to feel that what I did in the play would be felt, you *know* these things sometimes, but I didn't know to what extent," he recalls. "Sure, I felt good with the reviews. I felt as if the whole world had turned around, as if the veil had lifted. I felt that kind of excitement, felt it strong. It gave life dignity. And performing for an Italian audience was a marvelous experience."

It was little wonder that coming from complete obscurity, Pacino was overcome with his sudden jolting success. Although it was still limited to theatrical cognoscenti, including his peers, that situation was soon remedied.

A HIGHLY SUCCESSFUL entertainment manager named Martin Bregman entered Pacino's life after being advised to catch his performance in *The Indian Wants the Bronx* by one of his clients, Faye Dunaway. Just a few years older than Pacino, the brown-haired, craggily handsome Bregman was another Bronx boy, albeit from a slightly more salubrious area than his prospective client. A childhood bout of polio had left him with a brace that did little to restrict his mobility; with the aid of a cane the forceful Bregman was the equal of the fastest mover. He studied at the Indiana and New York universities before starting work as an agent, then as an insurance consultant. When the business became successful, it enabled him to moonlight in the area he really wanted to embrace, that of show biz representation.

Bregman was stunned by Pacino's tour de force. "I'll back you in anything you want to do," he told the baffled actor backstage after watching *Indian*. What was Bregman talking about? "I mean, I'll sponsor you," he clarified.

The untutored Pacino was none the wiser until he turned up at Bregman's Lexington Avenue office. There Bregman explained that he would act as a conduit between the acting and business side of Pacino's career, taking on the roles of manager and financial and career adviser. "Al still had no idea what I was going to do for him," says Bregman, "but we had trust in each other, and I had a tremendous respect for him as an artist."

Together with Laughton and Strasberg, Pacino now had a triumvirate of backers, gurus and father figures.

THERE IS A school of thought that all actors are incomplete creatures, filling a basic need by losing themselves in their roles and assuming the mannerisms of their characters. Pacino took the process a stage further. By taking on the roles of characters who were *unlike* him, he began to discover their traits in himself. The flip side of the coin was that for all his considerable gifts, he could never shake the feeling that the characters he played were so much more interesting than he was. If someone split Al Pacino in two, would he or she find nothing inside but a bland, hollow husk? For the time being the trade-off lay in the high that accompanied a satisfying performance. When he was in a play that worked, something about which he felt right, where he knew what he was doing, where he had been, where he was going, *why* he was doing it, and *who he was*, it was a tranquil respite from the real world, where none of these criteria applied.

The down side came with the letting go after each performance, mitigated only by liberal quantities of alcohol, then the end-of-run shedding of his character's painfully grown skin, followed by a sense of emptiness and uncertainty.

Clayburgh's contribution to the war chest, apart from $150 a week from her parents, was to appear as Grace Bolton in the long-running daytime soap *Search for Tomorrow*, as well as to work Off-Broadway. "I did the soap because we really needed the money," she explains. "And Al was very fussy; he wouldn't do that." (A solitary TV appearance was in fact made on *NYPD.*) "I'd be up at dawn, working in the soap all morning, rehearse the play in the afternoon and be onstage at six-thirty P.M. for previews. When I wasn't working, we'd stay home most of the time and listen to classical music. Or we'd go out for a drink to the Ginger Man's. I'd get all dressed up on these occasions, including high heels, and look ten feet taller than Al. He'd be wearing his army clothes with holes in the shirt." (Pacino's friend De Niro was another actor, among many famous names, who was unfussy enough to work on the indestructible *Search for Tomorrow*. So was another drinking pal, an intense young actor named Michael Hadge, recently discharged from the U.S. Coast Guard.)

Another favorite hangout was Jimmy Ray's on Eighth Avenue, where Pacino congregated with Clayburgh, Laughton,

Hadge, Ralph Waite, Mitchell Ryan, Joe McHarg and Charles Durning. The avuncular Jimmy allowed all of them to run up tabs, justifiably confident he would be paid when their ships came in. "Al would tell us he had a yacht," Hadge recalls. "He used to say the *theater* was his yacht!" (After witnessing Pacino's triumph in *The Indian Wants the Bronx*, Hadge overheard a woman in the foyer nervously ask her friend, "Do you think that guy was really an *actor*?")

There were many times when Pacino's alcohol consumption caused considerable unhappiness. After one three-day binge he lay soaking in a bath, utterly pickled and barely able to focus. Clayburgh came in and sat on the edge of the tub, looking melancholy. "I suddenly feel lonely," she whispered, "but you are drunk."

The two of them were discovered one morning, around eleven, in an otherwise empty, darkened East Sixty-first Street bar. "There's a certain power surging within you when you're in front of an audience," Pacino was overheard explaining to his distracted partner, the clarity of his articulation surprising even him.

"Shouldn't we go, Al?" Clayburgh asked. "I think we should eat something."

"What day is it? I'm twenty-eight and feel a hundred and eight."

"*Wednesday!*"

At first Pacino looked as if this news could not possibly be correct. Then he dropped off his stool and wobbled for a few steps. "Let's go, Jill," he said. "Three days on booze is enough."

Although Pacino told everyone he was "serious about Jill," there was always the rider "I don't think I'm ready for marriage. That's appropriate to a certain type of life, where reality is not always changing as it is for actors. Shows open, reviews come in, shows close. She'll be going away, and I'll be going away. It's just something we'll have to work out." On another occasion he stated, "I don't know what I want. I've never looked forward in my life." With little choice, Clayburgh stuck to more or less the same line: "We may get married someday. We want children, either our own or adopted. We really haven't decided."

When one reporter tracked them down in their apartment and pursued the marriage question, Clayburgh suggested, "Let's check with Al about that," and shouted through to him in the kitchen, where he skulked. "He's asking me about marriage, Al. Does that make you laugh or cry?" She waited a few seconds and grinned. "Did you hear that?" the reporter was asked. "He laughed."

With *The Indian Wants the Bronx* Pacino regained his fighting weight of 150 pounds. The underground word of mouth that continued throughout the run finally surfaced in February 1969 with the glowing reviews he received for his Broadway debut as Bickham, the sadistic psychotic of *Does a Tiger Wear a Necktie?*, Don Petersen's play about daily life inside a drug rehabilitation center. Pacino appeared only briefly in the first act, dominated the second, then was completely absent from the last act. This afforded him the opportunity for several stiff martinis before the curtain calls, with more to follow after the show.

Although the play opened to lukewarm reviews and closed after only thirty-nine performances, Pacino was singled out as having given one of the most brilliant displays of the season. Jack Kroll at *Newsweek* saw Pacino's Bickham as having "the choreography of a hood, with a poetic soul." Although describing his performance as "brilliant," he felt obliged to add that there was "a touch of the perfect academic demonstration. His performance misses the instant, total existential wallop of the early Brando and Dean." Clive Barnes wrote in the New York *Times* that Pacino was "the best young actor in town" before questioning Pacino's versatility and adding the damning praise of describing him as "an Italian Dustin Hoffman." Pacino himself realized that he was in danger of being typecast. And certainly he wanted to be simply *Pacino*, not the Italian version of anybody else. He empathized more with actors like De Niro, whose careers were still in the balance, rather than the fat cat

Hoffman represented after his vault to fame in *The Graduate*. Compared with Hoffman, he and De Niro were still upstarts, with all the disadvantages, as well as the few advantages, that come with the territory. A *Variety* poll of metropolitan drama critics that named him "most promising new Broadway actor" provided a boost, as did his Tony award for the Best Dramatic Actor in a supporting role.

Pacino was quietly delighted with the attention that was being paid to him after almost a decade of struggle. And just in case anyone confused the shy, soft-spoken individual with the Murphs or Bickhams he played onstage, Jill Clayburgh set the record straight. "Al is so gentle he won't even kill a cockroach," she assured everyone. "He's a very good man and a real artist. Oh, sure, he has a temper, especially when he's been drinking or working too much. But most times he's relaxed and completely at ease."

"I'm a notorious pacifist," Pacino agreed. "Everybody who knows me says that. My favorite color is passive. Maybe that's why I can get up onstage and do people like Bickham and Murph. They are violent, and I had to express that. Bickham kicks a door in, breaks a phone, kicks a desk, kicks a wall, pounds a desk with his fist and breaks a Puerto Rican boy's arm. Murph slashes an Indian with a knife. I guess I could be cliché and say that violence is in all of us. You can't help but feel it, just living today. I think everybody does have it in himself. It's just a matter of getting to it, like lyricism or comedy.

"But I don't necessarily think of violence when I think of Bickham. I consider him very, very lonely. The things that happen to him come from loneliness. He's a loner, a suicidal junkie at a narcotics rehabilitation center who is desperately afraid. He wants something but doesn't know what. *And neither do I.* He eventually kills himself, because his psychiatrist, David Opatoshu, isn't getting through to him. The shrink remains critical and aloof. That's why Bickham *kisses* him.

"I finally get to kiss someone onstage," Pacino said, grinning, "and it's a guy! But it didn't bother either of us. The only thing was that I kept getting these colds at rehearsal and David kept telling me, 'Close your mouth!' "

Despite his typecasting, Pacino claimed he would rather play comedy, which he described as his "first love": "I've always thought of myself as a clown. I love the circus, silent screen comedy, triple takes. So what do I get to play? Tough punks, drug artists—no clowns!"

The success of *The Indian Wants the Bronx* and *Does a Tiger Wear a Necktie?*, coupled with Pacino's total involvement in the roles, registered the onset of a new phase in his mental odyssey. The walk on the wild side the plays permitted also enabled him to view the world through different eyes. He referred to *Indian* and *Tiger* as "liberating and revealing," and although he was neither psychotic nor paranoid and far from being a junkie, Pacino caught a glimpse of how far he could take the "new life" the roles allowed him and how he might eventually find himself.

"There's a desire," he admitted, "to go through these experiences artistically. Let me give you an example: If you want to grieve, you have to step outside of yourself and let it out. If you hold on to it, it's there, it's inside you, and that's what it is with acting. You step outside of yourself in order to grieve, to be tragic. It's like losing yourself in your objectivity. As Michelangelo said, 'God, free me of myself so I can please you.' That's exactly it. It's confusing, and it's personal. I like to get caught up in a world and make it imaginative and alive. I *need* to do it!"

In the meantime, there was a perplexing series of physical injuries to contend with, including a wrenched back, sprained knee and twisted hip, that raised the question of psychosomatic inducement. Pacino reluctantly agreed to visit an analyst to seek answers, then, echoing his schoolboy reaction to the Stanislavsky principles he now embraced, gave up in disgust after just a handful of sessions. To swallow that he was punishing himself for his success was just too much. The after-performance "belts" he enjoyed began to assume ever more heroic proportions.

An appearance on *The Merv Griffin Show* during *Tiger*'s brief run proved a disaster. Pacino was thrown by the automatic applause that greeted the announcement of his name and reacted by executing an elaborate impromptu stage bow, the only one he knew. Halfway down he realized how ludicrous he must look, but by the time he straightened up and began to stammer out an answer to Griffin's first question, it was commercial break time.

To Pacino in the sixties the play was the thing, his three favorites being *The Iceman Cometh, The Seagull* and *The Master Builder*—O'Neill, Chekhov and Ibsen. "Chekhov was as important to me as anybody as a writer," he says. "Brecht, as well as Shakespeare, really helped in my life. Also Henry Miller, Balzac and Dostoyevsky. They got me through my twenties, gave me such a raison d'etre. The relationships we have with writers are quite a thing. They're different from the ones we have with actors or musicians or composers or politicians. Everything for me is the writer; without him I don't exist. An actor gets all the glory, but I don't know about enduring."

Already Pacino was publicly posing the question, "Can all this last?" And drinking—to forget the past and blot out the future.

CHAPTER 5

"THIS IS THE END"

AFTER THE SUCCESS of *Does a Tiger Wear a Necktie?* came the inevitable letdown. In *The Local Stigmatic*, a play by Heathcote Williams, which opened at the Actor's Playhouse in New York along with seven other one-act plays by Harold Pinter, Pacino was teamed with Michael Hadge, the cast list completed by Joe Maher and Paul Benedict. Yet again Pacino played a bully, who, together with Hadge, picks on an elderly, inoffensive actor to vent their bottled-up rage against society at large. "We had a hard time getting it put on," Hadge recalls, "and it didn't come into being until Al had won the Tony."

The resemblance to Murph in *The Indian Wants the Bronx* was just too much for the majority of critics. "If Pacino is an actor," *New York* magazine's John Simon suggested, "not merely a highly efficient robot programed for psychosis, evidence is urgently required."

"It was not received well," Pacino concedes, "and we were told to close after one night. Luckily Jon Voight happened to be around. He believed in the play very much and out of his own pocket gave us enough money to run for a week." It was a gesture Pacino never forgot.

He was plunged into despair when the play and its companion pieces closed after the eight performances Voight had made possible. He was convinced it had failed because of insufficient rehearsal time. "This is the end," he informed an anxious Clayburgh as he paced up and down their apartment, beyond consolation, absolutely certain that his career had peaked and that he was now on the slide.

A telephone call from director Milton Katselas persuaded him otherwise. Would he care to play the part of Kilroy, the all-American hero with the oversize heart, in a revival of Tennessee Williams's *Camino Real*? Would he ever! "I decided that was a good day for me whether I did the play or not," Pacino recalls. "It's such a beautiful piece."

Rehearsal time at Lincoln Center's Repertory Theater was again at a premium. "I don't even have time to find out about my role," Pacino grumbled. "I hate that opening-night deadline. It's like going out in the cold without a coat."

Although Tennessee Williams attended the previews and said it was his favorite production, specifically mentioning the sense of urgency he felt, the remark was lost on Pacino. "I don't know what he means," he admitted, "but he's a lovely man."

As he struggled with his own interpretation, others in the cast seemed out of tune. In his big love scene with Esmeralda, a prostitute who believes her virginity is miraculously renewed every full moon, Pacino at first played it straight. Unfortunately the actress was following Katselas's instruction to be offbeat and go for laughs, prompting Pacino, somewhat belatedly, to delve for humor as best he could.

In the New York *Post*, Richard Watts, Jr., wrote that Pacino's "touching portrayal" attested to his versatility. Jack Kroll at *Newsweek* was unconvinced and stated that Pacino "ought to be read the riot act" for relying on the same acting tricks that had earlier won him plaudits. Wasn't *Camino Real* meant to be an ensemble piece? What was with Pacino's stage-hogging attempt at a tour de force?

"This is the last play I'm going to do for at least two years," a humbled Pacino declared. "I've gotta take time out to learn more about myself. I'm confused." Instead, Israel Horovitz provided a welcome break when he invited Pacino to direct his short play *Rats* in Boston in March 1970. But more and more, however, Pacino felt that he was merely marking time. Through the auspices of Marty Bregman, that situation was about to change.

SEVERAL MOVIE OFFERS were sifted through and argued over for his first major screen role. There was no question of deserting the theater—although the theater seemed to have temporarily deserted him—but with a successful movie or two under his belt, Pacino's profile would be raised to such an extent that he would be able to pick and choose his theatrical roles, as well as be freed from purely financial considerations. Movies, in short, would be able to subsidize his theatrical outings, and if they could be artistically valid movies that stretched him as an actor at the same time, well and good.

Together Bregman and Pacino turned down a total of nine movie roles, ranging from Otto Preminger's *Tell Me That You Love Me, Junie Moon* (Pacino: "I didn't feel the part was right"; Bregman: "Part of a manager's job is persuading clients to avoid material that will bury them") to Mike Nichols's *Catch-22* (Bregman: "Paramount's own Catch-22 was their demand that Al sign a multipicture contract"; Pacino: "I wanted to do the picture, but I didn't want to be tied down by a contract"). For good measure the team also declined a guaranteed run on Broadway in *Zorba the Greek*.

They settled instead for a project entitled *Panic in Needle Park*, which the energetic Bregman pitched to backers in high-concept terms of "Romeo and Juliet on junk." Based on a book by James Mills, the screenplay had been written by Joan Didion and John Gregory Dunne and was being produced by Dominick Dunne.

The "Panic" in the title derived from street slang for a heroin shortage, the "Needle Park" location being New York's concrete Sherman Square, at the intersection of Broadway and Amsterdam Avenue, home to junkies, pushers and prostitutes.

Another of Bregman's clients, Jerry Schatzberg, an ex-fashion photographer who had one movie already under his belt in *Puzzle of a Downfall Child*, starring his girlfriend, Faye Dunaway, was chosen to direct *Panic*. Twenty-five-year-old Katharine ("Kitty") Winn was signed to costar with Pacino, having been named the "discovery of the season" after her performance in the American Conservatory Theater production of *Saint Joan*, in San Francisco.

Pacino, playing a seedy, sensitive junkie and drug dealer about to lead the girl he loves down the same deadly path he walks, researched the territory of hard drugs thoroughly. Before filming began, he hung around Needle Park. Kitty Winn accompanied him on several of these expeditions, absorbing with him the atmosphere of desolation and despair. Considerable tension was generated when a group of users decided they were undercover narcotic agents, necessitating a hasty exit.

On the first day of shooting, Michael Hadge was wakened by an urgent knocking on his door at 7:30 A.M. It was Pacino. "What the hell are you doing here at this hour?" asked Hadge.

"I'm in a movie we're shooting across the street," Pacino replied, "and I thought I'd come up and get some breakfast." By this time Hadge's wife had wandered through and began preparing eggs and bacon for all of them. "Gee, I'm so nervous," said Pacino, pushing his plate away. "Do you have anything to drink in the icebox?" His "breakfast" consisted of a single large glass of chilled white wine.

Pacino met a number of addicts at the Phoenix House and Reality House treatment centers. Each one, it turned out, did his thing differently. Just when Pacino would be saying to himself, "That's it, *that's* an addict," he'd talk to another and realize the variety and degrees of addiction that existed. "Man, you *never* make love when you're high," one addict assured him. "It's *great* when you're high," another swore.

Pacino sat in on one methadone session but was forced to make another exit when the leader divulged to the group he was an actor. Ex-addicts taught him the mechanics of using narcotics—heating up the heroin and improvising the tourniquet—which he practiced in front of a mirror. The intrepid Kitty Winn even took her research to the point where she learned to inject herself—minus the heroin.

There were several other occasions during the ten-week shoot when the borderline between real life and the plot became a trifle blurred. With the unit on a street-corner location and Pacino about to peddle his wares, a real heroin dealer arrived on the scene. As the two of them tried to outstare each other, the situation became confused, not to say downright dangerous.

Reliance on Jerry Schatzberg, the director as authority figure, was the most difficult personal discipline Pacino had to master. He stopped fighting it after three weeks, muttering, "You have to trust the director. He's got the scissors."

Displays of nudity and sex scenes bother Pacino. About to film a prison shower scene with several other actors, he turned to Schatzberg and pointed to the script girl, who meekly sat at her post. "Is she going to be there while we take our pants off?" he asked. A lovemaking scene between Pacino and Winn brought further problems, not so much related to the movie itself as to the principle involved of portraying the act on screen in a shallow or gratuitous manner. In the end he decided that the structure and form of *Panic in Needle Park* justified its inclusion, in that it moved the story along. He still pointed out that nobody in Shakespeare's plays even kissed, not even Romeo and Juliet. "With some of these things," he says, "they're just indulging in a lot of sloppy kissing and humping. And nine times out of ten, it's flat. It doesn't *have* to be there. I literally dread those scenes if I feel they are merely there to titillate and are not an integral part of the plot. I just want to get them over, close my eyes and finish."

Pacino says he was drunk when he turned up at the first screening of *Panic in Needle Park* but still claims to have discerned in his own performance "a talented actor who simply needed help" as well as "a vulnerability, a certain admission of my life, not just then but my whole life. Here and there are things I could say about my performance that I didn't care for, but certain things come through that I was glad about. You don't often see an *admission* on the screen, and it's a moving experience." Pacino seemed to be saying, "Swap the drugs for alcohol, and that's *me* up there, folks."

The reaction of his friends was that coming on top of his last few roles, Pacino had completed his "junkie" cycle. "Hey, look what happened to Pacino!" They laughed. "He went all the way on this one! He *mainlined*."

Panic in Needle Park did not prove to be Pacino's cinematic breakthrough, at least not to the general public, perhaps because of its grimly downbeat theme; one critic described it as "almost physically painful to watch." There was, however, sporadic acclaim, especially for the actors. "The entire cast, especially Al Pacino and Kitty Winn in the leads, create intensely real people. Their brand of realness feels close to documentary," Jacob Brickman wrote in *Esquire*. Pacino's performance was variously described as "remarkable," "marvelously alive" and "exceptionally successful." Kitty Winn was awarded the Best Actress prize at the 1971 Cannes Film Festival for her performance. "It doesn't preach," Pacino said of the film and its depiction of drug abuse. "It doesn't moralize about it. All it does is show it."

After the movie had been banned for several years in Britain, its release was greeted by Dilys Powell of London's *Sunday Times* in 1975: "Al Pacino belongs to a group of players linked not only by age, but by the essence of performance, a group whose members include Dustin Hoffman, Jack Nicholson and Gene Hackman. These are the players who have taken over as the interpreters of an uncomfortable world from Brando and

Newman. It is Pacino's astonishing ease which strikes one, the fluidity of his movements, the absolute freedom, or so it seems, from the conventions of acting. He doesn't look as if he's giving a performance. *It looks real.*"

Comparisons with Hoffman continued to be raised, only less flatteringly, and much to Pacino's chagrin, in John Coleman's *New Statesman* review. "Not a bad performance," he maintained, "but Hoffman was there first with his Ratso in *Midnight Cowboy*. Here you almost expect a limp from Pacino."

Since *Panic in Needle Park* and *Midnight Cowboy* had been shot simultaneously, affording Pacino no chance to view Hoffman's interpretation, or Hoffman Pacino's, for that matter, the comment was palpably unfair. And those who knew him were aware that Pacino would have bound his legs together rather than follow Hoffman in any way. In any case, hadn't the *New Yorker*'s ultracritic Pauline Kael given Hoffman's limp itself a bad review? "Dustin Hoffman is supposed to have a bum leg," she complained, "but his limp varies from scene to scene, at times giving the impression he is doing the Carioca."

It was Pacino the comedian who responded when one reporter asked him if it had been difficult preparing for his role in *Panic*. "Nope," he replied deadpan. "Just took dope for a year."

Then he produced a disarming mile-wide grin. "Kidding, of course!"

CHAPTER 6

SELF-DESTRUCTIVE BASTARD

PRODUCER AL RUDDY almost worked his way through the *Hollywood Directory*, first approaching Arthur Penn, Fred Zinnemann, Franklin Schaffner, Peter Yates, Richard Lester, Richard Brooks and Costa-Gavras before eventually settling on Francis Ford Coppola for Paramount's movie version of Mario Puzo's *The Godfather*.

At this stage *The Godfather* was on Paramount's B list, picked up for peanuts before the book became a best seller and blighted by the failure of its recent, similarly themed *The Brotherhood*, with Kirk Douglas. Dino de Laurentiis had originally been in line to coproduce *The Godfather*, with Charles Bronson in the title role, before the twosome backed out to make *The Valachi Papers* instead.

Despite Coppola's less than earth-shattering directorial track record—*You're a Big Boy Now*, *The Rain People* and *Finian's Rainbow*—his way with a script, as evidenced by the Oscar he had collected for *Patton*, was undeniable. Since Paramount was by no means ecstatic at Puzo's own first draft, this factor weighed heavily in its decision. As for Coppola, he had urgent need of a revenue injection, with his San Francisco-based Zoetrope Enterprises three hundred thousand dollars in debt to Warner Bros.

Coppola's first hard-won battle was to convince Paramount to accept Marlon Brando in the title role. Paramount and Ruddy had already looked at Laurence Olivier, George C. Scott, Rod Steiger and Richard Conte. ("Why didn't they ask Eddie Robinson?" Marlene Dietrich reportedly asked. Like Olivier, the superb veteran Edward G. was allegedly uninsurable because of health problems.) For years Brando had been box-office poison and considered the scourge of directors and their schedules. Ruddy privately bet Coppola two hundred dollars that Paramount would never accept him. The wager won, Coppola turned his attention to the other cast members.

He had been bowled over by Pacino onstage and felt strongly that he was right for the part of the youngest son, Michael Corleone. Paramount, wanted either Warren Beatty or Jack Nicholson, was unmoved. For that matter, Al Ruddy was pushing for Robert Redford, with whom he had just completed *Little Fauss and Big Halsy*, Ruddy's first big-screen effort following his TV stint as producer of the long-running *Hogan's Heroes*. Marlon Brando's advice to Paramount chief Robert Evans was simple: "Bob, the person who plays Michael should be a man who broods. He shouldn't be the usual kind of leading man. He should be a *brooder*." When Frank Langella was suggested at one stage and vetoed by the studio, Coppola insisted that Pacino be given further consideration. Mario Puzo was sold on the concept after watching a twelve-minute reel of *Panic in Needle Park*. "Above all," he wrote to Coppola, "*Pacino* has to be in the film." First a screen test was considered mandatory.

By this time Pacino and Bregman had another offer on hold, the part of Mario in MGM's projected adaptation of Jimmy Breslin's best seller *The Gang That Couldn't Shoot Straight*.

For *The Godfather* Pacino was under the initial impression that he was up for the part of Sonny, which James Caan went on to play. (Caan, in fact, tested well for Michael, as well as for the Tom Hagen role that went to Robert Duvall.) Then he was dismayed to find that his test as Michael was set during the wedding scene at the start of the movie, which he considered the dullest episode; basically it was all exposition and afforded him little opportunity to demonstrate the spark that Coppola had earlier watched ignite his stage performance. "I didn't know what he *expected* me to do," Pacino later complained to friends. "He tested me with the *wrong scene*!" Michael, he was convinced, had to start out ambivalent, almost unsure of himself and his place, caught between his Old World family and the postwar American dream represented by Diane Keaton, his WASP fiancée. Keaton, who tested with Pacino, had no illusions about her relative importance in the scheme of things: "They were mainly concerned about Al, and I think they finally got so tired of seeing me they said, 'Oh, for God's sake, give her the part.'"

"The self-destructive bastard" was the label Coppola applied to Pacino before the test was screened, for his chosen Michael had turned up without even bothering to learn his lines, then added insult to injury by partly improvising his own dialogue to fill the gaps, a device that betrayed a complete lack of understanding of Michael's character. Puzo was instantly turned off by what he saw as Pacino's lack of professionalism and demanded his letter of recommendation back from Coppola. Caan's test, he maintained, was ten times better. Robert Evans underlined the studio's now rock-solid opposition to Pacino. "Francis, I must say you're alone in this," Coppola was told. To an anxious Marty Bregman, Evans was even more forthcoming. "Your client will play Michael Corleone over my dead body," he snapped.

When Coppola persuaded Pacino to turn up for a second test, the results were the same: blown lines and another turndown. "This is ridiculous," Pacino raged. "These people don't want me, and I don't want to be around when they feel that way. Besides, I think they may be right."

To friends, he shrugged off Paramount's negative reaction, assuring them that he didn't really care whether he landed the part or not. If it was meant to be, it was meant to be. "If someone doesn't want me for a part," he said, "OK, I understand. I don't even get mad. But when they don't want me and they keep telling me to come back, well, under those circumstances, I'm not learning lines. A thing like that eats at your dignity. If that's being self-destructive, then OK, call me self-destructive." Negotiations lumbered on for an appearance in *The Gang That Couldn't Shoot Straight*.

As far as Marty Bregman was concerned, *The Godfather* was the only game in town, despite Robert Evans's attitude and his own client's recalcitrance. The agent appointed by Pacino thought differently. Half a loaf was better than none at all. "Take the money, sign with MGM" was the gospel he preached.

Charles Bluhdorn of Gulf & Western, Paramount's parent company, had his own dramatic overview of the endless tests Coppola was filming. "All of the actors' performances are bad," he pointed out, "and there is only one director. That must mean that it's not the *actors* who are terrible; it's the *director* who is terrible!" Fortunately, for Coppola, Bluhdorn's line of thought was never taken to its logical conclusion.

Coppola's will finally prevailed at Paramount after every executive had been forced to watch the *Panic in Needle Park* reel. Pacino was then approached to take a third test. By this time he had undergone a change of attitude. Having had ample time to study the character, he now desperately wanted to play Michael Corleone. "But please, Francis," he pleaded after the test, "*no* more auditions, *no* more screen tests. I can *live* without this part."

Despite his nonchalant attitude toward friends, the waiting had almost driven Pacino crazy, and Clayburgh along with him. MGM decided to sue Pacino, claiming he was already signed for *The Gang That Couldn't Shoot Straight*. His agent had indeed committed him, but subject to several approvals that were never finalized. MGM used as leverage knowledge that Pacino would not be allowed to make *The Godfather* until their lawsuit was adjudicated. "It was being settled in Los Angeles," Marty Bregman recalls, "and was all very high-powered. Al did not want to go out there to settle the matter. He was uncomfortable about the whole deal. He didn't understand why he had to go; he'd never personally agreed to do the film; he found the whole thing insane. I went to pick him up on the morning of the flight. He had two shots before he got on the plane, then became a little tipsy on the way. I had to drag him into that meeting. If I hadn't, he'd never have been allowed to do *The Godfather*."

In exchange for a settlement MGM managed to squeeze a property it coveted out of Paramount, as well as an agreement from Pacino that he owed MGM a movie. "I screwed them out of that," Bregman cheerfully admits. "He never made a movie for them. I kept ballooning it and postponing."

MGM signed a relative unknown to replace Pacino in *The Gang That Couldn't Shoot Straight*. His name was Robert De Niro.

ONCE HE HAD committed to the role of Michael Corleone, Pacino's doubts began gnawing away in earnest. It is part of an actor's basic insecurity that once he has worried his way through to actually being offered a role—and feigned insouciance is but one of the weapons in his armory—the next concern is with the role itself. With the primary doubt that he will ever work again temporarily removed, the actor now has to apply himself to fleshing out the development of the character he has chosen to inhabit.

Included in Pacino's research for the role was a visit with several leading Mafia figures that was discreetly arranged. It did little to help, since he was determined to create an enigmatic type the audience could never really be sure of, one who would start off as half-formed and uncalloused virgin clay. The key, he was convinced, lay in the clay's gradual hardening.

His first meeting with Brando, in the company of Diane Keaton, had the younger actors desperately trying to pretend their hero was just another movie star—and failing miserably. When

Brando said a simple "Hello" to Keaton, she nodded back nervously, as if unable to believe the whole episode was taking place. "Yeah, right, *sure*," she finally managed to mumble, while Pacino affected the aspect of a faun trapped in the headlights of an oncoming car. "Jeez, every time I'd run into Marlon Brando on the set, my face would turn red and I'd start laughing," Keaton later confessed. "I was *so* high school, so totally into self-loathing."

Al Ruddy organized a preshoot dinner for his director and cast at Patsy's, a trendy New York Italian restaurant. "Everyone was nervous about meeting Brando," Coppola recalls, "and immediately started relating to him as the Godfather. Jimmy Caan started telling jokes, Al Pacino looked tragic, and every time Brando turned his back, Bobby Duvall started imitating him."

On the first day of rehearsals Brando held forth on his pet topic, Indian rights, while Coppola, Caan, Pacino and Duvall hung around waiting to begin. "Oh, God, is this the way it's going to be for the next two weeks?" was the unspoken question going through their minds. After a while Duvall again began making faces behind Brando's back, breaking Pacino and Caan up, yet terrifying them in case the star would notice and think they were laughing at him. "Keep talking, Marlon, none of us want to work!" Duvall finally joked, breaking the ice. Brando laughed; he was comfortable with Duvall, having worked with him several years earlier on *The Chase*. Rehearsals were soon under way.

Brando turned up to watch Pacino's first scene with Keaton, the original test sequence, and stood by the camera while Coppola took them through their paces. During the take Pacino, without breaking pace, tossed away a leaf that fell from a tree onto his shoulder. "I liked what you did with that leaf," Brando informed him afterward. Pacino and Keaton went out and got drunk on the strength of the comment.

Pacino found particular difficulty in filming the scene set in the Luna restaurant in the Bronx, which also fell during the first week of shooting. It was, after all, familiar territory that released all his old ghosts. In the scene he had to enter the toilet, find a pistol behind the tank and reemerge to shoot down the police captain (Sterling Hayden) and Sollozzo (Al Lettieri) in cold blood. After the second take he turned to Coppola, wild-eyed and shaking, utterly drained. "Francis," he pleaded, "I don't want to do this anymore!" When Pacino watched the rushes, he saw his nervousness betrayed by a complete loss of focus in his eyes before the killings. As far as Coppola was concerned, Pacino had given the scene precisely the edge of desperation and determination he had sought.

Even after viewing the first dailies, the nervous studio brass still wanted to break the delicate truce and fire Pacino. There was no question of that, Coppola coolly informed them, even though his own position, with both Elia Kazan and Aram Avakian reportedly waiting in the wings, was still far from solid, despite Brando's assurance that "If they fire you, I'll quit, too." Pacino recalls arriving on the set and noticing absent faces on almost every occasion. He would ask, "Am *I* still here?" and heave a sigh of relief at the reply "Yes, Al, you're still here."

Pacino found his director to be an extraordinary individual, capable of delving into the personality of the actor in an almost voyeuristic way, yet possessing the ability to detach himself at will. That was why, he realized, Coppola understood the character of Michael Corleone, a chameleon as adept at isolating his emotions as he was at displaying them. Coppola became one of the models from whom Pacino drew his portrait of the Godfather's youngest son. In many scenes, when Michael Corleone almost appears to drift off into a trancelike state, Pacino had just finished listening to Stravinsky or Mozart on the set to ease him into the deep, abstract mood he sought.

Pacino's first scene to be filmed opposite Brando was the bedside vigil Michael keeps for his father following the assassination attempt. "Have you any idea what it was like to be doing a scene with him?" Pacino later asked, still every inch the ingenue. "I sat in the theaters when I was a kid just watching him. Now I'm playing a scene with him. He's *God*, man."

Brando's quiet support on the set helped considerably. "I felt that Brando really cared for me personally," Pacino acknowledged, "and that acceptance was a great thing for me. What can you say about someone that graceful?"

BECAUSE HE HAD worked with makeup man Buck Buchman on *Panic in Needle Park*, Pacino agreed to an interview with his journalist wife, Dian, in the apartment on Fourteenth Street he and Jill Clayburgh shared. Although he was in the middle of shooting *The Godfather*, Pacino came off fairly relaxed. "I'm happier than I've ever been," he assured her, clearly buoyed by the hospital scene with Brando that he had just finished and that he thought had gone particularly well. Buchman soon noted in Pacino a charming mass of contradictions. He walked miles every night, he told her; then in the next breath he claimed he would like to live and work in a radius of five or six blocks. His grandfather was described as "very inhibited" one moment, "very emotional" the next. When Buchman gently pointed out these discrepancies, Pacino blithely answered, "Sure, I hate to get married to one idea. I'm a philosophical anarchist."

He was adamant about his dislike of money or possessions: "I try not to want too much. I prefer work. The axle of life should be the work. There is nothing to *get*, for whatever you get is only *temporary*. I never buy things. I can't buy shoes, shirts or clothing without palpitations. Where I come from forking over money for shoes was a big thing, and I hate paying rent. And I have a lot of phobias, like not putting stamps on envelopes."

When the phone rang, the black and white kitten he had been fondling leaped up hysterically. The call having been answered, Pacino tenderly stroked the pet, then leaned forward, fixing Buchman with the full force of his flashing dark eyes. "You see this kitten?" he asked. "It was taken away from its mother. It wasn't properly weaned. It's very neurotic. *You can't be taken away from your mother!*"

Pacino paused and relaxed back into his chair. "I was taken away from my mother when I was three," he explained. "I never knew, or forgot it, until recently when an aunt reminded me after a show. It took me back! My mother loved me a great deal and gave me a lot of love, and that's very important. I don't know what would have happened to me if she didn't love me the way she did. It was tremendous, it was always there. I was my mother's whole world."

When Pacino and Clayburgh moved from Fourteenth Street to the upper Sixties, it was to a larger apartment left vacant by Candice Bergen on her return to Hollywood. Although grateful for the guiding hand of Bregman behind the scenes in the reassigned lease, Pacino would have preferred a move to a loft in the Village; it was Clayburgh who yearned for uptown.

IN CONVERSATION WITH Brando's makeup man while on location in Hollywood, Pacino denied he would ever desert New York and make California his base. "Don't worry," he was told. "I heard Marlon say that. You'll be out here in three years. You'll do very well in Hollywood. You'll get a nice place in a beautiful area. You'll be hailed as a good actor; you may even get to do nice work. *But don't hope for much more.*"

Brando's associate was drawing a distinctly wrong conclusion, unaware of Pacino's intense need to be around people on the ground, jostling, crisscrossing, intermingling. The longer he was away, the more he realized how much he missed every aspect of New York, from the traffic lights he had been able to time back in the old days so he never had to stop, to the walks he had taken from Ninety-second Street and Broadway down to the Village and back again, bopping like a trouper, his mind crammed with images of the roles he would play. "I love New York City," he said. "I don't think I'll ever move out. When I hit these streets, I want to walk. I got my places I hit, five or six bars, I bounce in, bounce out. Oh, I'll *visit* a farm, I'll look at a cow, I'll pet a sheep. But I love the city."

Much of Michael Corleone had been worked out as he had

jumped blocks and people-watched: the bag ladies, the cardboard shelterers, the kids in Chock Full o' Nuts, the bum stuffing a dozen crackers into his soup, the Times Square jiveasses. He desperately missed his workout at the Y, Picasso's *Woman in a Chair* at the Modern, the Ginger Man's for a drink with friends. L.A.? L.A. was for *oranges*!

CHAPTER 7

A COW IN KANSAS

THERE WERE SEVERAL aspects that made the shooting of *The Godfather* a misery for Pacino. Except for Coppola, Brando, Keaton, producer Al Ruddy and the occasional presence of his buddy John Cazale (playing his brother Fredo), he felt completely unwanted on the set, certainly by the multitude of Paramount executives. He mainly chose to stay out of the jocularity between Brando, Duvall and Caan, partly because he was playing an outsider, partly because he felt excluded in any case. "Really, Al and I felt like the creepy couple of all time," Keaton confessed.

Howard Newman, one of the few reporters given access to the set, summed the problem up: "Al was underplaying the part so much the rest of the cast thought he didn't know what to do. The feeling was that if the movie was a hit, it would be in spite of Pacino. Al was aware of the feeling, and off-camera he retreated even more. He wouldn't talk to people and refused 'official' interviews. He has a sense of humor, but it wasn't strong in those days. Let me put it this way: I'd rather go to a party with Jimmy Caan. For an evening of good conversation, I'd pick Al."

There were occasions later, although still just a few, when Pacino was able to unwind. He and Caan improvised together on a cops-and-robbers gun routine, Caan playing the cop first and drawing a gun on Pacino. "OK, let's go," he yelled. It was Pacino's cue to knock the gun out of Caan's hands and turn the tables on him. Then they would do a rerun of Pacino's old mental institution sketch, with its finger-biting finale, until it was time to get back to the serious business of mayhem and murder in the Mafia.

Coppola's bright idea to increase Pacino's height in some scenes by using elevator shoes quickly backfired. "What's wrong with you?" Coppola screamed. "You're walking like Donald Duck!"

"Get these lifts out of my shoes and I may walk straighter," Pacino informed him.

Gradually Pacino began to comprehend the basis for a comment of Brando's he had never understood: that acting was not an art. Brando had never returned to the theater after his success in movies and was referring to *movie* acting, which Pacino was rapidly discovering denied performers the chance for fluidity and the sense of musical dynamism that he had sought to bring to his theatrical roles. Onstage one move led naturally to the next, whereas in movies there was continual crosscutting from one performance point to another. The character of Michael Corleone was oppressive enough without the movie's being shot out of sequence. What chance was there to effect a smooth transition from Ivy League war hero innocence to cold-blooded killer? Pacino often woke up at 4:00 A.M. and lay worrying about the role and whether or not his whole performance was believable.

A visit to Sicily for location work had the most overwhelming and therapeutic effect on the exhausted actor. The wave of emotion that hit Pacino the moment he set foot on Italian soil continued in the ride through the streets of Catania and underscored his entire visit. How foolish were the friends, he thought, who chose to deny where they had come from. Having discovered a missing part of his personal jigsaw, he began to understand why Coppola had stuck his neck out for him in the first place. Somewhere in his loins, in his Sicilian heritage, the connection had been discerned.

Although the Italian Pacino speaks in the movie appears fluent, he had only a rudimentary grasp of the language. Back home his grandparents had spoken Italian only when they didn't want Pacino to know what they were discussing, leaving him perpetually suspended between the twin worlds of Sicily and the Bronx. For all he loved his mother and grandparents, he was never able to communicate with them in their native tongue.

Intensive study had to be undertaken for the sequence shot in Sicily, where Pacino faked it phonetically, aided and abetted by fellow cast member Richard Castellano. "What would a Sicilian say here?" Castellano was constantly being asked.

The end of filming produced a catharsis for Pacino that was like a dam bursting. It was partly relief at having gotten through the movie, together with the Italian experience and the painful evocation of the years he had spent as virtual prisoner of the Bronx. "I felt like I could open up and cry for years," he admitted. "It was hard for me to liberate these feelings. But I spent too much time alienated and lonely. I want to be a great actor someday, and I've decided there's no use philosophizing; the only way is to work."

THE COMPLETED MOVIE gives a clue to the difficulty Pacino encountered with the wedding reception test and why the Paramount brass had been less than enthralled: The scene not only is expositional but is written to be played ambiguously. Is Michael trying to win Kay over by telling her, "My father made him an offer he couldn't refuse. Either his brains or his signature would be on that contract"? Is he trying to put the poor girl off, or is he honestly laying his family situation on the line? Played even slightly off-key, the dialogue would have the ap-

parently clean-cut war hero basking in his father's reflected
notoriety; delivered off-kilter, it would not be so much expositional as downright confusing. Observing Kay's perturbed reaction, Michael hastens to put matters right. "That's my family, not me," he assures her, somewhat less than convincingly;
his acceptance of the situation has already provided the seeds
of his eventual downfall.

The news of the assassination attempt on his father brings
about the first change in Pacino's Michael, signaled by the
fierce resolve and raw intensity that glitter in his eyes when he
visits him in hospital. When the family friend he recruits to
help him guard his father begins to shake so fiercely he is unable to light his cigarette, Michael grabs his lighter and does
the honors. A close shot reveals his steady hand, a phenomenon he observes with cool surprise and quiet, private satisfaction.

In a further tightening of the screw, Michael tells the family
he will undertake the ritual executions of Captain McCluskey
and Sollozzo. "It's not *personal*, Sonny," he chillingly informs
his older brother; "it's strictly business." Before the killings his
face is a study, eyes darting this way and that, his nervous half
grins and tics distorting his features—until the "family business" has been bloodily resolved.

With his bride Appolonia murdered, Michael returns from
exile in Italy, somberly dressed for his meeting with Kay in a
black homburg, vest and overcoat. Although he assures her
that he loves and needs her, he speaks the words like a soulless
automaton. His transmogrification is clearly well under way
when he holds out the promise of legitimacy for the family:
"My father is no different from any other powerful men, like
senators or presidents." In Las Vegas Fredo is taken to task
with grim authority. "You're my brother and I love you," he
tells him, "but don't *ever* take sides with anyone against the
family again. *Ever!*'

The descent is all but final when he has a dozen enemies
wiped out while standing as godfather to his sister Connie's
baby; after the baptism ceremony he intends to have the child's

father killed as well. "Michael, is it true?" Kay asks him after Connie (Talia Shire) has accused him of her husband's murder.

He explodes, smashes his fist on a table, then relents and becomes calm. "All right. This one time I'll let you ask me about my affairs," he whispers.

Kay repeats her question: "Is it true?"

"No," he replies.

As Kay leaves after embracing him, Michael is shown in long shot, framed by the door to his den. Suppliants approach and kiss his ring, duplicating the movie's opening scene showing Brando granting communion to his flock. Kay stands there, unwilling to comprehend the truth of what she is witnessing, until a bodyguard quietly closes the door in her face. Michael's pact with the devil—and Pacino's icy, masterful transformation—are complete.

"The specter of Pacino's Michael," critic Gene Shalit wrote, "snakes larger and larger until it coils over the entire screen." In *The New Yorker* Pauline Kael was completely disarmed. "Pacino creates a quiet, ominous space around himself," she rhapsodized. "His acting, which is marvellous, big without ostentation, complements Brando's. Like Brando, Pacino is simple; you don't catch him acting, yet he manages to change from a small, fresh-faced, darkly handsome college boy into an underworld lord, becoming more intense, smaller and more isolated at every step." Larry Cohen wrote: *"The Godfather* belongs to Al Pacino. Everyone else is very good, down to the smallest part, but it's Pacino that's great—even better than in *Panic in Needle Park."*

Acting as part of a uniformly superb ensemble cast and in a movie Kael considered "the greatest gangster picture ever made," Pacino had managed to stand out and create a riveting, indelible impression.

ALTHOUGH *THE GODFATHER*'s impact on critics and audiences worldwide is now the stuff of cinematic legend, producer Al

Ruddy introduced an acerbic note into the general euphoria that greeted the movie's release in February 1972. "Making the movie was a miserable experience for everyone," Ruddy revealed. "There was not one good day on this picture." Pacino, it seemed, had been far from alone in his misery. Even so, Ruddy was now a rich man, Coppola's name was made, Brando's was reestablished, and a new star was born. "Brando is very fine," Mario Puzo wrote in his *Godfather Papers*, "but the great bonus was Al Pacino. As Michael, Pacino was everything I wanted that character to be on the screen. I couldn't believe it. It was, in my eyes, a perfect performance, a work of art. I was so happy I ran around admitting I was wrong. I ate crow like it was my favorite Chinese food."

Puzo was so determined to point out the error of his judgment that the seasoned Al Ruddy felt constrained to offer some advice on the workings of Hollywood. "Listen, if you don't go around telling everybody how wrong you were, nobody will know," he advised. "How the hell do you expect to be a producer in this town?" As for Coppola, he felt obliged to point out that the very factor Paramount wanted him fired over, the casting of Brando and Pacino, was precisely what had set the movie apart.

According to Paramount's publicity machine, an extraordinarily generous tribute, from one actor to another, came from Brando. "I didn't say much to Pacino when we were making *The Godfather*," he was quoted as saying, "but I not only consider him one of the best actors in America, but in the world. The picture just reinforced my opinion. That sounds like a put-on? Well, I never meant anything more in my life. I don't go around touting other actors, the profession means too much to me."

Pacino wasted no time in returning the compliment. "There's no doubt every time I see Brando that I'm looking at a great actor. Whether he's doing great acting or not, you're seeing somebody who is in the tradition of the great actor. What he does with it, that's something else, but he's got it all, the talent, the instrument is there, that's why he's endured."

He added another encomium, this time for Coppola: "If a director genuinely wants you, and the production needs you, then it's very good. That's what happened with Michael Corleone. Francis made it possible, that's all. I had personality differences with him, but those were his performances, he *made* them. And he knew it. He'd say, 'I created you, you're my Frankenstein!'"

Pacino's grandmother Kate Gerard was joyous at Pacino's success. She had seen him through all his plays, visiting him backstage in many a cramped dressing room, but a Paramount limousine driving up to her door to take her to *The Godfather* premiere was something else again. "They call me the celebrity around here now," she reported with a chuckle. "The man in the grocery wants me to get a signed picture of Sonny!" After the movie she told her grandson, "You were sweet, that suit you wore was really nice."

Ironically Pacino was accused of "doing a Brando" at the premiere by refusing interviews and dodging photographers. Robert Evans moved quickly to kill the gossip. "I don't see how Al could have been more cooperative with anyone," he declared. "He was gracious, modest, talked to the press, posed for pictures for hours. How do these things start?"

Evans was being just a tad disingenuous; Pacino, by his own admission, had turned up drunk. ("He was a wreck," says Bregman, "but I'm not sure it was booze. I think he was too nervous to get drunk.")

Although Brando was ostensibly the star of the movie, and despite their declared mutual admiration, Pacino still had enough sense of himself and what he had achieved to air his anger openly when Brando was nominated for a Best Actor Oscar, while he had to settle for a Best Supporting Actor nomination. He had, after all, been on the screen longer than Brando. Pacino decided to ignore the advice of friends who suggested that he should go to the length of repudiating the nomination. "Let it go," was his attitude, angry though he was. "Don't make waves."

Later it was claimed that he told the press, "People may

have come to see Brando, but they'll go away talking about Pacino." ("He didn't say that," says an unrepentant Bregman. "I did. It's amazing how these things get distorted. Al *revered* Brando.")

Handout puffs forgotten, Brando, clearly miffed, chose to tilt at Pacino over the affair. "At the end of shooting," he declared, "it occurred to Pacino that he wanted his name as big as mine on the billing. I had never made any trouble with such problems before, but this time I refused. I should have crushed the jumped-up little prick like a common or garden fly!" ("Brando must have misunderstood," Bregman insists. "His billing was contractual and agreed in advance.")

Now that the gloves were off, Pacino felt able to hit back, if not at Brando, certainly at the variety of Hollywood brass that had so pointedly made him feel unwelcome. "They said I was all wrong," he railed. "They said I would be a disaster, I was too meek and mild for the part. But when we finished the movie, the same people who were against me and put me down whenever they could were all for me. But then they couldn't understand why I didn't want anything to do with them. Well, I don't go for any of that. People are either for me or against me. They can't be both."

Pacino watched the Oscar ceremony on television, a contradiction in himself he acknowledged and cared little for. He was up against competition not only from cast mates Caan and Duvall but also from Eddie Albert for *The Heartbreak Kid* and the eventual winner, Joel Grey for *Cabaret*. When Brando won Best Actor, he created a sensation by having a Native American representative, Sacheen Littlefeather, refuse the Oscar on his behalf as a protest against America's treatment of its native citizens.

Brando also emerged the clear winner in monetary terms. Although he had been given only a token $50,000 salary for his role, and $100,000 more for his cooperation with publicity, a sliding-scale percentage of the movie's gross eventually landed him $1.5 million. And while Paramount claimed 84 percent of the profits, Ruddy 7.5 percent, Coppola 6 percent and Puzo 2.5

percent, Pacino's salary, by contrast, amounted to precisely $35,000, for a year's work.

But he had made his breakthrough. He was still only thirty-two years old, and the world was at his feet. As a bonus he had reestablished contact with his father, Salvatore, now resident in California and on his fourth marriage. In the company of Diane Keaton he also met his three half sisters for the first time.

Over the years Pacino had occasionally harbored deep resentment against his father, the bitterness at its peak through the fallow sixties, when he felt the need to expend that negative energy. Intellectually the only salve he could apply to the scars that still lingered was the knowledge that he was not the one his father had left.

After the visit there were signs of a new, lighter Pacino desperately trying to emerge. For every jest, however, the haunted side of his nature continued to struggle for domination. After he described himself to one reporter as "a Taurus/Aries cusp, with a moon in Sagittarius and a cow in Kansas," he felt obliged to add, "Success is relative, and I find it relatively frightening."

We'll spare the blushes of one well-known show biz observer by quoting his words but withholding his name. "No one doubts that *The Godfather* has opened all doors for Pacino," he wrote, "but it's unlikely that leading man roles will come his way. For one thing, he's too small at 5'7"; for another, he's no Paul Newman lookalike. His nose is too big and his skin is too pale. Maybe that worked wonders for Barbra Streisand. But Pacino can't sing either!"

CHAPTER 8

CRYBABY

Pacino opted to return to his first love, the theater, where his craft had been learned, after the frantic year spent making *The Godfather.* "I like doing both plays and movies," he explained, "but I'm not *crazy* about making movies. I don't want to sound pretentious. I've seen other actors, really fine actors, who prefer films. It's just a personal thing with me. I don't necessarily think the theater is better than film. I guess it's just that I haven't found my real *raison* for doing film. I mean, you learn something from it, but when I walk across the street and the camera follows me, it seems silly, I don't know why. Films are fragmented; they don't challenge you the way the stage does. I'll keep on making them, though, because I know they've helped me a lot."

One of the disadvantages of film that struck Pacino forcibly was having to watch his own performance and criticize it without the ability to change anything. Pacino saw film performances as butterflies trapped in amber, unlike the situation on-stage, where a performance was constantly fluid. Veteran Ethel Barrymore had detected as much difference between stage and films as between a piano and a violin and asserted that few performers could be adept at both. A generation later, following her stint in movies with *Come Back, Little Sheba*, Broadway's Shirley Booth quantified the main difference she found. "In the theater," she declared, "the audience is fifty percent of the performance."

In 1971 playright David Rabe's work had been introduced at Joseph Papp's Public Theater in New York with *The Basic Training of Pavlo Hummel*, which portrayed the travails of Vietnam conscripts, in particular the all-American foul-up Hummel. Pacino joined the Theater Company in Boston for a revival of the play early in 1972, under David Wheeler's direction, demonstrating his enthusiasm, amid rumors that the company was in dire financial straits, by working for two-hundred-dollars-a-week scale. At first Pacino and Wheeler had discussed the possibility of either reviving Bertolt Brecht's *The Resistible Rise of Arturo Ui* or a contemporary treatment of *Macbeth* but had abandoned both ideas when they ran into adaptation problems. When Wheeler suggested *Hummel*, Pacino attended Joe Papp's production and fell in love with the play. He recognized a lot of himself in Hummel. In place of his childhood saga of being a Texan dog owner, Hummel had his own howler, claiming an uncle on death row no less.

He saw the character of Hummel as complex and enigmatic, a man undergoing a complete personality refit from the beginning of the play to the end, a simpleminded, underdeveloped youngster maturing during his tour of army duty. By succeeding in fulfilling the army's expectation, he seems to have been exploited by the establishment. Or has he? Wasn't Hummel's "to-the-letter" compliance his own way of dealing with being cynically converted to cannon fodder?

Wheeler proceeded to put together a remarkably strong company for the revival, including New York actors Barry Snider, Walter Lott, Jack Kehoe, Lance Henriksen and Richard Lynch, with most of whom Pacino had worked and would work again.

During the run Pacino and Clayburgh were housed in a

rented apartment overlooking Boston Common. With the early-afternoon sunshine hitting the pile of submitted movie scripts lying on his study desk, Pacino openly reveled in his newfound clout. "I've always been interested in the artistic struggle," he said, "but I feel now as if I can be more interested. I've always said, 'Forget the career, do the work.' If you feel what you are doing is on the line, and you're going someplace and you have a vision and you stay with it, eventually things will happen. I'm a perfect example; I've been acting for years. But now I can do something. If I want to do a play, I can do it. I wanted to come to Boston to do this play, and somehow the play got done, we got money for the production. An audience came. There was a name they came to see."

With *The Godfather* just beginning its release, and Pacino's breakthrough to the public at large still several months distant, some performances were in fact attended by fewer than a hundred patrons.

Lured by Boston critic Elliott Norton's assertion that Pacino's Hummel "gave people a reason to return to the theater," reporter Chris Chase doggedly made his way to Massachusetts to check out the performance. Unexpectedly he encountered a situation that seemed calculated to ward off visitors. His hotel booklet had the play being performed out in Cambridge, yet when he tried the number listed, a recording indicated that the telephone had been disconnected at the customer's request. "Terrific," Chase fumed. "Greta Garbo's doing their publicity!"

Inquiries later revealed that the play was being housed in a small theater in Boston off an alley behind the Shubert Theater. The boy who answered the phone told Chase he didn't know if there was a Sunday performance. "If you want to see the play, you can't," Pacino laughed when Chase finally caught up with him. "That's the Theater Company of Boston!"

Chase had seen Pacino's Michael Corleone as a refinement of both his Murph and Bickham, still snake-eyed and dangerous despite the added dimension of sex appeal. Between the calculating Corleone and the eager superschnook Hummel, there lay a world of difference, bridged, in his estimation, by a virtuoso. He was reminded of an earlier comment of critic Clive Barnes after viewing *Does a Tiger Wear a Necktie?*: "I would like to see what else Pacino can do in this world besides scaring babies, old women and me." According to Chase, "what else" was currently playing in Boston.

"This play's the best thing that has happened to me in years," Pacino told Chase, who nonetheless put to him that he could be elsewhere, making fortunes on movies that would be seen by millions, rather than in a remote theater in an offbeat play. "Sure I could," Pacino countered. "But the core of the actor's craft, the real expression, comes onstage."

As Pacino waited in the wings ready to go on one night, it dawned on him, like a blinding revelation on the road to Damascus, why he liked to act. Here was a profession in which he could play a rookie soldier, a drug dealer, a psychopath, a Mafia overlord; there was no limit to the possibilities. And the play or film might be set at any time from the dawn of history through the Shakespearean era right up to the present, even into the future, limited only by the power of his own imagination. He thought of Laurence Olivier's *Henry V*, in which, before one of the actors goes on, he gives a little burp. "You see the whole thing," Pacino realized, "that he drank the night before, that he'll straighten up, go out there, make his first stroke, and that this is his whole life.

"My God, this is it," Pacino said to himself. "This is what it's going to be because this is what I want to do. *This* is my life."

He was unequivocal about the impact the characters he played made on his own psyche: "I don't see how they *can't*. I mean, you're living a part, and you try to absorb as much as you can. You're *thinking* in terms of the character. Actors have to keep these emotions alive, they have to take chances, and it makes for problems, neuroses." Fine, his friends agreed, but not something to be indulged in to excess. Remarks like "Jesus, Al, *relax*, it's only rock 'n' roll after all" went completely over Pacino's head.

The laying bare of emotions he was unable to expose in real

life demanded soothing, copious shots of alcohol after each performance. "I *need* that drink after the show," he insisted. "I really need it."

A local actor commented that Pacino had truly become a member of the company during Hummel's run, while remaining a totally private person. One of the cast, like Chris Chase before him, had the temerity to ask what he was doing in Boston performing to tiny audiences when he had so much going for him. "I'm an actor," he replied with a quiet smile and without the slightest trace of affectation. "I came to do a show. We are acting here."

During the run of *Hummel* the lectures he gave at Harvard University took him right back to his rebellion against discipline and authority, forcibly reminding him of his own school's confining atmosphere. Just as hard to take, as well as a throwback to an earlier reaction to having the law laid down, was a simple encounter with a driving instructor. "He was a perfectly nice guy," Pacino admitted, "but he's telling me what to do. After the lesson, I'm depressed, I'm out of my mind. *I've been told what to do*. I think I have a bit of a problem there."

Michael Hadge decided to tease his old friend a little about his movie success. "Al, what are you doing back in the theater?" he asked. "After all, you're a big movie star now!"

Pacino knew his leg was being pulled. "Michael," he said, fixing him with an amused stare, "I told you before the theater is my yacht. And I've no intention of giving up my yacht."

PACINO AND BREGMAN's decision to reunite with director Jerry Schatzberg for the star's next movie was taken only after director Mark Rydell had dropped out. This time they were working on a budget several times that of *Panic in Needle Park*, and for a major studio, Warner Bros. The move proved something of a step sideways.

Los Angeles playwright Garry Michael White's screenplay, "engineered" by Bregman into a "go" at Warner's, depicted the meeting of two gentlemen of the road. Pacino was cast as

Lionel, "the Lion," an almost feebleminded sailor making his way home after five years to visit the child born since his departure. Dustin Hoffman's early-days roommate Gene Hackman was Max, a violent ex-con with business aspirations. "That's a life I don't know," Pacino said of his role, "and I'm looking for what I can find out about that life through playing it." The actors spent a week together to get the feel of their parts, dressed in castoffs and soliciting handouts on the streets of San Francisco.

Pacino's joy in discovering that the movie would be shot in absolute continuity, as well as in having Laughton's wife, Penny, in the cast, was mitigated by the chill that soon developed with his costar. Much as he admired Hackman as an actor, there was no camaraderie between them. "Gene and I are two people not very similar," he noted. "We had to play a very close relationship, but I just didn't think we were as connected as we should have been. We seemed apart. We didn't have altercations, but we didn't communicate, didn't think in the same terms. We didn't *hate* each other, but I had a stronger connection to Brando. Gene and I were thrown together, but under ordinary circumstances we'd never cavort or be friends. It was two worlds—but I have to say that I was as much responsible as he was."

Reading between the lines of this movie speak, one may discern that there were in fact *constant* altercations among Pacino, Hackman *and* Schatzberg—in between the bouts of silence, that is. One of the reasons may be that in *Scarecrow* Hackman indisputedly had the showier role and therefore stood a far greater chance of dominating the film than Pacino. (Hackman later included *Scarecrow* in his list of favorite movies.)

Max's taunt to Lionel, "You're not playing with a full deck, you've got one foot in the great beyond," held resonances for Pacino outside the script, since Lionel's passivity began its spectacular descent into catatonia only near the movie's climax. In one scene Hackman all but consumes the furniture as he hilariously performs a striptease, coyly removing endless items of his on-the-road apparel, while the other occupants of the bar cheer him on—and Pacino beholds the spectacle disbelievingly. "Why ain't I doin' that?" his bemused expression seems to suggest.

Pacino still managed to turn in a heartbreaking performance as the simple, easy-to-please Lionel, sporting an eager smile that would yield him coffee and a Danish at any door, yet forever doomed to be the innocent foil and tragic victim.

Most U.S. critics deemed *Scarecrow* a pretentious plod, chock-full of heavy-handed symbolism. "This crow ain't for eatin'," Judith Crist headlined in *New York* magazine. "The script is phony from word one," Stanley Kauffman agreed in the *New Republic*. David Thomson described its attempt at "poetic hoboism" as "a solemn disaster." On the other hand, Charles Champlin of the Los Angeles *Times* hailed it as "one of the new year's best movies" and lauded the "astonishing performances" by Hackman and Pacino.

The cast emerged not only unscathed but with considerable credit. Crist described Gene Hackman as "a master of timing" and found Pacino "completely endearing." Throughout his career, she pointed out, he had been blighted as "a second Dustin Hoffman," but in *Scarecrow* she found him "more Hoffmanish than ever before—but this is no denigration—he makes the role very much his own." Penny Allen she found "superb." Don Lyon praised both Hackman and Pacino for their "excellent performances."

"Hackman takes over the script," *Cosmopolitan* still thought, unwittingly echoing his costar's thoughts during filming, "and Pacino is left with very little to do." *Time* magazine concurred: "Hackman's fine . . . but he gets in so far that no other actor can reach him. Pacino's characterization remains unresolved. The two never really react off each other because Hackman remains self-absorbed."

Audiences stayed away from what came to be regarded as an art house movie. It nonetheless went on to garner a considerable degree of critical recognition outside America, sharing the Palme d'Or at Cannes in 1973 with *The Hireling*, while faring no better commercially than on its home turf. (Both the awards, it was pointed out, owed much to the performances.) The main souvenir Pacino took from *Scarecrow* was Lionel's prison shoes, which he wore until they fell apart. As Pacino put it, "They walked away and said, 'I'm tired of you.'"

IT WAS BACK to the stage after *Scarecrow*, working once more for scale with David Wheeler at the Theater Company of Boston. This time Shakespeare was on the bill, Pacino's first attempt at the bard. When the production of *Richard III* he was heading failed to work satisfactorily, the company moved to a local church. There it really took off, with up to three hundred people congregating at each performance. Again Pacino proved his dedication; although sick with the flu and seeing double, he missed only the final run-through rehearsal. Critical reaction was mixed. "One of the most credible—and creditable Richard IIIs ever to limp his way across the stage," one review ran. Others were less flattering.

Since the notion of himself as an actor of ever-expanding capabilities clearly appealed to Pacino, as it would to any emerging artist, the leap he had made from the relative monosyllabism of Michael Corleone to the glories of Shakespearean text was particularly thrilling, as was his second return to the stage after striking movie fame. "I have a very strong musical sense," he told another brave reporter who had battled his way through the wilds of Massachusetts, "and in a movie, there's no chance for that rhythm to build. I really feel that I was meant to compose music, and in a different environment I might have done it. It's still my first love, by far. I know more about music than I know about what's happening in the theater. That's why I love Shakespeare, because I can get into a rhythm of the words and the whole rhythm of the thing. I fear doing things in translation, because words are notes to me and I play them. This is an area of myself nobody knows about. Michael Corleone didn't have many words."

PACINO'S PARRYING OF the question of marriage to Clayburgh became increasingly confused. "I don't entertain thoughts of marriage," he told one scribe. "If it comes, it'll come. I've always known I'd want children, but lately it's been with me a lot. I even think about adopting. I'd have ten kids, make 'em all actors too. Life goes on, it happens, we'll just have to give it room to breathe." To another reporter: "Yes, I'd like to marry Jill and have children, or maybe we'd adopt them. Or it's possible we'd have children without marrying."

As if in answer to the puzzled expression his contradictory remarks produced, he admitted there were quite a few items about which he himself was unclear. "But while I'm thinking about them," he suggested, "what do you say about having another drink?"

When he finally reached the point at which he refused to discuss their affair, friends read between the lines and drew their own conclusions. "Even in the good articles," he complained, "the writer throws a light on the relationship that just isn't there. For want of a better word, the article *distorts* the relationship. And it's upsetting to both of us. Because, you know, we do our business, we have our thing, and we have our feelings, and suddenly, it's in public—the public knows about it, and that has a way of affecting the relationship. And I value it too much at this point. I don't want to sound like a crybaby, but it's not fair to Jill."

After five years of living together, and with the ink barely dry on this interview, Pacino and Clayburgh split up in 1972, torn apart by their careers, Pacino's success in particular and personal problems that had developed in their relationship.

Pacino is the first to acknowledge his own culpability. "I wasn't very aware of things at thirty-two," he concedes. "It was like swimming, like trying to get out of a barrel."

While Pacino had rocketed to success, Clayburgh's career had progressed in fits and starts. She had scored on the New York stage in *The Rothschilds* and *Pippin* before being called to

Los Angeles for her first major movie role in *Portnoy's Complaint*. In California she agreed to appear as Desdemona to James Earl Jones's Othello. "It was a troubled time in my life," she recalls, "and not one in which I did my best work." With the breakup imminent, friends "close to Al" had the temerity to inform her she was a mediocre actress and "should stick to soap opera."

Following the disastrous opening of *Othello*, she went to her manager in tears and told him she intended to give up acting. "I can't imagine what those 'friends' had in mind," says one close associate, "except to show Al they were on his side. As for poor Jill, her confidence was shattered; she never knew what happened." Although the end was characterized as "painful," there was one ray of sunshine on the horizon for Clayburgh—*Hummel*'s author, David Rabe.

"He fell in love with Jill when I was with her," Pacino said later, adding that he was unsure whether Clayburgh herself was aware of the attraction at the time. "I don't know. She didn't tell me. I guess she didn't know." By his own account Pacino had been "half in the bag" with Clayburgh, yet unable or unwilling to continue. "I said, 'My professional life is going to go fine, that's clear, but the personal stuff, that relationship isn't going to last.' At a particular point I understood that there was something in myself that was lacking."

"I'm feeling sad about it," said Clayburgh. "It was not my wish to part. I was happy enough, but that's the way things go."

The talk around town was that Pacino had jilted Clayburgh, led astray by a new love, the blond actress Tuesday Weld. Although there is no record of who led whom, Pacino was but the latest figure in a long line of turbulent love affairs Weld had conducted since her emergence in the fifties as the latest "teen sensation" in *Rock, Rock, Rock!*. He found himself with a tiger by the tail.

Even before her teens Weld had claimed a nervous breakdown at nine, heavy drinking at ten and a suicide attempt at twelve. "As a teenager I was a wreck," she admits. "I drank so much I can't remember anything. My teens passed by in drink." She had brawled publicly with an early Hollywood beau, John Barrymore, Jr., and tried to run down another, Gary Lockwood, speeding down Sunset Boulevard with him clinging to the hood. "Tuesday's done some wild, wild things," said one longtime friend, "and screwed up many, many guys. She's highly sexual." With a career perpetually on the verge of happening, Weld finally achieved critical acclaim in Noel Black's *Pretty Poison* in 1968 and *Play It As It Lays* in 1972, for which she garnered the Best Actress award at the Venice Film Festival. For the most part the rest of her movies are best forgotten. "No actress," says another friend, and her costar in *Lord Love a Duck*, Roddy McDowall, "was ever so good in so many bad films."

In a determined effort to sort herself out after a failed six-year marriage to writer Claude Harz, dissolved in 1971, and the birth of a daughter, Natasha, in 1968, Weld had tried hypnosis, psychotherapy and psychoanalysis. Now, it seemed, she was trying Pacino. "We're very much in love," he continually reassured friends, and perhaps himself, Clayburgh apparently forgotten. "Tuesday's good for me. I'm the kind of guy who's always needed to have a woman around. I guess it's the companionship I like."

Their idyll together, if yet another union of the walking wounded can be so described, was short-lived. Pianist actor-comedian Dudley Moore had taken over within a year, rekindling an affair that had begun with a one-night stand a decade earlier; this time it culminated, for a while, in marriage. Pacino's views on the marital state began to sound ever more militant. "I don't understand the officialdom behind it, the law behind it," he declared. "I don't believe that's a commitment. You know what Brecht said, 'Who will protect us from our protectors?' Not that I'm married to *not* being married. If I have kids, I'll get married. And I do love kids."

Sally Kirkland, Pacino's friend from his struggling Off-Broadway period, together with old flame Susan Tyrrell—nominated for Best Supporting Actress for her performance in

John Huston's *Fat City*—and Candy Darling, threw a party for
him after the opening of *The Godfather*. "There were five hundred people there," Kirkland recalls, "and every single girl
came to look at Al Pacino, to try to get a shot at him. Let me
tell you, women find Al fantastically sexy. It's sort of incredible
when you think about it, that this little guy should be so sexy.
But believe me, it's true." (At an earlier bash security men had
been alerted that two bums were outside talking in the bushes.
They turned out to be Pacino and Bobby De Niro.)

PACINO MADE UP his mind to dispense with the services of the
agents who had advised him to forget about *The Godfather* and
make *The Gang That Couldn't Shoot Straight* instead. After a
decent interval he set about appointing new and, he hoped,
more prescient representatives. "Can I speak to someone in
charge?" he asked the lady who answered his call at William
Morris. "I'm looking for an agent," he added.

"Oh," she said. "What's your name?"

"Al Pacino."

"Are you *sure*?" she asked.

For someone with a rapidly emerging identity crisis, the
question was a tough one.

CHAPTER 9

"TO THE DOOR"

B Y THE EARLY seventies Marty Bregman, at one time or another business manager to Barbra Streisand, Raquel Welch, Diahann Carroll, Sandy Dennis, Bernadette Peters, Faye Dunaway, Liza Minnelli, Woody Allen, Michael Douglas and Alan Alda, as well as Pacino and several producers and directors, was securely installed as head of Artists Entertainment Complex. The public company was devoted to investing in and producing motion pictures, together with furthering Bregman's own production ambitions. Already the company had Raquel Welch's *Kansas City Bomber* under its belt, an unpretentious but profitable start.

To follow Pacino's enormous success in *The Godfather*, Bregman had in mind an adaptation of Peter Maas's *Serpico*, the account of New York cop Frank Serpico's fight against police corruption that had culminated in the setting up of the Knapp Commission. Maas had scared off all the major studios by demanding $450,000 ahead of publication for the movie rights to his book. Bregman hawked the project, still in outline form, the length and breadth of Hollywood. Since the movie was at the end of a long line of cop movies produced over the previous two years, he found no takers. Ultimately only the court of last resort was left—the volatile independent Italian entrepreneur Dino de Laurentiis, who had produced *The Valachi Papers*, the movie adaptation of Maas's last book.

Unknown to Bregman, the recent émigré was financially on his ass, deep in serious problems with Dinocittà, the studio he had left behind in Rome, and persona non grata with the Italian government. De Laurentiis's answer to Bregman's submission was to persuade Charles Bluhdorn at Paramount, one of the studios that had already turned him down, to pick up the tab, for both the book and the production of the movie. He succeeded where Bregman had failed because of the extraordinarily close personal relationship he had with Bluhdorn, the type of powerful connection the fledgling producer Bregman could only dream of at that stage.

With a budget set at a tight three million dollars, de Laurentiis became Bregman's "production company," to all intents and purposes his "studio," his conduit to Paramount—and the source of their profit points, if any materialized. On his ass or not, de Laurentiis negotiated a terrific deal with Paramount in which he and his partners were to share 50 percent of the gross rental from the first dollar *Serpico* earned.

(Just for the record, de Laurentiis's long-discounted version of the story, which features a prize for anyone who can trace any mention of Bregman's involvement, is that he was at the rough-cut stage with *The Valachi Papers* when he phoned Maas. "Peter, what are you working on now?" he claims to have asked. *"Serpico,"* came the reply. De Laurentiis's interest was "instantly piqued." "An Italian name, no? What is it about?" Although Maas had only a few pages written, the much-vaunted "outline," de Laurentiis insisted on reading it. There and then he claims to have offered Maas $450,000 for the movie rights. "Dino, are you crazy?" Maas asked him. "Look," was the reply. "Why take a chance? If the book is no good, what then? Take the money!" [Even as he spoke he was thinking, "If it's no good, I change it!"] The version according to Dino de Laurentiis is that Maas sold him the rights that very afternoon. "Only de Laurentiis can make a decision like that," he said of the incident.)

Back in the real world, Bregman had already more or less sold Pacino on *Serpico*, on the basis of just a story outline. The deciding factor was a meeting Pacino had with Frank Serpico in New York. The moment he shook his hand and looked into his eyes, Pacino understood what the movie could be. Peter Maas watched, gratified, as the two men interacted. "Within twenty minutes," he marveled, "Al was absorbing Serpico through his pores. It was like he was inhaling the guy!" What clinched it for Pacino was the slice of the action, on top of his salary, that Bregman dangled.

Pacino and Serpico spent several days together in a house the actor had rented in Montauk, Long Island, for the summer. Pacino found himself fascinated by the ex-cop, but nothing he had read in the book or in Bregman's outline had satisfactorily explained to him why a man would throw away his career and security by blowing the whistle on his colleagues. One evening, when the two of them were sitting at the lakeside, gazing out over the still water, Pacino decided to put the question. *"Why, Frank?"* he asked. *"Why did you do it?"*

"Well, Al, I don't know," Serpico whispered. "I guess I would have to say it would be because . . . if I didn't, who would I be when I listened to a piece of music?" Pacino was bowled over by the reply and became more than ever committed to making the movie.

WHILE IN MONTAUK, Pacino came up against another consequence of his newfound fame. When he visited a local store to purchase a table, the owner invited him to charge everything. "Anything you want," she told him, "charge." Pacino had never charged anything in his life and was nonplussed. "Fill out an application," she urged.

"Well, I don't feel like it," he replied, hedging. "Why don't I take it home and fill it out? I just don't feel like writing my name down and doing it now." Pacino reflected that it was perhaps fortunate that the big bucks had failed to materialize earlier in his career. Now, in his early thirties, he was better able to handle his finances.

The way he avoided being overwhelmed by material possessions was to keep his eye on more important matters. "Things that are more personal," he said in explanation. "Work is one. I don't know yet; this is beginning for me. I don't know what the hell is going to happen. I've got a lot of money, and more's gonna come. You know, I could say to my uncle Frank, 'What do you need?' and that's a good feeling. I don't get my cookies from it, but it makes me feel good."

NOW BREGMAN NEEDED a script; Waldo Salt was set to work. The star's initial reaction was unfavorable; he, Bregman, Maas and de Laurentiis did not consider the first-draft screenplay satisfactory. They seemed to be stuck with the Salt of *The Gang That Couldn't Shoot Straight* (which had turned out disastrously) rather than the Oscar-winning writer of *Midnight Cowboy.* "To me, Salt's first screenplay made no sense," says Bregman. "It was very political and had very little to do with the story we wanted to tell. At a meeting between myself and Salt I had him go back and start from scratch. He never forgave me for that. I brought Peter Maas in; we outlined these elements in the book that we wanted Salt to bring out in his screenplay." Although the second draft was a considerable improvement, to Bregman it still refused to "sing."

For a while Pacino's attention was diverted by an offer from Bob Fosse to star in his movie adaptation of *Lenny*, Julian Barry's account of the turbulent life of comedian Lenny Bruce. When he chose to turn it down, after a considerable amount of dickering, the ubiquitous Dustin Hoffman seized the opportunity.

The director de Laurentiis and Bregman initially chose for *Serpico* was John G. Avildsen, who had made his name with the Peter Boyle vehicle *Joe*. Unfortunately Avildsen and Waldo

Salt failed to meld satisfactorily, on either a personal or an artistic level. Matters reached a head when Avildsen threatened to withdraw. In an effort at appeasement Bregman allowed the director to call upon the services of Norman Wexler, his writer on *Joe*, to "adjust" Salt's screenplay. Avildsen and Wexler were dispatched to Switzerland to spend a week with the self-exiled Frank Serpico. With the adrenaline flowing freely, a new treatment was hacked out.

Two months before production was due to start—the timing strictly mandated by the impending *Godfather II*—Avildsen began to threaten to walk out every time Bregman disagreed with him. "I made a decision I did not want to make the film with Avildsen" is Bregman's recollection. "I told Al, and he said he wouldn't make the movie without me. Avildsen and I totally disagreed about many, many things. We were having big problems with the script and getting close to our production date, and he hadn't made a single decision. The crunch came over the choice of locations. I told Dino he had to replace him and arrange a meeting where he would quit—but in front of several witnesses."

For authenticity, Avildsen wanted to film inside Serpico's parents' original Brooklyn apartment. Bregman scheduled a meeting at de Laurentiis's offices with Avildsen to sort the matter out once and for all. De Laurentiis sat at one end of a long boardroom table, flanked by several enormous Italian associates. The spaghetti bolognese started to sizzle as Bregman pointed out that Serpico's ex-home was far too cramped as well as too frail to support the crew and equipment that would be required. "His apartment is *not* the Arc de Triomphe!" de Laurentiis boomed to an increasingly agitated Avildsen. "It is *not* the Champs Élysées! No one will know the difference!"

Avildsen stood up and, as was his wont, launched into the third person. *"Avildsen* decides where he shoots his pictures," he yelled. "If Avildsen decides to shoot in Serpico's pad"—so saying, he pointed his index finger heavenward—"Avildsen *shoots* in Serpico's pad. *Avildsen* decides locations! Not you"—

the finger was jabbed at Bregman—"and certainly"—now it was the startled de Laurentiis's turn—"not *you!*"

De Laurentiis decided that a spot of reciprocal digital calisthenics was in order. Drawing himself up to his full height, though still dwarfed by his seated associates, he extended his own index weapon at Avildsen and intoned, *"To the door!"*

"Fuck you! I quit!" was Avildsen's parting shot as he stormed out.

Bregman swears Avildsen's agent had a telegram on his desk terminating their association by the time his client hit the ground floor. The expertly programmed meeting had produced exactly the desired result. With equal dexterity a "hired gun" replacement director was drafted in.

Bregman's choice of Sidney Lumet was nothing if not adventurous, as well as expeditious. A small, energetic, determinedly good-humored bundle, whose film career stretched all the way back to *Twelve Angry Men*, 1956's taut courtroom drama, Lumet was the son of Baruch Lumet, a distinguished member of the New York Yiddish theater, who had read his son *Hamlet* when he was six years old—in Yiddish! Young Sidney became a radio actor in 1928 at the age of four, attending a school for professional children where the pupils earned more than the teachers. In 1935, already the veteran of eight Yiddish plays, he acted in Sidney Kingsley's *Dead End*. Because Lumet was too small for his age to play one of the Dead End Kids, Kingsley wrote Lumet's role specifically for him.

After World War II Lumet made the leap from acting to directing for both TV and Off-Broadway shows, his TV adaptation of O'Neill's *The Iceman Cometh* receiving special praise. *Twelve Angry Men* was followed by the film version of Tennessee Williams's *Orpheus Descending*, retitled *The Fugitive Kind*, and starring Marlon Brando, Anna Magnani and Joanne Woodward. *The Pawnbroker*, featuring an award-winning performance by Rod Steiger, was another Lumet landmark. Although commercial success in movies had thus far eluded him, his reputation as a "get-the-job-done" professional and a skillful handler of actors was second to none. And the buzz was good on his most recent assignment, *The Anderson Tapes*, featuring Sean Connery.

Lumet was never given details of the falling-out with Avildsen and chose not to inquire too closely. He had a movie to make, and when Lumet is "on the case," the job is the job. Luckily he knew New York's locations like the back of his hand. "I knew that shooting *Serpico* was going to be physically brutal and emotionally tough," he recalls, "but I was determined to get all that intensity up there on the screen."

Pacino's absorption in his role was so complete that he tried to arrest a truck driver halfway through shooting. The incident began one cruelly hot New York afternoon while he was in a taxi, stuck behind a truck pouring out exhaust fumes. "Why are you putting that crap in the street?" Pacino yelled.

"Who the hell are you?" the driver yelled back.

"I'm a cop," Pacino claimed, "and you're under arrest. Pull over!"

The fantasy lasted only until Pacino extracted his Serpico badge and mumbled something about a citizen's arrest.

Later he was refused a table in his favorite New York restaurant when he turned up in Serpicos "hippie" regalia, the deferential treatment he had received up until then strictly off the menu. He made little fuss because the incident perfectly summed up the dilemma he perceived in stardom. "Right now," he said, "I'm trying to work out how to be a star and at the same time manage to live a quiet life. That's important to me. The only part that really counts away from the camera is how I play Al Pacino. The fringe benefits of stardom leave me cold."

With 107 speaking parts and an almost identical number of Gotham-based locations (one of which was playwright Sidney Kingsley's Fifth Avenue loft, used for a party scene, as well as Harlem, Bedford-Stuyvesant and, close to home for Pacino, the South Bronx), Lumet wrapped *Serpico* in a remarkable fifty-one days, right on budget.

Always a director who responds to social protest and moral fervor in his subjects, Lumet was, and remains, wholehearted in his praise for Pacino: "Al felt the same sense of obligation to the material that I did, which was part of the reason for his sensational performance. The other part is built into him as an actor. There are only a handful of actors who are literally incapable of doing anything false, and Al is one of them. He never says, 'I can't do what you ask because it would not be true to me.' He simply gets into a character and doesn't come out.

"He's a complicated man and uses himself brilliantly, so there's complexity in everything he does. He is an instinctive animal but makes slow decisions. Maybe it's because he's a street person that he likes to keep his options open. He is totally consuming, totally committed, and you have to match his dedication. He doesn't give a damn for anything; he just wants to do good work.

"I know very little about his life. I never ask personal questions. One of my cardinal rules is never to invade the actor personally. If he's got sexual problems, hang-ups, whatever, I don't want to know about it, and I certainly don't want to use it. If he's got problems about knowing who he is, the same. I want to work it out of craft, and if we can't do that, fuck it. I never ask personal questions. The little Al has volunteered, like being in the house alone for years, being brought up by his grandmother, that's all I know—and that I could work with him forever."

The female point of view was presented by Barbara Eda-Young, a cast member Pacino had worked with before at the Lincoln Center Repertory Theater. "Al's a very easy guy to like," she declared, "warm and friendly, not at all as serious offscreen as he seems on. But he isn't simple; he's a very complicated person. He's a self-involved, inner-directed man. That's as it should be for an actor, but it's also the reason why I'd rather work with him than live with him!"

EARLY IN 1973 Pacino had uncharacteristically chosen to ruminate on his sex life. "I've always been partial to girls," he admitted. "Women brought me up. When I was younger, I had fantasies of being sought after by the world's most glamorous women. Sure, there are starfuckers. My experience is that you can go with something like that, it can be very tempting. But I take a *relationship* seriously. I'm a romantic. And somewhere along the line, deceit sets in. It's not the act of fucking, it's the giving of *oneself* that's deceitful. I've never been terribly attracted to that. I've had it happen where a woman comes up to me and says, 'I want to go to bed with you.' I'd say something like 'I'm flattered, you're very nice yourself.' "

Pacino broke into a grin at this point. "You know, maybe I'm paranoid, but I have to say it, there's something really hostile when a woman does a thing like that. In many respects they frighten me. They are not liberated. They are the opposite. They are slaves to something they cannot control."

With *Serpico* completed, he chose to unburden himself further in the fall of 1973, when he was discovered valiantly knocking back vodkas in the relative anonymity of New York's Downey's restaurant. Clad in a wide-brimmed beach hat, sandals and a muted print shirt, he still affected Serpico's thick black beard and mustache. "I had a thing with Tuesday Weld," he acknowledged, "but it's over now. Let's just say that Tuesday Weld is now my favorite *drink*. Sometimes I walk into a bar and really throw the bartender by ordering a Tuesday Weld. It's something I invented, a Brandy Alexander poured over an Oreo cookie. Tuesday and I used to laugh a lot about that.

"You know," he continued, "it's amazing what a cloistered life I lead. I don't go to many parties, and when I'm working, who is it that I meet? *Actresses.* Every time I get started with an actress I say, 'Hey, maybe we shouldn't enter into this.' Then I get that classic thing where they'll say, 'I'll give up acting.' Then I say, 'What the devil do you mean? Don't give up anything for me.' What I'd really like to do is meet a sculptress. I've lived with women since I was sixteen, and they all seem to have been actresses."

Pacino mourned the end of a relatively carefree era in his life. "When I was young, I'd walk down the street, see an attractive girl and start to follow her. Sometimes I'd catch up with her, we'd look at each other and before long I'd be making out. I haven't done that for a few years because everyone who does that sort of thing has got to be crazy, right? But just recently I spotted this really beautiful girl, and I decided to see how far I could get with her. We reached a stoplight together. I looked over at her, gave her a big smile and said hello.

" 'Hiya, Michael,' she said. It was then that I knew it was all over for me. I slunk off and tried to hide behind a building, but the girl followed me. 'Come on out, Michael,' she said. 'No,' I answered, 'it's all over.' 'What do you mean, it's all over? It's just beginning,' she said. 'No, you're making a big mistake,' I told her. 'I'm *not* Michael Corleone!' "

Pacino swallowed his final vodka, smiled and pushed a tip across the counter for Downey's barman. "I don't think you'll be seeing me in too many movies," was his parting shot as he got up to leave. "I still want to play Hamlet, and time's running out." Then he turned at the door and shrugged. "Ah, hell," he muttered, "who wants to play Hamlet? I just want to go home to bed."

The women who waited around when Pacino got home at night, and constantly phoned him, served only to deepen the identity crisis he had delineated. He wanted to remain Al Pacino, not Michael Corleone, and be desired for himself, not for the parts he played. What he failed to appreciate was how much worse the syndrome would become when he no longer had to compete with Michael Corleone alone—but with Al Pacino, superstar. Without mentioning names, he admitted to friends that one of the reasons he had broken up a long-term relationship was that the woman in question had insisted on splashing his pictures all over their bedroom walls.

Pacino's determination to assert his own identity continued in an encounter with a male admirer. In a restaurant bathroom one day the guy next to him looked around and said, "Hey, man, what's this? Michael Corleone taking a piss?"

"No," Pacino replied.

"You mean to tell me you're not Al Pacino?"

"Yes, I am," he admitted, "and *that's* who's taking a piss!"

CHAPTER 10

THE UNKINDEST CUT

SIDNEY LUMET VIVIDLY remembers viewing the final cut of *Serpico* with Pacino and Bregman and, seated alongside them, Dino de Laurentiis and his wife, Silvana Mangano. After the screening Silvana leaned across her husband to talk to Bregman. "It's brilliant," she told him, "but Martin, don't let him"—nodding at de Laurentiis—"touch one frame of it." Her husband beamed graciously, while Pacino, Bregman and Lumet laughed, a trifle nervously.

"I didn't have final cut in those days," says Lumet, "and I sensed trouble. I knew for sure there'd be trouble with the score. I didn't want any music at all, and I knew that Dino would take it back to Italy and get Nino Rota to score it, which would have been wrong for that movie. We got a tremendous break. Mikis Theodorakis was released from prison and flew to Paris. I got hold of him and explained the situation and asked him to come and see the picture. He arrived in New York at midnight and was leaving the next morning, and I screened the film for him at one A.M. on Forty-fourth Street. He took a cassette out of his pocket with a song he thought would be wonderful for the movie. He was just about to go on a four-month tour with his orchestra because he needed the cash and hadn't time to arrange the song, so I got the jazz musician Bob James to go on the road with him and do the score on his days off. It worked out perfectly, fourteen minutes of music, most of it at the beginning."

Bregman found himself with an even more formidable challenge to circumvent Dino. "He didn't understand all that political stuff with the Knapp Commission and wanted it all cut out," he says. "I went to see Paramount's Frank Yablans at his home in Westchester and put the problem to him. Thankfully Frank loved the movie as it was. We plotted together and decided to move the release date to December, locking in the opening, so Dino didn't have time to make the cuts. We put him in a box, *finessed* him."

Serpico was released on December 5, 1973, just three months after shooting ended, to generally enthusiastic reviews. Jerry Oster in New York's *Daily News* regarded *Serpico* as "a triumph of intelligence, compassion and style, an uncommon movie about an uncommon man." Particularly pleasing to Pacino was Oster's comment on his comedic skill, overlooked so often throughout his career: "He is a fine comedian, and when he's being funny he resembles Charlie Chaplin; his clothes seem too big all of a sudden and his feet are not where he expects them to be."

Vincent Canby in the New York *Times* saw *Serpico* as "a disquieting drama. Lumet and Pacino manage to suggest so many things about Serpico that we wish they could have enjoyed greater freedom in exploring the character of this unusual man."

OK so far, but lying in wait was Pauline Kael, the *New Yorker*'s great cat, who stealthily inched her way to the very last comment Pacino wanted to hear. "Pacino doesn't seem to have the moral conviction that would make us take his character seriously. His poker face and off-hand fast throwaways keep the character remote" was the opening. Worse was to come.

Kael conceded that Pacino was "chirpy and brisk" in the role, before pouncing on the fateful blot on his performance, the worm she detected at the apple's core. "He is often indistinguishable from Dustin Hoffman," she wrote. "He uses a high, nasal whine and wrangling New York speech, and as he got longer-haired and more bearded, I began to lose track of who it was under the foliage. There are scenes in which I actually thought I was watching Hoffman and had to remind myself it was Pacino."

Kael continued to pile insult upon insult. That Pacino had not "turned into Hoffman" in *The Godfather* was all due to Francis Ford Coppola, in her estimation: "He probably exercised more control over his actors than Lumet, whom many actors love to work with because he lets them do what they want. Without much guidance in *Serpico*, and with a short shooting schedule and a character who's written to be played on the surface, Pacino must have fallen back on hero-worship of Hoffman."

Pacino's reaction was predictable. "Why was she pissed off at me, I wonder?" he asked, clearly angry. "Sometimes the things that piss people off!" Then he calmed down. "Well, I piss myself off too sometimes," he admitted. "When I've seen myself on-screen from time to time, I've said, 'Who does he think he is, smirking like that?' or, 'Why doesn't he take a bath?' But *Serpico* seemed pretty good to me." As for Kael's Dustin Hoffman comparison, "Is that before she had the shot glass removed from her throat?" he asked.

Kathleen Carroll provided an element of common sense that demolished Kael's spurious comments. "Pacino gives a masterful performance," she declared. "He proves that, although there is a strong resemblance, he is no rubber stamp Dustin Hoffman. No longer does he have to stand in Hoffman's shadow. He is an important actor in his own right." Carroll was also perceptive enough to detect the similarities between Pacino and the character he portrayed. "With fellow humans, especially women, Serpico has difficulty sustaining relationships. Too often his intense preoccupation with his work gets in the way."

SERPICO WENT ON to become Pacino's personal launching pad. He was the star of a major commercial smash, the linchpin that had made the whole deal possible. It was also the first time he became interested in film as a medium: "With *Serpico* I was more on the *inside*. I found out how to *act* a scene, what you do when you *write* a scene, what it's like to work together with people like Lumet, Marty Bregman and the editor Dede Allen."

He gives extra credit to Bregman, maintaining that the movie was "completely his idea." Apart from being his triumphant debut as a major producer, the movie holds even greater significance for Bregman. During the shooting he fell in love with Cornelia Sharpe, who soon became the second Mrs. Bregman.

With the film still playing on Times Square, where the Paramount publicity machine had erected a building-size picture of Serpico's melancholy, brooding face that invoked comparisons with a pop art image of Christ, Pacino was asked how he felt about such hype. "I don't make the connection," he replied. "It's me, but it isn't me. *I'm* me—here. It's a picture of me blown up so all those people can go to see the movie."

"Here" was Bregman's Lexington Avenue offices, where reporter Helen Dudar was about to witness for herself the show biz world of three-minute intimacies. Just as Pacino was busy describing Lumet as "a director with an ear," in walked Lumet, bubbling over at the movie's success. The two men embraced and kissed cheeks soundly, in a decided mixture of both European and theatrical fashion. "You look beautiful," Pacino was told by a beaming Lumet.

"You look a little fat," Pacino replied, nodding with a sly smile at Lumet's tightly packed midriff section.

A few moments later Lumet was off to pack for Europe and his stint on *Murder on the Orient Express*.

Pacino relaxed and continued his interview with Dudar, who

observed his Salvation Army thrift shop attire with interest. He was wearing clean old jeans, a shiny brown shirt-blouse, a half day's growth of beard and a Winnie-the-Pooh gold emblem on a chain around his neck, a souvenir from *Serpico*. Plunked on his head was a bottle green knitted cap. The ensemble was topped off by a pair of silver-rimmed glasses.

In the middle of the conversation Bregman came barging in. "What's with the cap and glasses?" he wanted to know. "You won't like it when you see the photos!" Both were momentarily removed, although the cap was replaced a moment later. Pacino admitted that his outfit put the fear of death into storekeepers. When he was in one Fourteenth Street store to buy a sweater, the owner, fearful of a rip-off, followed him from bin to bin while Pacino raced up and down the aisles, grabbing sweaters. "I had four of them in my hands," he told Dudar, "and then I pulled fifty dollars out of my pocket to pay for them!"

As Pacino talked, he cradled a heavy black cane, a Christmas present from his actor friend Jack Kehoe. Slowly and dramatically he unscrewed the top, to reveal an empty test tube capable of holding several hefty belts of his liquor of choice. Bregman reentered, this time with a present of his own for Pacino, a computer wristwatch with an illuminated dial. "Al," he said, winking at Dudar, "just remember who made whom!" Pacino smiled. "He's always telling people he discovered *me*," Bregman explained.

Despite the festive levity and the fact that Pacino's professional career was in excellent shape, his personal life was rapidly developing into a shambles. An affair with Diane Keaton was on one minute, off the next. Even as he blithely agreed how heavily he was hitting the bottle, he masked the true extent of his continuing addiction. The pressure of living up to the image being created for him was becoming intolerable. He felt unable to relax or talk to anyone unless liquor was being offered. Bars, rather than sound stages or theaters, were his favorite places.

Nominated for Best Actor for his performance in *Serpico*—

no supporting role this time—Pacino attended the Academy Awards ceremony with Keaton and sat alongside Jeff Bridges and his companion. Up against Jack Lemmon for *Save the Tiger*, Jack Nicholson for *The Last Detail*, Robert Redford for *The Sting* and Marlon Brando for *Last Tango in Paris*, Pacino was highly nervous. He chewed Valium as if it were candy and tried desperately to affect a look of chilly indifference to cover his anxiety. With his hair unnaturally bobbed and teased for the occasion, Pacino not only looked odd but sounded it as well. "Hey, looks like there won't be time to get to the Best Actor awards," he gabbled to Bridges as the evening wore on. Bridges gave him a strange look. "Well, it's over, the hour's almost up," Pacino explained.

"The ceremony is three hours long," Bridges crisply informed him, deadpan.

Pacino felt like an idiot; he had watched only the TV-edited version of the Oscar evening before and had assumed an hour was all of it. By the time the Best Actor award was about to be announced, he was a nervous wreck, despite the Valium. And he was desperate to take a leak. "Please," he claims to have prayed, aware he would never make it to the podium, "don't let it be me." A feeling of tremendous relief swept over him as the winner, Jack Lemmon, was announced. Ironically, Lemmon's award-winning performance had been directed by John ("To the door!") Avildsen, prior to his brief flirtation with Pacino, Bregman, de Laurentiis and *Serpico*.

De Laurentiis provided a typical coda to *Serpico*'s enormous success. Bregman was astonished to find a budget of seven million dollars—not three million dollars—preceding the profit statement. What was this? Closer investigation revealed that the three-million-dollar budget had been padded out with an abundance of personal items, like furniture and paintings for de Laurentiis's apartment, as well as a massive "overhead figure" that had never been discussed, all of which served to decrease the profit points painstakingly negotiated by Bregman for himself, Pacino, Lumet, Maas and Dede Allen. "You can't do this," he told de Laurentiis.

"Sue me!" de Laurentiis coolly suggested.

Together with Pacino, Lumet and Allen—Maas declined involvement—Bregman proceeded to do just that. The case was settled out of court, heavily in favor of Bregman and his team. "*Serpico* was already a big score for Dino," he rationalizes. "He just wanted more."

A few weeks later the wily de Laurentiis sprang another surprise. "Marty, I don't know how to tell you this," a friend from Rome began his call, "but Dino's taken your name off *Serpico*. In Italy it's billed as a Dino de Laurentiis production."

When an indignant Bregman called to check, de Laurentiis played innocent, insisting it was an error. "Dino may be one of the great salesmen of all time," says Bregman, "but George Washington he is not!"

Asked if there were any circumstances under which he would ever work with him again, Bregman hesitates for a split second. "Maybe if he kidnapped my child," he replies. "And even then I'd have to think about it!"

PACINO CONTINUED TO display his "stage actor available" sign at every opportunity, anxious to protect himself from the down side of success in movies that quickly emerged. "As soon as you've made one hit movie," he lamented, "people think you're a star, and they don't send you plays to read anymore. There was a time when you didn't become an actor unless you loved to act. Actors today get to a certain point where they become affluent and cavort with kings and queens and oil barons and all the fashionable people. They become political, investors, businessmen, sportsmen, they hunt elephants in Africa, they own farms and build lakes and mountains—but they don't act, or else they do the same damned thing over and over again. Shoot the elephant! You know what I mean? I don't cavort. I lead a simple life. My life-style is pretty much the same as it's always been. I'm an *actor*. Those people who say success went to my head, they make me sick. I'd been down-and-out with nothing for so long."

An associate readily agreed with his friend's life-style analysis and maintained that its origins were only too obvious: "Al had such a lousy early life. There were such fears, he was such a drifter before he began acting professionally, and such an utter failure, that I think he's afraid that if he expands himself, it will all just deflate, vanish, and everything good that's happened to him will only seem like an illusion. The way he was brought up, the way he lived, he could easily have become a basket case. The fact that he didn't is a miracle."

AFTER BEING REUNITED with his father, who had looked at him as if he were a son rather than a movie star, Pacino had gained a new sense of family, enabling him to cling to a sense of his own identity. "After a while in this business, you really long for that," he said soon after the visit with his father. "The thing I miss most is having people look me in the eye in a certain way, the way your mother looks at you, no matter what you've done. You can tell when people aren't really seeing you, when they're just seeing the image. I can't tell you how many times at parties I'll be sitting there in the dark talking to somebody, and it's wonderful until the lights go on and they see you're Al Pacino, and a new look comes into their eyes, and suddenly everything's different.

"When I was with him, I somehow felt the family, the blood tie, the bond that all of us have, the reason we all identify so strongly with *The Godfather*. I wrote him a letter and told him how I felt about him. It's a funny thing, but being with him brought back my mother to me and made me realize how deeply I miss her."

Pacino's sense that he had let his mother down, and even contributed to her early death, had never left him. If only she had lived to see and share his success with him, how much sweeter it all would have seemed. Following the reunion with his father Pacino was able to talk more freely about Rose, referring to her as hypersensitive and well read, as well as to reveal the analysis she had undergone for years. He hinted, without quite saying, that she had suffered several nervous breakdowns and painted a picture of a loving, brooding, erratic woman who was often difficult and unwell. Then there was his grandfather, "a great man, the greatest man who ever lived, an emotional man with incredible wit. I loved him so much. He gave me an image which is very strong."

A saying of Marlon Brando's, "Guilt is a useless emotion," had made a profound impression on Pacino from the moment it was uttered. Recovery from the condition could only begin, however, when its origins were recognized, articulated and properly understood. This it would take him several more years even to partially achieve. The biggest barrier was his refusal to fully accept the very concept of responsibility. He was above all that, he tried to persuade himself. "Everything gets so aborted with me because of my pride," he confessed. "I've done this sort of thing all my life, and I'm so tired of this abortion. I'm making a conscious effort to stop it."

For a while he planned a unique form of self-therapy to release the demons that still haunted him. He swore that he would write and direct a movie about the first fourteen years of his life, a movie to be told through the eyes of one kid, showing him learning about life, sex and eventually leaving the neighborhood. Sadly, this particular rites-of-passage tale has yet to be made.

CHAPTER 11

IN DEEP

ACUTELY AWARE OF the thieves' bargain it had negotiated in Pacino's thirty-five-thousand-dollar fee for the original *Godfather*, Paramount offered him a hundred thousand dollars for the sequel. Pacino knew it was time to flex his muscles and turned the offer down.

"How about a hundred and fifty thousand dollars?" the studio countered.

"Well, I don't think so," Pacino said.

"How about if Puzo writes the screenplay?" the studio cajoled. Pacino agreed to look at the script, which he deemed "OK, but not definitive." Again he declined the studio's offer.

"They went up to two hundred thousand dollars," Pacino recalls. "I said no. Then they went to two-fifty, and three, and three-fifty. Then they made a big jump and went to four-fifty. And I still said no. Then they called me into their office in New York. There was a large bottle of J and B on the table. We began drinking, talking, laughing, and the producer opened his drawer and pulled out a tin box. I was sitting on the other side, and he pushed it over in my direction. He said, 'What if I were to tell you that there was a million dollars in cash there?' I said, 'It doesn't mean anything—it's an abstraction.' "

The meeting concluded with Pacino more or less apologizing for not taking the million. When his agents took over negotiations, the stakes went up even further, even though there was less up front. The eventual agreement was for six hundred thousand dollars in cash, together with no less than 10 percent of *Godfather II*'s profits.

Pacino says it was a meeting with Coppola, rather than the money, that made him decide to close the deal. "He would have inspired anybody," he claims. "The hair on my head stood up as I listened to him. I usually say, if you feel that from a director, go with him."

He admitted that the salary and points he was getting on *Godfather II* were beyond anything he had ever dreamed possible. "Not that I'm just doing it for the money," he hastened to add, "but when one thinks about it, I wouldn't do it for *nothing*!"

Coppola had initially written the script for the movie on his own; then Puzo had made a few significant changes. When Pacino saw the results and declared himself dissatisfied, Coppola completed a rewrite in three days. Pacino continued to show his mettle after suggesting Lee Strasberg to Paramount for the role of the Jewish godfather Hyman Roth. Initially the studio executives offered the acting guru a paltry ten thousand dollars for his participation. Pacino may well have been looking over their shoulders when the offer was finally raised to an acceptable fifty-eight thousand. Strasberg's performance—strangely enough, his first since a Clifford Odets one-act play in the thirties and his first time ever before the cameras—proved to be one of the movie's highlights.

Another was the big-screen breakthrough of the actor who had made his film debut in *The Wedding Party* with Jill Clayburgh and then replaced Pacino in *The Gang That Couldn't Shoot Straight*. Just as *The Godfather* had made Pacino's name, so *Godfather II* made a star of Robert De Niro, signed to play Vito Corleone as a young man embarking on a life of crime.

"He and I have gone through similar things," says Pacino. "There was a period in my life when it was very important that I get together with somebody I could identify with. Bobby's always very quiet; it's an inherent thing. He does talk with me, though."

As WITH THE original, the months of filming on *Godfather II* took a heavy toll on Pacino. Living with the complexity of Michael Corleone, his isolation and loneliness, was all-encompassing. "I couldn't be that guy and have a good time," he says. "I wanted to, but I couldn't. At the end of Part One there's a kind of bounce to Michael, that subtle joy of what he's doing, that newness and that kind of taking it on. When we pick him up in Part Two, he's been doing it for five years, and the bounce has gone. That's what I went for. There's such a dichotomy in Michael, he's so ambivalent. It's this dichotomy that finally leads to his madness. He is lost at the end of this film. He's a beaten man, a desperately sad person.

"We worked for twenty weeks on *Godfather Two*. I was living with that weight all the time, and it was suffocating, it was hurting. In a film it's much more difficult, especially Michael Corleone, it's a film performance, a character done on film. You don't do that on the stage. In the theater there's a chance to step outside of it, to become artistic, objective, and not take it out on your own time. The more experienced you become, the more aware you become, you start taking less and less out of your own hide."

Actress Fay Spain witnessed the female devastation Pacino continued to leave in his wake. "Al is quite touchable," she observed, "but he is *selective*. It must be really tough if you haven't been that famous before and suddenly you're *Al Pacino*! On location in Florida, and the Dominican Republic, the girls were just everywhere. Psychologically it must have been difficult. Imagine, there he is working, and he had to have a bodyguard outside his hotel room because the girls were always around. Boy, do they really dig him!"

Blond, blue-eyed Ms. Spain, who had made her debut as Darlin' Jill in 1957's *God's Little Acre*, was playing Hyman Roth's wife, Marcia, in *Godfather II*. She herself was not immune to Pacino's allure. "I'm a married lady," she pointed out, "and I was terrified to go on location because I just dig Al so much. Those tremendous eyes! He's a very warm person. He's so involved, so intense about everything. I mean, you could say it's a nice day, and Al would want to know why it was and what about it. He's so curious about everything. He's not a 'grand' person, not 'A Star.' He's—well, when I say his name, I smile. I can't help it, because I love him."

One of the girls who slipped past Pacino's bodyguard dreamily described the experience to *Film World* in language worthy of a Paramount handout: "He's the kind of man who takes you to great heights of ecstasy and knows what to do when he gets you there. He's gentle, sure of himself and very considerate. I think he's a real man, because he made me feel like a real woman." Pacino had his own, rather more down-to-earth expression for the willing hordes, describing their attempts to occupy his bed as "like buying a bus ticket."

In one of the final scenes of the movie, where Michael Corleone, now fully transformed into the iceman, closes the door forever on Kay, Pacino decided he needed something extra to complete the portrait, the prop that would whisper volumes, the equivalent of the black homburg outfit in the original. This time he picked the stiffly formal elegance of a magnificent camel hair overcoat and matching scarf. "I got lucky there," he agrees. "The touch removes Michael in a way, it's something distant, and the formality of it felt good." (Brando had, in fact, beaten him to it, although his camel-colored overcoat in *Last Tango in Paris* looked more like cashmere.)

Pacino's favorite scene occurs when Michael and his brother Fredo are in Cuba, watching the Superman show in a nightclub. The moment when Cazale as Fredo tells him, "Johnny always used to take me here," Michael realizes that his brother has betrayed him. Pacino was rushed to the hospital in Santo Domingo after shooting the scene, his nervous and physical exhaustion having led to a bout of bronchial pneumonia that was stark proof of the toll the movie had extracted.

As with his portrayal of Serpico, the payoff for Pacino came in the sense of achievement he gained from having produced a rounded, complete character of Michael Corleone, yet one devoid of false emotional appeal. He had burrowed inside the character and allowed it to flow of its own volition, without opting for the sympathy or understanding that was gratuitous of the character: "I wanted people to like Michael, to like him in the sense that I wanted them to see him, to understand him and his dilemma, *without* asking them to identify with him. *That's* what I was after. It's a very difficult thing to do, and I think I did it. I'm most proud of that."

Coppola is the first to concede the extent of Pacino's input. "I wanted to take Michael to what I felt was the logical conclusion. He wins every battle; his brilliance and his resources enable him to defeat all his enemies. I didn't want Michael to die. I didn't want Michael to be put in prison. I didn't want him to be assassinated by his rivals. But in a bigger sense, I also wanted to destroy Michael. There's no doubt that by the end of the picture Michael Corleone, having beaten everyone, is sitting there alone, a living corpse. He's doomed; there's no way that man is ever going to change. I admit I considered some upbeat touch at the end, but honesty—and Pacino—wouldn't let me do it. Michael is *doomed.*"

LIKE PACINO IN the original, De Niro was nominated for an Oscar for Best Supporting Actor in the *Godfather* sequel, pitched against cast mates Lee Strasberg and Michael V. Gazzo. Unlike Pacino, De Niro won the award. Pacino received his second nomination for Best Actor—that is, his third Oscar nomination —for *Godfather II*, the competition on this occasion being provided by Art Carney for *Harry and Tonto*, Albert Finney for *Murder on the Orient Express*, Jack Nicholson for *Chinatown* and Dustin Hoffman for *Lenny*, the role Pacino had declined. Again Pacino was passed over, with the award going to Carney. *Godfather II* won awards for Musical Score, Art Direction, Script, Direction and Best Film, registering an unprecedented triumph for Coppola, who had performed the hitherto impossible feat of producing a sequel universally regarded as superior to the original. Theater owners still complained about the running time of three hours and twenty minutes, which drastically reduced the number of shows they could run daily. Although the film was successful, the worldwide gross of *Godfather II*, even when given a much-needed boost by the Oscars, came to just a fraction of the original's take.

Jill Clayburgh, whose star was once more on the ascendant after a series of personal and professional setbacks, paid tribute to Pacino, the actor and the man. "I'm speaking as an actress, not Al's former lover," she first made clear. "I think he projects such power because of his total lack of egocentricity. A lot of actors want to be sexy, cute, adorable . . . do anything to win an audience to their side . . . cater to every cheap, trendy, obvious appeal that will make them laugh. *Al couldn't care less. He's too honest,* and he *loves* the characters he plays too deeply to go in for that sort of thing. That's why he can turn acting into poetry. In that generation of actors working around New York in the 1960s, it was always Al and maybe one or two others they spoke about when they dared talk of genius and the kind of actors who might make it big."

In 1975 Clayburgh went on to win an Emmy for Best Actress for her performance as a prostitute in the TV film *Hustling*. Although she was turned down by David Rabe for a part in his play *In the Boom Boom Room*, the two of them finally married in 1979 after several years of living together. By this time the remarkable Clayburgh had survived *Gable and Lombard* and *Semi-Tough* and had two Oscar nominations of her own, for *Starting Over* and *An Unmarried Woman*. "She was excellent, wonderful," Pacino said of his ex-lover's performance in the latter role. "She became one of us, in a sense." He confirmed that he still saw her occasionally and regarded her as a friend —unlike Rabe, who was *persona non grata* for several years.

Clayburgh allowed that she had dipped into her inner resources to play her role in *An Unmarried Woman*: "The character was only partially autobiographical, although I definitely drew on some of my experiences with Al."

PACINO'S VISITS TO psychoanalysts began shortly after he started seeing everything in monochrome. The condition had quickly escalated. "When the panic button is pushed, when your nose suddenly looks like a banana and you start peeling it—well, then you go for help," he rationalized. Soon one psychoanalyst wasn't enough, for Pacino felt too embarrassed to return after a single visit. He made appointments, then failed to show up. Romantically he was on his own again—and drifting.

"I don't think analysis is for me," he told one reporter, "but I could change my mind tomorrow. I hope, eventually, as I straighten out personally, that I can deal with the pain of it all. But now my personal life is in trouble, and I think the more I align myself personally, the better it will be for my work. You need to have that foundation in life before going into the chaos of work."

Pacino came perilously close for a while to losing his battle with the bottle. "I still belt the booze," he blithely admitted in 1974. "Laurence Olivier was right when he said a drink after the show is the best thing about the theater. Whiskey is *very* underrated. I know, because I've been to psychoanalysts and they didn't calm me down as much as a good belt. I socialize better and talk better with it. I'm open. But I never touch a drop when I'm working, and I've given up three-day binges. Coming out of them leaves me too depressed; they're strictly downers."

Pacino's problems were evident to many of his friends: the continuing pain of guilt deriving from his mother's death during their estrangement, his seeming inability to sustain a stable romantic relationship, coping with the pressure of his sudden fame—all of them magnified by the mercurial mood changes his bouts with alcohol produced. Pacino was in denial, the stage when many heavy drinkers become almost unreachable.

Never having enjoyed a "drinking buddy" relationship with Pacino, Marty Bregman was unable to reach his friend and client—try as he might. The situation was discussed many times, with Pacino always maintaining that his work was unaffected. Bregman had to admit was true. So far.

Only his closest and oldest friend, Charlie Laughton, was in a position to penetrate Pacino's stonewalling defenses and dare to make him face the truth. A year earlier Laughton had disciplined himself to stop drinking, and he knew Pacino had to be shocked into following suit.

"You're *drinking*," he told him. "Nightly. Heavily. *Look* at it, and recognize it for what it is, *an addiction*. Do it *now*, Al, before it's too late. Otherwise it might be all over for you."

It was a powerful moment for the actor. "I *didn't* know it," he later claimed, "and I didn't know that other people knew! Facing the truth was difficult because denial kept trying to gain the upper hand, and defiance as well. What was the use of all the fame if you couldn't enjoy a drink like everyone else?" It took him a full year before he was able to stop.

Pacino sat one day with a friend on the patio of an East Village restaurant across from the New York Shakespeare Festival Public Theater. A bunch of actors were laughing and talking at another table, with coffee, croissants and glasses of wine resting on the red-and-white-checkered tablecloth, as sunlight filtered through a rainbow-colored umbrella overhead.

It was like something out of a Renoir painting, Pacino marveled. He saw the group as chroniclers of their time, as if they had existed for hundreds of years in their ancient and familial world. Through overheard snatches of their conversation, he felt he could trace their roots. The feeling of belonging to a family was overwhelming and something he desperately missed in his own life.

"You see them?" he said to his companion. "I can't take my eyes off them!"

CHAPTER 12

METHOD IN THEIR MADNESS

P ACINO IS SOMETHING of an authority on the life of the legendary nineteenth-century Shakespearean actor Edmund
Kean, whom the poet Byron once described as "the sun's
bright child." Pacino regards Kean as the first acting superstar. "Someone said that watching his act was like watching
bolts of lightning cross the stage," he points out. "But he had a
tragic life; he couldn't cope with fame. It's funny, at first he
couldn't get work. He had these dark features, and he was
considered too short. But he dethroned John Philip Kemble
with his first Shakespearean performance at Drury Lane. Actors were *scared* to share the stage with him."

Author Julius Berstl, who took upon himself the task of com-
piling Kean's "memoirs," inadvertently spelled out several
parallels between his hero and Pacino. Kean was abandoned
as a child, although by his mother, and sent to live with in-laws
when his twenty-three-year-old father fell off a roof in a
drunken stupor and killed himself. His mother reclaimed him
when he was four years old.

Like Pacino's, Kean's upbringing was penurious, and at

school he "hated the set pedantry of the teacher and the gloomy atmosphere of the classroom." After hours he "roamed about in old and poor quarters of London and played hide and seek in the nooks and crannies of decayed and tumbledown houses." He became a "child spouter," a young actor who delivered Shakespearean tracts as after-dinner entertainment, much in the manner of Sonny's movie party pieces.

Kean was also estranged from his mother, and his training in booths and fairgrounds was the equivalent of Pacino's Greenwich Village cafés and storefronts, just as his reaction to supporting roles was similar to Pacino's. "Can you measure," Kean wondered, "what it means to be obliged to watch others play themselves into favor with the public while the beginner is forced to stand aside and fret like a circus horse champing at the bit?"

There was Kean's obsession with work, his total involvement in the characters he played, and his desolation in between assignments: "I was a flame consuming myself. If I were not performing, I was hanging over a bottomless pit." A "feeling of utter loneliness, of being at the mercy of fate" tormented him and could be stifled only in drink. "Perhaps," he mused, "it is the fate of the actor to submerge his personality in the multitude of his disguises. He who sees in every episode the germ of another part, he who gets into the skin of a character, however fictitious, shedding his own with delight; he who, with fatal facility, can change his ego into a multiple of egos, must need become a prey to self-estrangement. He lives on the extreme edge of a precipice." Kean began to dread being faced with what he saw as the futile and meaningless intervals between his performances.

He signed with a rival theatrical house while under contract to the Drury Lane Theater, leaving the proprietor and "Napoleon of the stage" R. W. Elliston to anticipate MGM's contractual tussle with Pacino by a century and a half. "To any man with the smallest gift of intellect," Elliston admonished, "it must appear that you deemed yourself engaged to Drury Lane and that subsequently, a more attractive offer having been made, you held it convenient to consider your pledge as idle words uttered in a dream. All *my* engagements are made and fulfilled with honor on my part, and I expect an equal punctiliousness from others."

Then there was Kean's involvement with the ladies. Maidens and matrons, snub-nosed shopgirls and grand ladies—all lost their heads at his approach. "What actor or man," he demanded to know, "could disdain the easy fruit dropping into his lap, as befell one, when women, young and old, constantly invaded my house, when they climbed through my windows on rope ladders? A man ruled by his sex instinct is only too readily possessed by any woman appealing to that instinct. He becomes like one intoxicated or ridden by a fever of the worst kind."

There followed the same intermingling of public and private life with which Pacino wrestled. "The mystic bond between me and my public did not confine itself to the theater alone," Kean agonized. "It also exposed my private life to the glare of the footlights. This perplexed me. Fame became my armour, the armour became my prison."

Kean even had his own Dustin Hoffman, in the form of one Junius Brutus Booth, whose "name was on everyone's lips" and was "astonishingly like me in build and voice." When the two rivals played together on stage, Kean as Othello partnered by Booth's Iago, Kean "recognised that this double provided for me by nature was in every respect worthy of being reckoned with as an equal."

Truly, there is nothing new under the sun.

BERTOLT BRECHT'S *The Resistible Rise of Arturo Ui* was written while the playwright was cooling his heels in Norway in 1941, awaiting his U.S. visa. The play parodied Hitler's rise to power in Germany, beginning in 1929 and climaxing in 1938 with the capitulation of Austria. Brecht's *Arturo Ui*, a two-bit Chicago gangster boosted to power by wealthy capitalists, provided the Hitlerian parallel, exposing the Führer to down-to-earth ridicule along the lines of Charlie Chaplin's *The Great Dictator*, with a hefty added dose of hysterical menace.

In 1974 impresario Joe Papp gave Pacino forty thousand dollars to develop a staging of Brecht's play with David Wheeler's Theater Company of Boston. Following its out-of-town birth, Papp expected to present the production at his New York Public Theater.

What Pacino had in mind from the outset was to do full justice to Brecht, not just with any old bunch of hired actors but with an ensemble company and months of rehearsals. Papp's conception of a quick and cheap success, to follow his previous season's Lincoln Center hit with Liv Ullmann in *A Doll's House*, clearly placed him at odds with his ostensible partner's "workshop" concept. Four weeks were spent in rehearsals by Pacino and his company before he had to take a break to film *Dog Day Afternoon*.

By the spring of 1975 Papp had become restive. "The workshop's fine," he told Pacino, "but where's the show?" The actor shrugged his shoulders and, armed with fresh backing from ex-Brandeis University students back in Boston who were willing to reinvest their profits from a local production of *Lenny*, continued his apparently endless rehearsals.

Charlie Laughton remembers the day Pacino began to get a handle on his character. "He spilled some coffee at rehearsal and started to wipe the table. He did this fastidiously, then cleaned the cup in the same manner, then the table legs, then moved on to the floor, working obsessively all the while and saying his lines. Onstage you really get that opportunity to work things out. A happy accident is fine, but the ability to *recognize* it and *use* it, that's quite another. Al has that ability."

For a while Pacino toyed with the idea of not opening the play at all and performing free for students instead. He opted in the end for an eight-week limited run at the Charles Playhouse, the Hub venue in the heart of the red-light district of strippers and porn movies where he had first worked with Wheeler. Changes of policy continued even after the run was sold out in advance. There was talk of not having an opening night for the press, which eventually translated into local reviewers only, and at the last minute the play was drastically pruned from five hours' running time to three.

Papp was furious. He had written off the forty-thousand-dollar investment when it seemed Pacino was unwilling to go public. Now the show had opened after all, with three new producers and Papp apparently squeezed out. At the very least, he railed to reporters, he had certain rights. "I started the project," he pointed out. "I gave him forty thousand dollars and the costumes. Then they came to me and said they wanted to go to Boston. I said OK. But if they decide to bring it to New York, I have the option to produce it." Nothing was final yet, Papp hastened to add. "Al and I have been talking, but mostly it's the way he feels about it. If he's enthusiastic, we'll bring it to New York, but he didn't demonstrate much enthusiasm the last time I talked to him. In fact, he's very dubious right now. I don't know why."

One of the reasons, thought the *Village Voice*'s Ross Wetzston, was Papp's perceived attitude toward the production. When Wetzston mentioned that he personally had some problems with Pacino's performance, but that on the whole the production was magnificent, Papp retorted, "It *should* be good by now; they've been working on it for seven months." Later he changed his position, claiming it was *not* a good production: "I went up to Boston last week. Al was great, but the production wasn't any good." A sentiment better calculated to aggravate the situation, with Pacino firmly in his loyalty-to-the-ensemble mode, was difficult to imagine.

It was baffling in particular to the *Voice*'s correspondent since the sterling cast included such Off-Broadway veterans as Penny Allen, Sully Boyar, Garry Goodrow, Jack Hollander, Jaime Sanchez, Brad Sullivan, Taylor Mead and Pacino's buddy John Cazale, most of whom were giving what he considered the finest performances of their careers. Cazale he singled out in particular as "stunningly Brechtian," adding, "He may well be the finest actor in America today. As Givola, the Goebbels figure, he coldly, impassively limps on his club foot, murdering with a glance, conveying motivation without a trace of internalizing, and combining comedy and menace, banality and malevolence, with a brilliance that made me want to see him as Ui himself."

Although Wetzston found Pacino "superb on his own terms," he disagreed with Papp's judgment. The leading actor, it seemed to him, was in another, non-Brechtian production, his style totally out of synchronization with the rest of the cast. Instead of seeing Pacino as attempting to invoke primitive passion, Wetzston considered Pacino's early appearance as the Hitler symbol merely dumb, withering the credibility of his later ascent to dictatorhood, "the disparity too great even for this most gifted actor to overcome."

The problem went even deeper than that, in Wetzston's view, all the way down to Pacino's mumbling diction: "under oat" for "under oath"; "nuttin" for "nothing"; "frens" for "friends"; "troot" for "truth." Pacino, he thought, should have heeded Brecht's completely sterile ideal of the *tout comprendre c'est tout pardonner* school of ironic detachment, rather than his Method-style mesmerizing naturalness. Instead of a menace at the heart of the play, Pacino's Ui came over as a neurotic.

Arthur Friedman of *The Real Paper* proved to be no great admirer of either the production or its central performer. For that matter, he had been totally turned off by Pacino's earlier Boston appearance as Richard III, which he termed "one of Boston's major cultural disasters, one of the two worst Shakespearean performances by an actor of note I've seen, a dubious laurel Pacino shares with Jason Robards' wool-mouthed catatonic Brutus."

Friedman saw the problem back then as lying in Pacino's "limited technical repertoire." With *Arturo Ui* he wondered if an actor could be sued for plagiarism if he were stealing from his own previous work. "If so," he pronounced, "Pacino should be hauled before the Court of Theatrical Good Taste and booked on charges of thespic pilfering. For his Arturo Ui is a faded carbon copy of his Dick Crookback. He moves from small personal gestures to what passes in Pacino's theatrical lexicon for grand acting—screaming." Small wonder, Friedman noted, that several matinee performances had been canceled because of the star's laryngitis.

Carolyn Clay was another whose admiration for what she called Pacino's "stumbling his adenoidal way through *Richard III*" had been strictly limited. Unlike Friedman, however, she had considerable respect for his Arturo Ui: "Pacino's internalized Ui chills despite his clowning in a way no ham actor donning the mask of Hitler could." David Wheeler's "fluid production," in Clay's view, fully lived up to its *Godfather*-fanned hype.

"We never really got the play right," Pacino admitted, "but the time away from it helped a lot. It's the same reason why John Gielgud and Ralph Richardson were so miraculous together onstage. They'd work together, then go away, then work together again on another play."

Pacino's later suggestion that the procedure be adopted on his movies—"We take two weeks off after finishing and then come back fresh and look at what we have, perhaps even reshoot things"—received no takers. As for Brecht's neglected masterpiece, never produced in the author's lifetime, intractability on both sides finally held sway, denying New York theater audiences what many felt was one of the finest Brecht productions ever staged by an American theatrical company. Joe Papp's disgruntled "It's up to Al" cut little ice, since everyone knew Papp hadn't got where he was by leaving things "up to Al."

"I've always gravitated towards doing plays in out-of-the-way places, away from the flak of Broadway," said Pacino. "You should be free to fall on your face. But you know, I have a strong dichotomy about my career. In some ways, I don't want to work at all, and I'll do almost anything to avoid it.

"Yet when I get into a play, it consumes me. I've been accused of fanatical relentlessness in my drive. It's a strange love-hate relationship I have with the theater. There has never been a play I've done where, at some point, I didn't get sick and say, 'I can't stand this, it's all wrong for me, get me out of this.'

"After performances of *Richard III* in Boston I'd go into the dressing room, pound my fists against the wall, bang my head against the table. Because it's all so crazy. You spend three hours onstage and your own life becomes secondary. If you don't have a source to go back to, a family, you're left with just that three hours, and it's very lonely."

Marty Bregman's attitude to Pacino's stage forays has been consistent from the beginning. "The stage is where Al lives," Bregman insists. "It's where he goes to recharge his batteries. He needs these outings to fulfill himself. The man's an *artist*."

THE TERRITORY PACINO longed to explore was that which lay between great acting as generally perceived—that is, an actor playing a part he knows and has polished to perfection—and *really* great acting, which in his Method terms, the gospel according to Strasberg, has the actor regressing to an emotional parallel in his own experience. Was this acting, Pacino asked himself, or psychoanalysis in public? Was that what acting was anyway, and if so, wasn't the Method by definition *quintessential* acting?

Confusingly, different schools advocated varying brands of the Method, although the two leading lights, Lee Strasberg and Stella Adler, both claimed to interpret Stanislavsky's concept of the actor's *becoming* his character, his emotions real, not pretended, the action happening, not indicated. Strasberg's belief was that internalization, the use of affective memory, held the answer, with the actor drawing from within to find the key that would unlock his character and endow his interpretation with a prior existence beyond the boundaries of its time span onstage. Surely, his argument for regression ran, characters thus became three-dimensional, acquiring a past as well as a present and future.

Stella Adler professed to achieve the same result, but by preaching the gospel of externalization, the actor empathizing with and creating a character from the outside in, the exact reverse of Strasberg's philosophy. In her pantheon the actor would remain within the author's confines of time frame and setting, absorbing the signposts of art and architecture, props and physical action laid down. Sparked by these external stimuli, he would then be able to arrive at his interpretation by stepping outside his own experiences and allowing his "creative imagination" to soar, *creating* a past that belonged to his character. "Your life is one-millionth of what you know" was Adler's belief. "Your talent is in your imagination; the rest is lice. Acting is action; action is doing. Find ways to do it, not to say it."

Strasberg, therefore, much more than Adler, was arguably responsible for the most common and frustrating argument heard by the collaborators of Method actors, "My character wouldn't say this," a red flag to many a directorial bull. Strasberg's regression theory provided in advance the perfect answer to the question then posed: "How do you *know?*" Since our previous experiences are unalterably engraved on our consciousness and as individual as a fingerprint, the question, in Method acting terms, would be logically answered, "How could I *not* know?" (Director Robert Altman provided one answer when confronted with the problem. "Never mind the drugstore philosophy," he told one actor; "just say your goddamn lines.")

Distinguished man of the theater John Houseman had his own view of both Strasberg's and Adler's efforts. "For many years," he pointed out, "American acting was an honorable branch of the British theatrical tradition. Then, with the rise of native American drama, there gradually developed an unfortunate and ever-widening chasm between the classic and realistic schools of performance in this country. In the past two generations more of our best young actors have been concerned with the inner mechanics of expressing emotion—the much-discussed 'Method.'" Houseman was clearly out of sympathy with the "unfortunate and ever-widening chasm."

Director Elia Kazan is himself a survivor of the original

Group Theater formed with Strasberg in the thirties, an enterprise forged by the Depression, Freud, Stanislavsky and the concept of "poetry from common things," of liberating realism and naturalism. He argues that to consider that true acting revolves around Strasberg's "emotional recall" tends to turn the craft into a competition to prove which actor can produce the greatest emotional fireworks display. With the widespread knowledge today of the effect Proust's madeleine engendered, and the reactions of Pavlov's dog, the concept is no longer esoteric. Neither, Kazan maintains, is it Stanislavsky's method, which he interprets as concerning itself with the *reason* for the character to be onstage, within the framework of the scene envisaged by the writer.

"Emotions differ," Kazan points out, "they have different qualities; they are part of a characterization; they are specific. We don't feel alike, nor do we always feel at top pitch. In life most of us conceal our feelings; we don't want them to be seen. Many actors I know, especially Lee Strasberg's pupils, brandish these emotions as if they were the only measure of talent." Strasberg's retaliation combined candor with vainglory. "I don't teach the Stanislavsky method," he claimed. "I teach the *Strasberg* method!"

If Pacino was Strasberg's "baby," Stella Adler was, for the most part, De Niro's "mama," although De Niro is on record that he does not believe one "method" is better than another. He does, however, see Adler as remaining more faithful to Stanislavsky's principles and Strasberg's interpretation as "another thing." Pacino is even vaguer. "I really don't know what the Method is," he claims. "I remember doing scenes in the Actors Studio, and then, when everybody would talk, I would count numbers so I wouldn't hear it. Good actors are made, and great actors are born. Either you've got something to say, or you don't. And you try to get to the point where you *say* something as an artist. I've seen actors who've studied the Method who have become better from it, but I've seen others who've become worse."

As one of the "new generation" thirty-six-year-old John

Malkovich denies the Method any credit whatsoever when discussing the style of the Chicago-based Steppenwolf Company of which he was a founder member. "It's nothing to do with Method acting," he claims. "None of us would know what Method acting is, nor would it interest us. The other day I read that an actor had done the time-honored thing of hanging out with some people on whom his play is based. That seems to me the most mindless thing imaginable, because right away it assumes it is not an act of imagination, but rather of impersonation. Personally I can always tell when an actor is over-researched."

As for Brando, the original star exponent, who shot to fame in Kazan's *A Streetcar Named Desire* and *On the Waterfront*, his "method" for the last twenty years has amounted to little more than reading his lines from a prompter—for added spontaneity, he says. Go figure.

Critic Pauline Kael counsels caution above all in any assessment of the Actors Studio and its Method dictum. She concedes that its exponents are terrific at portraying gloom, defeat, manic joy and desperately troubled psychiatric states. "But they're so inward," she concludes, "that you can't see them getting through a competently managed average day!"

CHAPTER 13

OUT OF THE CLOSET

PACINO'S HABIT OF acquiring clothes from his movie roles, even to the extent of his prison shoes from *Scarecrow* and Serpico's far-out threads, is far from unique. Added to his other frugalities, however, it has earned him a reputation as a tight man with a dollar.

The flip side of the coin is his willingness occasionally to forgo astronomical Hollywood sums to pursue his theatrical career: "The big item when I do Off-Broadway is the fact that I'm getting only two hundred and fifty dollars a week. In that area you can anger people no end—you start talking about how you don't care about money, yet there you are, pulling in one million dollars or whatever. I feel kind of funny about that because it really can grate on people's nerves."

Now that Pacino was a relatively wealthy man, he acknowledged that the problem of managing his money paled into insignificance beside the years of financial insecurity. His only uncertainty now was what to do with his wealth. "It would be different if I had a family, a wife and children to support," he claimed, "but now the money provides me with a certain privacy I need. I try to keep it as simple as possible, to find out about my money, what it means, how it's invested. It's all very complicated. It took me a while to take on the responsibility. I give it away here and there. I'm a poor kid from the South Bronx, and there's certain things about money I don't understand and never will. I always *felt* I had money, even when I didn't have it. I always had a dollar in my pocket. I knew I could get that Chianti wine if I wanted to, and a knish. Just the other day I looked at a loaf of bread and realized how much money it is. Cigarettes are very expensive; I realized I hadn't looked at a pack of cigarettes in a couple of years. I don't know how much a container of milk costs. But when I *had* to know how much it cost, that was a different story.

"I'm not sure, but I think I'm rich now. I've got a manager and an agent who gets twenty-five percent and the government gets fifty percent. That only leaves twenty-five percent for me. Still, I know I must be getting rich."

He confirmed that friends borrowed from him, while pointing out that nothing could be better calculated to ruin a relationship. "I'll lend it to them, sure. When I'm lending it, I'll preface it by saying, 'Look, if this affects the relationship in any way, forget it.' Invariably, it does, though."

Althoughly avowedly apolitical, Pacino remarked at the time of *Serpico*'s release that the movie was not just about crooked cops. He compared it with Watergate, as an examination of multileveled corruption. "I don't want to sound too pessimistic," he declared, "but I don't think things are going to change that much. There always will be graft and corruption in politics. It'll be modified, perhaps; the *degree* of corruption will lessen as a result of the Watergate disclosures—at least, let's hope so. We have a lot of problems, but God, it's *still* a great country. I'm going to have it put into all of my future contracts that any picture I do will not be done in a fascist country. I just couldn't go there.

"I've seen political repression, and it makes me appreciate very much how lucky we are here in America, despite Watergate. I can't claim to have my finger on the pulse of the whole country, but where else could you do a film like *Serpico*? Certainly not in countries where the political parties control films and television."

LIKE *SERPICO* BEFORE it, progress on Marty Bregman's production of *Dog Day Afternoon* was made only after considerable initial difficulties were overcome and after several false starts. Bregman had acquired the rights to the property, which was based on a real-life robbery committed by Sonny Wortzik, a bisexual "married" to a transexual. An article in *Life* magazine detailed the heist that had taken place in Brooklyn in August 1972, the proceeds of which were intended to pay for Wortzik's lover's sex change operation. The robbery had been doomed from the start, with the manager and staff held hostage throughout a sweltering afternoon and night while the police laid siege to the building and the press and television crews—as well as scores of onlookers—ogled the proceedings. Wortzik had ended up as both spectator and participant in his own outlandish telethon, a Marshall McLuhan media nightmare run riot.

The only individual interested in developing the material was Dick Shepherd, an ex-agent who was an executive at the time at Warner Bros. "No actor was attached to it at first," Bregman explains. "I couldn't go with Al hand in hand. First of all, I still represented him; then you're never going to get a firm commitment from anyone until you have a screenplay. Al may have said, 'Well, that's an interesting idea, let's check it out further down the line,' but that's all you can expect from anyone at such an early stage."

When Frank Pierson's script was finally at Warner's, and with Sidney Lumet back as director, Pacino first agreed to do it, then backed out. Word came down that Dustin Hoffman might be interested in playing Wortzik. "Nothing came of it," says Bregman. "I never had a conversation with Dustin. He's a wonderful actor, but I believed that only Pacino could bring the sensitivity and the vulnerability we needed here. Al and I

opened up the subject again. It took a tremendous amount of
courage because he was a leading man, not a character actor,
and he's being asked to play someone who is gay. It was a big
risk. When you play a character, you become the character,
especially when you're Al, and that might have been a world he
did not want to explore. You have to remember that back then
no major star had ever played a gay; he was the first. Imagine
if someone like Bogart had suddenly played in a movie where
he had a male lover. It was a big jump, and he was nervous
about it. But I didn't want to make the movie with anyone
else."

After agreeing to play the role for a second time, Pacino had
a further change of heart and announced he was out. A multitude of excuses was offered. He simply did not want to make
another movie, he told the startled Bregman. He preferred
stage work and had come to the conclusion he would never
make the adjustment required for movies; it was a medium he
would never feel comfortable in. Coming from a veteran of
four starring roles, three of which had won him Oscar nominations, the explanation rang distinctly hollow, especially after
his avowed conversion to movies following *Serpico* and the
association with Lumet and his team. Pacino later admitted to
a tantrum, brought on by a mixture of drinking and exhaustion. And he was desperately lonely. "I need a life outside
work," he declared. "I feel the lack of such a life can destroy a
person, even kill them. It is not valid for everyone, but God
knows I must escape into something other than my daily
chores."

Sidney Lumet echoes Bregman's explanation for Pacino's
self-styled tantrum. "We weren't just talking about a major
star playing a homosexual," he says, "but also portraying that
whole insane framework of life. Al came back in. Then the
week before we were meant to go into rehearsals, he, Marty
and I were talking with Frank Pierson, and I really thought Al
was going to pull out *again* that night! What he was asking for
was so wrong, a basic modification in the guy's behavior—his

instincts are marvelous, usually he's never wrong—but it was just the sheer terror of getting into this.

"Since none of us ever know how an audience is going to react, I usually ignore them. However, on *Dog Day Afternoon* I was as terrified as Al, because the subject matter was so sensationalized. The freaks are not the freaks you think they are; we're much more closely associated with even this extreme behavior than any of us dare admit."

Tantrums, reservations and misgivings behind him, the fears of Bregman's main man seemed finally to be assuaged. *Dog Day Afternoon* now encompassed the three elements Pacino looked for: the ideal director, text and role. An added bonus was having his friend John Cazale play second lead, as well as Laughton's wife, Penny Allen, as one of the cashiers. The casting of Judith Malina in a key supporting role, at Pacino's suggestion, represented part of a debt repaid. He had never forgotten the help and inspiration he had gained back in the sixties from Malina and her husband, Julian Beck, the cofounders of the Living Theater. The fine cast was rounded out by Charles Durning as the detective trying to break the siege and Chris Sarandon as Sonny's lover.

Despite the three weeks of rehearsals that had gone before, Pacino was unhappy as he sat in the preview theater with Bregman, watching the first day's rushes. "Marty," he murmured as the screen darkened and the lights went up, "we may have to do these over."

"Whaddya mean?" the no-nonsense Bregman yelled.

"I don't have the guy," Pacino replied. "Let me find the guy."

He sat up all that night on his own with the script, downing half a gallon of white wine in the process and dealing Laughton's temperance campaign a considerable blow. In the morning, however, he had his answer. In all the time he had spent discussing the story line and motivations with Lumet and Pierson, he had tended to overlook the essential Sonny Wortzik. "What I watched in those rushes," says Pacino, "was someone *searching* for a character, but there wasn't a *person* up there on the screen. For example, Sonny comes into the bank wearing glasses. And I said, 'No, hold it, he *wouldn't* be wearing glasses.' *Ordinarily* he would, but on the day of the heist he would have forgotten them, because subconsciously he wanted to get caught."

After a talk with Bregman and Lumet on the set the following day, the director agreed with Pacino's assessment and reshot the scene. From then on the movie led a charmed life. "It's out of my hands," a delighted Lumet declared a few days later. "It's got a life of its own."

Lumet's preoccupation continued to be the audience's reaction to the drama. One false note in the movie, and the whole structure would fall apart. "When you deal with sex and death and get into real working-class districts, you never know how people are going to react," he says. "I'd have been deeply upset if the material had become oversensationalized and people had laughed in the wrong places. I said to Al and the cast on the third day that I didn't want them to create the characters from the outside. I wanted them to use themselves to the fullest degree they could, their tears, their sweat, their tiredness, their humor.

"The phone call in the barbershop between Al and Chris Sarandon was completely improvised; the dialogue was entirely Al's and Chris's. Some of the stuff in the bank with the hostages and a lot of the stuff between Al and John Cazale as well. I think that allowed Al to take that character into himself in a way that was thrilling. There's nothing homosexual in Al, I'm sure he hasn't got a homosexual thought in his head, but being able to improvise to some extent enabled him to connect with his character."

After Sonny emerged from the bank yelling, "Attica! Attica!" and was instantly adopted as a media star, Lumet helped Pacino put across the feeling that it was *his* day in the sun. Pacino watched as Lumet created a similar impression with the pizza delivery boy, who, realizing he is on camera, cries, "I'm a star!" He could understand Lumet's McLuhanistic argument, the notion of a media circus that was plugged into imagery of fantasy and film and how the concept stretched the movie's boundaries. "We don't know enough about the media yet," it dawned on Pacino. "We don't know its effect on us. It's new. It's got to do something to us." And Lumet, he felt, had tapped into that energy source.

The interplay and mutual dedication between Pacino and Lumet were to produce a couple of scenes that neither will ever forget, Wortzik's phone calls to his "wives." "I wanted to shoot them in one take so Al would build up a head of steam," says Lumet. "The only problem was that the two scenes together ran fourteen minutes and the camera only holds nine and a half to ten minutes of film. So I got a second camera in, and we got a fourteen-minute take of the two most emotional speeches I've ever seen in a movie.

"It was extraordinary what he did. When he finished the take, I could see he'd let it all out. I said, 'Cut. Let's go again, Al.' His eyes flashed at me in disbelief, I thought he was going to kill me, but exhausted as he was, he knew what I was after. I wanted him to start on the level that he'd finished these two speeches. I said, 'Roll,' and he began again. I really pushed him, I just knew he had another take left in him because he's got an emotional reserve there.

"At the end of the second take I was positioned between the two cameras and our eyes met. Usually this breaks an actor's concentration, but fortunately I'd been so moved there were tears running down my cheeks. He burst into tears himself when he saw me and covered his eyes up. It was an amazing moment, which we left on the screen, as good a moment of directing as I've ever had in my life."

With the movie finished and critics' screenings scheduled, Lumet was startled to get a call from Marty Bregman. "Al saw the movie last week," Bregman informed him, "and he wants a cut in the scene with the reading of the will. I've told him I don't want to do it, but you're going to have to talk to him. I've told him I won't cut it if you say no."

Pacino explained to Lumet that he had a problem with the line ". . . and to Ernie, whom I have loved as no man has ever loved another man," and begged the director to take it out. Only after a gallon of black coffee and some highly persuasive fast talk was it agreed that the scene play as it was.

When Charlie Laughton saw Pacino's performance in the finished movie, he pushed any remaining doubts aside. "Al, do you know what it's like?" he asked. "It's like pulling a pin out of a hand grenade and waiting for it to explode!"

A relieved Pacino made it bouquets all around, particularly for Sidney Lumet, who had once again fired his enthusiasm for the art of film: "On *Dog Day Afternoon*, he was the one who made me understand the camera and get comfortable with it. Lumet is a genius at staging, much more of a stage-orientated director. He's 'stagy' in a good sense. He frees the actors instinctively by setting up his cameras and lighting, then allowing freedom within that framework. He never tells you a word, but just by the way he has you move, the scene comes alive. He pointed me in a direction and said, 'Go here, go there.' It was extraordinary."

"Extraordinary" is the word for Pacino's entire performance in the movie, from the first sight of Sonny Wortzik as he sits in his beat-up car before the robbery, psyched up to the eyebrows, the pupils of his eyes dilating with excitement. His master plan begins to fall apart almost before the robbery is under way, with one member dropping out and taking the subway home, leaving Sonny and Sal (Cazale) to make all the running. Sonny's "OK, we're movin' right along, folks," and "I'm a Roman Catholic and I don't wanna hurt anybody" manage to be ludicrous, droll and tragic all at the same time. Pacino conveys frenzy, determination, concern and idiocy within seconds of each other yet still manages to pull together these disparate strands into an utterly credible performance. When everything is lost and he sees Cazale being wheeled away on a stretcher, the camera lingers on a man watching his dreams swirling down the drain. There was ample evidence of the "strong feelings" Pacino had felt for Sonny in every frame of the movie.

If Pacino is superb, so is Cazale. With his wide, high forehead, cleft chin, sad-sack expression and long, center-parted hair, Sal looks like a cross between a disconsolate spaniel puppy and a morose Mohican. "Your body is God's temple," he solemnly informs one of the tellers, trying to persuade her not to light a cigarette. Yet Sal is no mere cipher, resigned to his fate, as Cazale powerfully illustrates in his explosion of rage when Sonny makes one idiotic proposal too many.

The movie opened to mixed reviews, with Vincent Canby in the New York *Times* deeming it Sidney Lumet's "best-ever film outside *Long Day's Journey into Night*." There was no pleasing Jon Landau in *Rolling Stone*, however. "Tired, creaky stuff, that winds up a bore," he complained, adding, somewhat astonishingly, "Its almost total failure rests on Al Pacino's shoulders."

Variety would have none of it. "An outstanding film," it raved. "Frank Pierson's excellent screenplay combines warm, human comedy with solid underlying dramatic pathos that ranks with the best of Frank Capra and Robert Riskin. One cares about Pacino, Durning, the bank tellers, the pizza boy who becomes an instant celebrity, the lover, the wife, even Judith Malina, Pacino's mother who proves his lover's statement that the marriage of his parents was 'like a bad car wreck.' The entire cast is excellent, top to bottom. *Dog Day Afternoon* is, in the whole as well as in the parts, filmmaking at its best."

Richard Schickel, although finding much to praise in "Pacino's electric performance," panned the picture. "One tries to be sympathetic," he wrote, "but the audience leaves the theater with that most devastating of verdicts, *this has nothing to do with me!*"

As usual the public proved itself unwilling to have its judgment pre-empted and voted with its feet, enabling *Dog Day Afternoon* to emerge as the second worldwide smash hit for the Pacino-Bregman-Lumet team.

Pacino received his fourth Oscar nomination for his role, competing with Jack Nicholson in *One Flew over the Cuckoo's Nest*, Walter Matthau in *The Sunshine Boys*, Maximilian Schell in *The Man in a Glass Booth* and James Whitmore in *Give 'Em Hell, Harry*. What gave him an equal boost were Best Supporting Actor nominations for John Cazale and Chris Sarandon, as well as for director Lumet, writer Pierson and the movie itself.

Many believed that this time Pacino would end up the recipient of the coveted award. In Sonny he had created a character from nowhere, resisting the obvious temptation to play him stereotypically gay and investing the role instead with a unique mixture of bewilderment and warmth that was wholly his own. He truly *became* Sonny, out of the closet and onto the streets.

"To do anything is scary for me," Pacino said after his experiences on *Arturo Ui* and *Dog Day Afternoon*. "To do a movie or a play, you're as good as the chances you take, so it's a chance to fail. Also, it's a little frightening to go into yourself and commit yourself, take the responsibility of it, take hold of the reins and say, 'I'm somebody, I've got this to say and that to say, and here it is.' The most exciting thing about it is that opportunity to change, to go through an experience and come out of it different."

He still expressed a preference for the ambiance of the stage: "I like working in the theater at night because it makes my day. It's a focal point. I read more; I see more people; I have a better time. Of course, I *die* when I have to go there at night. I want it to end, I want the run to be over, but every time it is over I miss it, and I go back to it. The change and routine makes for a life."

From his ringside seat Marty Bregman had a deeper awareness than most people of the dichotomy with which Pacino had to live. "Being an actor and acting are two separate existences," he maintains. "An actor hoping to land a job is playing a passive role. That state of being is very destructive; it's living in a vacuum all the time. Existing onstage or on film is a very positive, almost aggressive thing. You're *creating* something. But waiting for that work to be offered is living in a void. It's a frightening role, and that's why most actors, when they finish a project, become depressed. The depression's normal. There is suddenly the prospect of huge inactivity. Even though you're exhausted, it's stopping a force."

Pacino's constant goal remained the integration of his stage and screen work with his personal life. He recalls Brecht's being asked about an actress, "Is she happy she's working?" The maestro had replied, "She's working, she's happy." The concept placed Pacino at the opposite end of the scale from journeymen actors, going from one rent-paying role to the next. The window of opportunity had to exist of finding "the vehicle of expression you didn't know was in yourself."

A NEWS ITEM in January 1976 carried details of Pacino's wedding to an actress named Joanne Alex Skylar. The couple had just returned from New York, Marty Bregman was alleged to have reported, and they had been married at his home in Beverly Hills.

Within hours Bregman was frantically denying the false story, which had been telephoned in by the Associated Press. "That's the biggest bullshit story in ten years," he declared. "Al hasn't married anyone, much less someone called Joanne Alex Skylar, whoever *she* is, if there *is* such a person. It beats me how such a completely untrue story can get started. Al hasn't been on the Coast for months. How could he get married out there?"

Report of Pacino's Marriage a Hoax, the Los Angeles *Herald-Examiner* duly headlined.

WHILE JACK NICHOLSON was being presented with the Oscar for his performance in *One Flew over the Cuckoo's Nest* (John Cazale, too, had lost out, and *Dog Day Afternoon* won only a Best Original Screenplay award for Frank Pierson) Pacino sat the ceremony out in sweat shirt and jeans several thousand miles away in a Greenwich Village restaurant. His only companion was the stage manager with whom he was involved in yet another "workshop" production, this time a revival of Heathcote Williams's *The Local Stigmatic*, for the ubiquitous man of the theater Joe Papp, with whom he had reconciled.

Pacino stoutly maintained that the performance of the play he had just given, for specially invited guests and for no money, constituted a "more important previous date" than the Academy Awards ceremony. "Fame is a perversion of the natural human instinct for validation and attention," he told a photographer, before abruptly turning down a request for a picture.

While maintaining that he would never personally campaign for an Oscar, Pacino later admitted that he understood why some actors did just that: "There are certain manipulations that go on, certain favoritisms, partialities. I don't know where specifically, but I can sense this. I've experienced having lost four years in a row. It's strange. You feel good being nominated; then you get turned into some kind of loser when you don't win it. You've been feeling terrific, and suddenly you've got all these people consoling you. Real strange."

There was a further element of sour grapes in Pacino's reaction to Nicholson's win, the third occasion he had been pitted against the actor. In one breath, he conceded that Nicholson deserved the award: "He's been out there awhile, made a lot of different films; he's been great." The next, he was claiming he would have turned the role down: "I thought *Cuckoo's Nest* was a kind of trap. It's one of those built parts; I don't think it has much depth. Commercially it's very good, but as far as being a really terrific role, I don't think it is. If I won the award, that's terrific. I've won awards. And they didn't make me feel bad winning them, I'll tell you that. They made me feel pretty good. But it also did not make me feel bad *not* winning the Academy Award. I will honestly say I felt—the same. I didn't feel as though I was cheated or that I deserved something and didn't get it. That's honest. That's true. Now, if you ask me whether Jack Nicholson deserved it or not—if he got it, he deserved it."

CHAPTER 14

LOST WEEKEND

For almost a year Pacino enjoyed being out of work, sunk deep in a personal twilight world on his longest-ever "lost weekend," shrinking from the spotlight, haunted by memories of his mother's and grandfather's deaths, brooding on his own mortality. The offers that poured in were rejected for a variety of reasons.

At Sam Spiegel's behest, Harold Pinter forwarded his adaptation of F. Scott Fitzgerald's *The Last Tycoon*, offering the role of Monroe Stahr. The movie was to be directed by Elia Kazan, filling the breach for Mike Nichols, who had bowed out.

After a decent interval, and no response, Spiegel personally forwarded a second copy. Again no reply. Finally "an associate of the actor" telephoned to say the script "wasn't right" for him. Quite apart from the courtesy aspect, Pacino's stance was puzzling. Spiegel's track record stretched all the way back to *On the Waterfront* and the partnership with Brando and Kazan that had helped inspire Pacino as a kid in the Bronx.

Spiegel appeared to have the last laugh when Robert De

Niro accepted the role, although the film emerged as a major disappointment. "There were times in my life when I didn't even read what was being offered to me," Pacino concedes. "Sometimes I can smell something that's not right for me." Maybe *The Last Tycoon* was one of those times, although his olfactory senses might also have picked up that the original director's choice had been Dustin Hoffman and that Spiegel's own preference was always for Jack Nicholson.

For a while Pacino became interested in a project entitled *Slapshot*, the story of a tenth-league ice hockey team that decides to go for the big time and play dirty. Word was leaked to director George Roy Hill, whose project it was, that Pacino was ready to talk. Hill's response infuriated Pacino. "Can he ice-skate?" he was alleged to have asked.

"I should have made that movie," Pacino complained years later. "The hockey player was my kind of character. Paul Newman is a great actor; it's not a matter of that." It was all down, it seemed, to Hill's reported concern over Pacino's ice-skating prowess. "That's all he was interested in" was Pacino's interpretation. "That was a certain kind of comment. He didn't want to talk about anything else. It was like he was saying, 'What the hell, it would work with anybody.' The way in which he responded said to me that he wasn't interested."

"Al's sulk cost him a good movie," said one close associate of the episode. "It was the mood he was in at the time."

Gradually Pacino accepted that Charlie Laughton had been right all along about his drinking. After *The Godfather* he had almost became an alcoholic. At last he began to analyze the tidal wave of success that had almost drowned him: "When you've been down so far you catch pneumonia because you don't have a warm place to sleep, success throws you. I'd been down and out for so long that I began to wonder how much further I could slip. Then all of a sudden I'm the costar in the biggest movie of all time, acting alongside Marlon Brando, one of the world's biggest actors—I couldn't *adjust* to it. Fame is like candy: You want to keep it, but you can't. I've had some bad times with it. I mean, all the changes you have to go through to get yourself animated. One day you're a struggling actor, the next a success. The changes really shook me.

"There's a term in the drinking world which is called reaching one's bottom," says Pacino. "I don't know if I ever got to my bottom; I feel I've been deprived of it! But I stopped earlier than that. Still, there's a pattern in drinking; it can lead to other things, a downward spiral. I took access to AA for a while; it was for a lot of reasons; I asked to go there. I didn't pick up the program, but I found it very supportive and meaningful."

Instead, Pacino found a sympathetic ear in another therapist he visited. From what little he knew of Catholicism, which he roughly equated with psychotherapy, he expected a positive avalanche of hellfire and brimstone to rain down on his head as he expunged his deepest feelings, reopening scars that had never satisfactorily healed. "The amazing part of it all," he marvels, "was that I didn't *disappear* and that nobody *killed* me or said I was *guilty*. It was a *tremendous* relief.

"There is only one way of surviving all the early heartbreaks in this business," Pacino suggests. "You must have a sense of humor. And I think it also helps if you are a dreamer. I had my dreams all right. And that is something no one can ever take away. They cost nothing, and they can be as real as you like to make them. You own your dreams, and they are priceless. I've been a lavatory attendant, a theater usher, a panhandler, all for real. Now, as an actor, I can be a journalist today and a brain surgeon tomorrow. That's the stuff *my* dreams are made of."

THE STRIKING SIMILARITIES to his own situation that he perceived in the character was one of the main attractions for Pacino when he considered the title role in producer-director Sydney Pollack's new project. *Bobby Deerfield* was a superstar racing driver of humble origins, from Newark, New Jersey, rather than the Bronx, who had graduated to an ivory-tower existence in Europe.

The fragile story line, adapted by Alvin Sargent from an Erich Maria Remarque novel, *Heaven Has No Favorites*, had the emotionally closed-off Deerfield meeting and falling for a life-loving European woman, who turns out to have incurable cancer.

What brought the role eerily close to home for Pacino was Deerfield's mid-life crisis, which he felt echoed his own constant struggle to cope with everyday life. He was convinced he could reach inside himself and illuminate the character of the lonely expatriate.

With Marty Bregman reverting to a purely managerial role and negotiating Pacino's $1.5 million fee for *Deerfield*, there was a sense that the partnership was breaking up. Pacino wanted to be his own man and do his own thing. For that matter, so did Bregman. For Pacino, therefore, *Deerfield* became an even more personal project, his own symbolic breaking away. "I didn't want Al to do *Deerfield* because I didn't like the screenplay," says Bregman. "I thought it was a character he should not play. For him to do Bobby Deerfield after the series of great roles he'd played, that stuck in my throat. But he wanted to do a love story, and that's what started the split between us."

In the absence of steady female companionship but determinedly on the path to sobriety, Pacino permitted himself a good, old-fashioned verbal wallow, briefly highlighting aspects of his personality that constantly fought, in his still-confused condition, to gain ascendancy. Now that he was on his own again, the self-pitying: "It gets lonely." The immediately contradictory: "Sometimes it doesn't, but it's a novelty to me and I like it." The bathetic: "The loneliness is something that I have to deal with. It's very deep." The mysterious: "My loneliness has to do with other things, not just being alone. The fact that I get lonely has to be something I'm holding on to." The idealistic: "The other day I was saying to someone, I would give it all up as long as they didn't take my work from me. I would give up fame and most of my fortune." The pragmatic: "Not *all*."

The reasons he provided for all this introspection appeared

to belong to the *Bobby Deerfield* school of navel gazing: "One grows tired of certain inconsistencies, certain alienations, isolations. I do have friends I am close to, but just a few. If I had a home, a family I felt a part of, that would supply me, I guess, with enough whatever it is that makes one go on, and it would be easier for me to balance my success."

Pacino was paying the price for a choice he had consciously made back at the start of the decade, when he had turned his back on the opportunity to develop his personal life on parallel lines with his career. If the alienation from the world and society in his early life had given him the juice to go on, to be the outsider he was, what would happen if the alienation were removed? Would the juice evaporate? It was a risk Pacino had felt unable to take. "I was afraid I wouldn't want to act anymore, that I'd lose my talent," he said. "You don't, but it took me a long time to realize that."

MARTHE KELLER, THE blond thirty-four-year-old costar proposed by Sydney Pollack, was on a roll. She had completed two major Hollywood movies, *Marathon Man* and *Black Sunday*, in the previous eighteen months. After her first film in 1968 the Swiss-born Keller had a four-year affair with the movie's director, Philippe de Broca, with whom she had a son, Alexandre. "We didn't love each other when the child came. I think a man and a woman should love each other, and that marriage should be forever." A brief entanglement with director Claude Lelouch had followed, before the actress, now the veteran of fifteen films and fifty stage roles in Europe, had fallen into what she described as "the big happy accident" of her American film career. She had already come close to costarring with Pacino in *Marathon Man*, when he was John Schlesinger's first choice for the role of Babe, before being overruled by producers Robert Evans and Sidney Beckerman, who plumped for Dustin Hoffman instead.

Pacino's first encounter with Keller was inauspicious. Having towered over Hoffman in *Marathon Man*, the five-foot-eight-and-a-half-inch actress turned up for their lunch appointment in New York wearing flat shoes. Nervous at meeting Pacino, she arrived first and remained seated when he made his entrance. She had informed Hoffman of the meeting, and he had asked if he might join them. He was a great admirer of Pacino's, he explained, and since they had never met, this seemed like the perfect opportunity. "Everything went fine until Dustin walked in," Keller recalls. "He and Al *hated* each other on sight. Then I had to go to the bathroom. With Al watching, I stood up, crouching a little to de-emphasize my height, and began to leave the table. 'Is there something wrong with your legs?' he asked."

For his part Pacino kept the tone light when asked about his initial impressions of Hoffman. "I love his work and think he's brilliant," he claimed, "but when we met, I think a whole different thing came across. And he *is* older. And shorter!" Once his system had recovered from the shock of the introduction, he went on to approve Keller's casting. Marty Bregman is adamant that Keller's *"hated* each other on sight" view is inaccurate: "It's not true. No, they didn't know each other, they've never been close, but he has great respect for Dustin. They're different kind of people. Al was a good boozer, a barhopper. Dustin came from another kind of life. There's an awareness of each other, a competitiveness invented by the media, but they're very different. There are lots of short men in the world!"

Filming in Europe began smoothly at first on *Deerfield*, with Pollack and his leading players seeming to mesh well. "Al's questions are of a very, very detailed and minuscule nature," the director observed. "Like 'How long has it been since Deerfield raced last?' or 'How long does it take him to come down after a race?' He's very hard on a director. In a nightclub scene he wanted to know, 'Is this the first or second time we've been here?' He wants to know what day of the week it is for a scene. He wants to know the entire background to the relationship with the girlfriend he's with before he meets Marthe. 'Did I pick her up? Did she pick me up?' He does not ask broad-stroke questions about what a man wants out of life. Once he starts on the track of a character, it's like a dog picking up a scent."

He had sought Pacino out for the role because of the character's passivity, which he felt could best be conveyed by an actor whose emotions were close to the surface. With an inexpressive actor like Clint Eastwood, Pollack had thought that Deerfield would come across as merely stolid.

Pacino observed a strict fitness regimen during the four months of filming. "In this picture I've got to drive a couple of cars that you've got to be a contortionist to even get into," he explained. "I've also got to run a lot, like jogging in the park, because that's what Bobby Deerfield does in the movie to stay in shape. When you've got to jog a couple of hundred yards in a scene, and the director keeps saying, 'Let's do it one more time,' you know very quickly what kind of condition you're in." He admitted that the schedule would have been even stricter had he chosen to observe it *every* day. "But with guys like Sydney and my trainer breathing down my neck . . ."

The trainer in question was a giant named Al Silvani, who towered over Pacino as he beat on a small punching bag. Silvani had trained twenty-two world champions, including Rocky Graziano, Rocky Marciano and Jake LaMotta, and while there was no intention of launching Pacino on a new career, his sworn duty was to toughen the actor up.

Shortly after Pacino arrived in Paris to begin rehearsals, he and Silvani—or Big Al and Little Al, as they soon became known—set off to explore the city on foot. Together they scaled the Eiffel Tower, Notre Dame Cathedral, ran through the Louvre, trotted around Montmartre and walked almost every street in the city. Pacino enjoyed every minute of it, especially when Silvani allowed him to sit at a sidewalk café and catch his breath.

Later, in Leukerbad, Switzerland, a tiny town forty-five hundred feet up in the Alps, the sight-seeing was over an hour after the two arrived. Silvani set up a gradually accelerating schedule for Pacino, which involved early-morning hikes in the fresh spring air of the resort and setting-up exercises in the sun on the terrace of the sedate Maison Blanche Hotel.

Silvani reminisced to Pacino about the day in 1940 when a scrawny kid had begged to be taught boxing. "He had lots of guts, but he sure was skinny," said the trainer.

After a few months the kid came to Silvani with a strange request: "Al, you know everybody in boxing. I wonder if you could get them to let me sing the national anthem at Madison Square Garden next week?"

Silvani replied, "Why not? Somebody's gotta sing it."

Since then Frank Sinatra had never forgotten Al Silvani, who often served as the singer's bodyguard and companion.

The skirmishing between Keller and Pacino that soon developed was one of the most intriguing aspects of *Bobby Deerfield*'s filming. There were evening games of tennis between the two that were extraordinarily combative. According to Pollack, "We didn't know if they would end up loving or hating each other."

While his two stars teetered on the brink, the relationship between Pollack and Pacino began to cool, as the director was exposed to a hitherto unappreciated aspect of the actor, his rampant insomnia. Since he did not take kindly to delivering psychiatric advice at 4:00 A.M., there was soon a total falling-out. "And Pollack quickly lost patience with Pacino's turtle-slow acting style," one observer noted. "He nearly flipped out over the time Al wasted 'getting into' his role."

"Al and I saw the movie in a slightly different way," said Pollack, "but this is the kind of story that's too personal for anyone to agree absolutely. It's like looking at a Rorschach test. Obviously what I see relates to my own past, and what Al sees relates to his past."

Pacino acknowledged the split and gave his own version of it. "It's because we're different," he explained. "Sydney had a genuine idea for the movie; it meant something to him. We had different views, and in a movie like that you need to be together on it. We were a *mess*. Maybe we would have been better off if I'd listened to him more. . . ."

Filming moved on to Italy's Lake Como, then Florence and finally Le Mans in France, where Pollack assembled a dozen cars, drivers and teams at the celebrated track, together with all the backup equipment, track officials and medical services necessary to simulate races. Pacino's double, Carlos Pace, a Brazilian on the Martini-Brabham team, had already been photographed racing all season in a Bobby Deerfield uniform, with the U.S. flag prominently displayed on his car.

As soon as Pacino reached the location, he spent hours on the phone talking to veteran drivers and watched racing documentaries and newsreels, as well as TV footage by the mile. He wanted to find out how a driver looked, felt and talked, what he talked about, whom he talked to and how he walked, sat and stood, whether at the track or on the street. He took lessons on the Bugatti circuit from the resident pro, all so he could convincingly portray a Formula One driver. Although the movie was not about car racing, Pacino was determined that at least this aspect of the movie would be authentic.

If neither Pacino nor Pollack looks back on the making of *Bobby Deerfield* as an exultant experience, and the finished product seems only to confirm their differences in approach, at least Pacino and his costar went on to find common ground, with Keller moving into his New York apartment soon after filming was completed. There was still a love-hate relationship involved, with both emotions present in equal measure, according to one friend: "Al wanted to be the boss, and Marthe wouldn't do anything to upset him."

In this, as well as in the field of discretion and loyalty, Keller had much in common with Pacino's previous women. "What I feel about Al belongs to me," she said at one point. "It's so beautiful that even talking about it seems like playing striptease with my soul." In a lighter moment she shrugged off her five-foot-eight-and-a-half-inch height to Pacino's five feet seven inches. "You'll never notice in the love scenes in *Bobby Deerfield*," she predicted. "We're all the same height lying down."

She was prepared to talk about professional matters, even to the extent of entering the Hoffman versus Pacino debate, upon which she was in a better position than most to adjudicate. "The only thing they have in common is their hair color, size and talent," she declared. *"Both* are real geniuses. I never saw two people so different, the way they work, the way they act. Al works from the inside, Dustin from the outside."

Hoffman has recalled whirling her around, as if on a dance floor, to prepare for a scene in *Marathon Man* in which they both were supposed to be exhausted. Pacino, she revealed, had his own psychological exercises, a private program he observed before every performance: "I don't suddenly *become* violent," Pacino confirmed. "I *psych* myself up to become violent."

Before Keller's arrival on the scene, Pacino's outfits consisted of T-shirts, rain slickers, jeans, trainers and an accompanying five o'clock shadow. In their place he had taken to wearing Bobby Deerfield's stylishly tailored Meledandri suit and shaving regularly. Pre-*Deerfield* Pacino had been unable even to drive a car, although his lessons stretched back for years; now he was the proud owner of a gleaming BMW.

When he and Keller turned up together at Lee Strasberg's seventy-fifth-birthday bash, fellow guests at New York's Hotel Pierre beheld a transformed Pacino, resplendent in tuxedo and newly styled short haircut.

CHAPTER 15

"ARE YOU AL PACINO?"

His fee for *Bobby Deerfield* safely stashed away, Pacino scheduled a revival of David Rabe's *The Basic Training of Pavlo Hummel*. Apart from acquainting Broadway audiences with what he considered a major work—and with his feelings about Rabe on a personal level clearly shunted to one side—Pacino intended to introduce David Wheeler's Theater Company of Boston to New York.

Rabe, presumably at a discreet distance, was taken aback by the kaleidoscope of different interpretations Pacino gave one scene at rehearsals: "He played it twenty different ways, whimsically, passionately, angrily, grievously, childlike, befuddled, hardly taking a breath between them. This emotion and that. It was like putting on suits."

The startled playwright realized he was watching a man possessed, intuitively sifting and seeking for an ever-shifting "definitive." Pacino continued to allow his interpretation to grow and change as the Broadway premiere approached.

The opening-night party at Sardi's seemed to mark a reversal in PR terms. Pacino and Keller kept the press waiting for more than an hour, then insisted that no photographs be taken. "Is it that bad, Al, being on the front page?" columnist Earl Wilson asked the next morning.

Wilson had listened disdainfully to the advice from Pacino's aides at the Longacre Theater, who had earlier advised the writer, "Oh, don't *talk* to him; he's *so* sensitive, *so* dedicated, *so* immersed in his work." In all this Wilson detected a strong scent of bullshit. "Don't be a Garbo, Al," he advised. "Give out some interviews, pose for some pictures. You might not feel so immersed. You might even find there are newspaper guys who are just as dedicated to their business as you are in yours." He dubbed Pacino "the male Greta Garbo."

Wilson was also unimpressed with the three guards with walkie-talkies, hired with Pacino's approval, two of them from nightly duty at the Longacre. When the actor was questioned about them at Sardi's, Pacino's already frayed first-night nerves snapped. "I don't need *no* bodyguard," he snarled. "I'm from the *South Bronx*. I can *handle* it."

Pacino's grandmother Kate Gerard gave the lie to this particular piece of braggadocio. "Sonny was a very *refined* boy," she confirmed. She was also less than enthralled by the graphic "horrors of the Bronx" account that her "little dude" had given of his upbringing: "A lousy back apartment in a scummy, bad neighborhood." She says: "He always says the *bad* things, my grandson. He sounds like he comes from the slums. It was very nice, a nice section."

ALTHOUGH *PAVLO HUMMEL* was seen by some as the weakest of David Rabe's Vietnam trilogy, *Sticks and Bones* and *Streamers* being considered tighter and tougher, the play remained a powerful and eloquent indictment of the waste, stupidity, corruption and implied cheapness of life the conflict had visited on an entire nation. "Pacino's performance is compounded of an inner power that surmounts questions of time and datedness," Alan Rich wrote in *New York* magazine. "Overlook this at your peril," the New York *Daily News* advised. Nominated for his second Tony award for the play, Pacino chose to lunge at those critics who regarded Hummel as a cipher; Walter Kerr had been particularly dismissive, terming the character a "wistful zero" and describing Hummel as Pacino's "Dustin Hoffman performance."

"He said that a character like Hummel was unimportant," Pacino grumbled, "and nobody would be interested in a person like that. Nobody cared, why do a play like that? Well, Pavlo Hummel is as 'unimportant' as Willie Loman in *Death of a Salesman*! He is *not* a loser. He has an incredible will to live. He has courage. I'm very positive about him. He's a character that I'd like to be around. Hummel always leaves them laughing. The thing I loved about him was this kid was inept at everything, but he had this great hope. I loved him for that!"

Mel Gussow of the New York *Times* was in tune with Pacino's views, with a single rider. "Acted badly," he pointed out, "the weak, cipher-like Schweiks, Wozzecks and Pavlos in dramatic literature *can* seem boring exercises in futility, shadowy figures. Pacino plays Pavlo *incandescently*. He takes a battle statistic and humanizes him by showing us all aspects of the man, his eagerness, gullibility, weaknesses, especially his vulnerability. His Pavlo is pathetic, a man who courts his own victimization, and he is also a grand clown."

Before Gussow made this connection, Pacino had already viewed Pavlo as a mixture of, among others, Charlie Chaplin and Harpo Marx. As the run of the play progressed, the character became even weirder and more unusual, acting as a counterbalance to the realism of the play around him, while Pacino sought to convey the deprivation and hurt of a man against whom the deck was well and truly stacked. In this, Pavlo Hummel was a character with whom Pacino closely identified.

WITH KELLER OFF to Europe to film *Fedora* for Billy Wilder, Pacino blasted *People* magazine for printing an unauthorized picture of the two of them. "I didn't pose for it," he complained, "and it did damage. Our relationship became crazed by it." In far-off Munich all Keller would add was "It's hard to have a relationship with someone who does what you do."

When she was rushed to the hospital after suffering a series of blackouts, Pacino closed his play for two weeks and flew to be by her side. "I started feeling crazy," the emotional Keller told him. "I didn't recognize myself in the mirror." The prospect of a tragic real-life echo of her role in *Bobby Deerfield* was defused by the eventual diagnosis of circulatory problems.

Pacino undertook a side trip to East Berlin to visit Bertolt Brecht's original theater and watch the Berliner Ensemble at work. The story of one of their rehearsals had always intrigued him. The actors arrived late, then wandered onstage and began exchanging jokes. They drank coffee together and cavorted around the set, chatting and jumping on and off boxes. Then they sat around talking for a while and left. "Rehearsal" was over.

Back in New York Charlie Laughton saw further affirmation of his friend's commitment to his craft. The entire cast of *Pavlo Hummel* was startled when a full dress rehearsal was called—on the afternoon of the final performance! "He felt a certain slackness had crept in," says Laughton. "He was living that part, it meant so much to him, everything had to be right. After the show he looked at himself in the dressing room and said his farewell to Pavlo."

Pacino's dedication was rewarded with a Tony, Broadway's top accolade, this time for Best Dramatic Actor.

WITH *FEDORA* COMPLETED, followed by a huge success onstage in Paris with Chekhov's *Three Sisters*, Keller was reunited with Pacino in New York. "Al has changed in a year," she told friends. "When I met him, he would walk with his head down. Now he's gotten taller, or I've gotten smaller. He's opened my eyes. He's started to see more things. He's always working, even when he's not working, and he doesn't always know it.

He constantly talks about characters. He plays so many parts every day."

Keller filled her own day with domestic chores, escorting her daughter to school, coaching with Lee Strasberg, taking ballet classes, playing tennis and reading a book a day. Her apartment on the Left Bank of Paris was kept on, together with her chalet in the Swiss mountain village of Verbier. Although Keller loved the energy and electricity of New York, she professed to be scared of America and the pace of life there. "Without Al I wouldn't do it," she admitted. "Some people get married because they are afraid to be alone. I'm not; you're born alone, and you die alone. However, I believe one should have a man in one's life, someone you always go to and share with."

Since his pre-*Deerfield* profundities, Pacino had lightened up, if only just a little, with the advent of Keller in his life. "Let me tell you something about the power that I feel," the born-again romantic suggested. "The power one feels when one is with love, when one loves oneself and someone else, and is loved. The *power* of being loved. Loving *is* a power. If you have that, you really don't need much else in worldly power. The fact that someone would give their life for you and that you would give your life for them, that is incredible."

He still looked decidedly uncomfortable when he and Keller were interviewed together. Dressed in beige jeans and a T-shirt, he shifted his weight edgily from one foot to another as Keller held forth. "There are those who think we're together only because of the film. They're wrong. This is a real love story. With Al it's everything, without him it's nothing. We are really, really, really in love," she stressed, lingering over each "really."

She wrapped her arms around Pacino's waist and squeezed him tenderly. "He's my only man." Pacino's response was a nervous, positively embarrassed half-smile. Never one to shout his feelings from the rooftops, here he had a partner happy to do just that.

"I need to admire somebody," Keller added. "I lived alone

for two years before I met Al. Why? Because I prefer to be with myself rather than with someone stupid. And I could never have somebody who is younger or who doesn't make as much money as I do. Al has the most incredible talent and energy, and I need both from him. Al feels comfortable when he's immersed in one-to-one relationships. He's never been one to run from a relationship. We are very similar that way. I belong to Al, nobody else. Whatever he wants—marriage or no marriage, children or no children—he can have."

Pacino's only comment was given in a quiet, almost inaudible whisper: "We just want to be left alone together. We're happier that way. We just want to fade into the night—unrecognized, unnoticed and by ourselves."

Keller shrugged off the addition of a Dior wedding dress to her wardrobe, trilling, "A girl doesn't know when she'll need one." If she had Pacino in mind as a candidate for the altar trip, she was soon to be sadly disabused of the notion.

IN CONVERSATION WITH critic Mel Gussow, Pacino still contended that ultimately he found movie acting unsatisfying. He quoted the late actor Leslie Howard on Hollywood: "In an atmosphere of indescribable din and well-meaning chaos, actors succeed in giving a superficially proficient performance, with its glaring shortcomings irrevocably fixed for prosperity." In the theater, on the other hand, there was, again quoting Howard, "the sublime satisfaction which is the immediate reward of a perfect communication between both sides of the footlights, as the actor leads his audience from the beginning to the end of a fine play."

"I'm just at that beginning," Pacino argued. "I'm still struggling. I'm just beginning to understand what technique is, being able to let go of some of the things you are secure with. The freer I am, the lighter I am. You want to get to the point in acting when you don't have to act. You hope it stays with you like lint. Duse worked on her voice so hard that when she spoke it seemed to come from the audience."

Pacino was on an unprecedented career roll, the only major actor successfully straddling the world of stage and movies simultaneously, with *Pavlo Hummel* on Broadway in the summer of 1977 and *Bobby Deerfield* set for a fall premiere. Behind his rhetorical question to Mel Gussow, "What can you say about a profession where you can be anybody and do anything?" there lurked a quiet pride.

He laughed when asked about the bewildering range of characters he chose to play, stretching onstage from the psychotic Murph in *The Indian Wants the Bronx* to the zealous blockhead who tries his limited but level best to become "Good Soldier Hummel."

"These two guys would never get together," he told Gussow. Asked if he could imagine a meeting of minds between any of his other characters, he replied, "I don't think so, except for Lionel in *Scarecrow*. He could get along with anybody. The rest, I don't see it."

He laughed off the notion of Michael Corleone sharing afternoon tea with Frank Serpico. "OK, I'm going to have a party this week," he joked finally, "invite them all and see if it works out." The one common binding agent between all his characters, he pointed out, was the empathy they, or their situation, evinced in him.

"There should be a stamp on an actor's work," he claimed. "People went to see Junius Booth enact Richard III just as they went to see Toscanini or Caruso. Too often an actor is put in a position of doing a part he can't really speak through. I have to *connect* with the material. My training was on the boards in the early '60s. And my training continues. When you look at John Gielgud in *No Man's Land*, one of the great performances of all time, or when you look at Sam Levene making his entrance in *The Royal Family*, that's *50* years on the boards!"

Nor was his respect confined to those legendary names, for Pacino had by now acquired his own group of traveling players, including Jack Kehoe, Penny Allen and Richard Lynch. And he was loud in his praises for thespians as diverse as Olivier, Brando ("We are all indebted to him. There has been an American style of acting since Brando"), George C. Scott and Walter Matthau. ("I love Matthau. He liberates me.")

He later named Gary Cooper as "kind of a phenomenon, his ability to take something and delegate it, give it such dignity. One of the great presences." Charles Laughton remained his "favorite," while Jack Nicholson had Laughton's "kind of persona; he's also a fine actor." Robert Mitchum and Lee Marvin were "great, terrific actors." Other performances he singled out included Brando's in *Viva Zapata*, Gielgud's in *The Charge of the Light Brigade*, Vanessa Redgrave's in *Isadora* and Nick Nolte's in *North Dallas Forty*.

Bang the Drum Slowly was his "all-time favorite film." He described the baseball motif and the quality of the relationship between Michael Moriarty and Robert De Niro as "beautiful." He also liked Fellini's *8 1/2*, loved *La Strada*, wasn't crazy about *Amarcord*. His favorite actress in the world was Julie Christie, "the most poetic of all actresses."

Later still the list was updated to include Meryl Streep—"I always go to see her. It happens once in a while that somebody like her comes along who has that kind of alacrity"—Diane Keaton—"just the greatest"—Barbra Streisand—"I wouldn't mind doing something with her"—Gérard Depardieu—"I love that guy"—Richard Gere—"When I saw him for the first time, I knew he was a movie star; it's written all over him. He has an unusual charisma"—and William Hurt—"He's got it; he's really got it. He's a major actor, the same as Kevin Kline."

Pacino emerged as a fan of actors in general: "We're all so different, probably more varied than any other profession. I can always spot an actor. He's usually looking for work, and he's dieting! There are actors who are strong in suggestibility. There are actors who are intellectually attacking material. There are actors who are very instinctive and operate completely on tremendous believability. There are actors who are able to find the humor in a situation immediately and get right to the essence of a play."

Asked what he would be if he were not an actor, Pacino

replied, "I wouldn't be me. You would be asking someone else that question. I'm an Elizabethan person. I've got one foot in the Elizabethan age. But people have this other image of me." The determination in his voice was unmistakable as he added, "Time will take care of that."

Pacino revealed he was looking at the possibility of a *Pal Joey* remake for his next stage role. Then there were various productions of Strindberg, by now his favorite playwright, he affirmed, as well as Shakespeare to consider, possibly a Broadway *Hamlet* or *Richard III*.

In Marthe Keller's absence, Gussow witnessed one of Pacino's most pressing problems as the two men sat down for dinner at the actor's favorite neighborhood restaurant. "Are you Al Pacino? *Are you Al Pacino?*" a young woman demanded after flying across the room to their table. Pacino was flustered and, after a slight hesitation, stumbled for the door. He looked back for a few seconds, seemed to consider staying, then left anyway, with Gussow following his confused trail.

Back at Pacino's apartment, dinner was a large slice of pie and a glass of milk. "The apartment is in transition," Pacino explained, waving at the sparsely furnished living room. Through a large hatch lay a modest kitchen; there was a bedroom largely taken up with an unmade bed and a bathroom with a constantly running toilet. "I look around at places I think I should be living in; then I come back and move the couch or the piano and I'm satisfied. This is a pretty nice place."

Gussow noted with some amusement that the name of the apartment's previous occupant was still on the door, as "C. Bergen." Not only that, but with neither a guard nor a doorman in evidence, Pacino had left the name of long-departed tenant "Goldman" on his downstairs buzzer.

If Pacino's purchase of not one but two houses at Snedens Landing, New York, can be seen as a step nearer security, or at least a striving for that goal, it was two full years before he felt secure enough to move in. And even then he still kept up the humble New York apartment.

CHAPTER 16

BREAKUP

Pacino was intrigued by an approach from Francis Ford Coppola to consider either the role of Willard or Kurtz in the director's adaptation of Joseph Conrad's *Heart of Darkness*. Since the script for *Apocalypse Now* had been written specifically for Steve McQueen, who subsequently rejected both roles, Pacino asked that it be rewritten before he gave a definitive reply. Even then he still refused to commit. "Al," the astounded Coppola was told by an emissary, "can't fit it in."

Pacino tells a slightly truncated version of the incident. "I told Francis that I hadn't been in the army, and if I were to go, I wouldn't want to go to war with him!"

Coppola had perhaps misinterpreted Pacino's enthusiasm for *The Basic Training of Pavlo Hummel*; it had been the universality of Hummel's theme, rather than the play's Vietnamese setting, that had captured his imagination. Another factor, of course, may have been *Hummel*'s stage-bound location, rather than the hellhole in the Philippines Coppola intended. "Al would have done the film if we could have made it in his apartment," Coppola told one scribe. ("I doubt it," says

143

Marty Bregman. "Al simply wasn't hooked on the characters, whether it was being shot in his apartment or in the depths of the jungle.")

After further rejections, from Jack Nicholson, Robert Redford and James Caan—and a falling-out with Harvey Keitel during production—a chance meeting in an airport lounge with Martin Sheen finally landed Coppola his Willard. He was particularly bitter about the turndowns from Caan and Pacino, the "young whippersnappers" whose careers he had helped launch in *The Godfather*. Perhaps Brando's participation as Kurtz, together with Robert Duvall's return in a supporting role, eased his indignation.

"Things come along and I look at them," said Pacino. "They're good films with good directors, yet I feel that's six months of my life. I can't give myself to something unless it presents some kind of challenge or stimulation. I can read a script, and it can be very good, but I wouldn't want to do it. I've been as discerning as I can be in the picking of my films. At this point it seems to be one of the few things I've been consistent at."

Undaunted by all this, Marty Bregman thought that ex-Marine Corps Sergeant Ron Kovic's intensely moving autobiography, *Born on the Fourth of July*, would hold enormous appeal for Pacino. He secured an option on the rights with his friend and star client in mind. Privately he felt the movie would be "almost impossible to make," because of its supposedly noncommercial twin themes, the Vietnam conflict *and* paraplegism. Still, he relished the challenge.

Kovic remembers both Pacino and Bregman telling him at their first meeting that they thought his experiences could be turned into a great movie. The project seemed to be gaining momentum when Bregman hired a screenwriter, who turned up at Kovic's house in a limousine, impressing his mother no end. When the first submitted script failed to work, Oliver Stone, a Vietnam veteran himself, was given the job by Bregman. He had first heard of Stone during a holiday in Africa with his wife. Stone's mother was staying with them in the home of a mutual friend and kept going on about this son she had who was a terrific writer. When Bregman met with him on his return to the States and asked to see an example of his work, he was presented the script for *Platoon*. Bregman liked it enough to option it, then sent it to every studio head. Although they all turned it down, Oliver Stone's name had had its first airing in Hollywood's executive corridors.

Having rejected *Platoon* at Columbia, Peter Guber commissioned Stone to write the screenplay for *Midnight Express*, the movie he was producing independently after leaving the studio. Meanwhile, Bregman and Stone had become close buddies. "I was his rabbi," says Bregman with a grin.

Born on the Fourth of July proved a tough sell for Bregman from the beginning. "I approached everyone in town," he recalls, "but it was just me and Stone, still a relatively unknown writer." For a while Paramount picked up an option, which then passed to Universal. When it put the movie into turnaround, Bregman was left with no alternative but to develop it himself.

After months of tricky negotiations and several exhausting trips to Europe, Bregman returned in triumph. Preproduction money had been secured from a group of West German investors, with the promise of more to come. With Daniel Petrie scheduled to direct, and a distribution deal set up with Orion, the picture moved from the status of a dispiriting "no-no" project to a heartening "go."

Pacino was enthusiastic enough to grow a mustache, just like Kovic. He also turned down *Coming Home* and the role of the paraplegic that went to Jon Voight, on the basis that he was making Kovic's story. A decision to pass on Terrence Malick's *Days of Heaven* landed Richard Gere a major role.

Pacino spent a lot of time getting to know Kovic, who was lodged in a plush New York hotel courtesy of Bregman. Kovic began staying out all night dancing at Studio 54 in his wheelchair, sleeping till noon, then getting down to work with Pacino while forty-five-dollar hamburgers were wheeled in from room service.

To the exhausted veteran it was a stark contrast with the misery of the rat-infested VA hospital he had endured on his repatriation. He was living it up in Grace Slick's suite. He was *somebody;* his book was about to be filmed and Bregman and Pacino were the catalysts who were making it possible. Why, rehearsals were already well under way, with location filming due to start in Puerto Vallarta, Mexico, in a matter of weeks.

The team, as Kovic read it, could hardly be closer. "Oliver was wounded in Vietnam five days before I was, in January 1968, so we understand each other," he enthused. "Dan Petrie was wounded in action in World War Two. Marty had polio as a child and walks with a brace. And Al and I have become good friends."

The end of the honeymoon began as Kovic sat one day in the bustling Drake Hotel awaiting Pacino's arrival. Their last meeting had been four days earlier, when Pacino had hosted Kovic's thirty-second-birthday party, with a host of stars, including Robert De Niro, in attendance.

Eagerly sitting forward as the actor walked through the revolving doors, Kovic slumped back into his wheelchair as he noticed the fateful change in Pacino's appearance. "I knew I was going to get the hug and the kiss on both cheeks before they do you in," he recalled. "I knew my dream was dead because Al had shaved off his mustache. . . ."

The movie, it seemed, had been canceled for financial reasons, the follow-up finance from Germany having fallen through. Kovic rejects this explanation. "If Pacino had really hung in there, it would have been done," he insists. "My feelings when I left New York were 'Why are you telling me the money isn't there?' If he had wanted to make this, they would have made it. He had the name; he had done *Dog Day Afternoon, Serpico* and *The Godfather*s. He *must* have been the one that backed out."

Oliver Stone agrees. "Al got cold feet. If he'd gone ahead, any money problems would have been taken care of. It was a heartbreaker for everyone involved. Marty Bregman was in for a million dollars of his own." ("More," says a tight-lipped but philosophical Bregman.) "I just gave up at the thought that a studio wouldn't make a six-million-dollar film," adds Stone, "not a lot for one starring Al Pacino. I became semicomatose, and Ron became a complete basket case."

With the movie's cancellation and the immediate withdrawal of Bregman's largesse, Kovic was given two days to leave his hotel and denied further admission to Studio 54. The attitude of the disco's owner was simple: "This movie isn't happening. Now, who *are* you and what are you doing in my place?"

The extraordinarily individual account Pacino later gave of the cancellation throws another name into the plot, that of director William Friedkin, and seems to confirm Stone's and Kovic's theory that Pacino was indeed the one who jumped ship. *"Born on the Fourth of July* was a 'go' project," Pacino told Laurence Grobel of *Playboy.* "Billy Friedkin and Oliver Stone wrote a terrific screenplay, but Billy couldn't do it for some reason. Apparently it was a studio that wouldn't let him out of a commitment. When a director is taking on a picture of that size and dimension, it's his picture. I had an interest in making it with Billy. So suddenly, Friedkin is out of the picture —now what? I wasn't going to make that movie!"

Bregman is uniquely placed to sort out the red herrings on display. "Friedkin did *not* cowrite," he says. "We had a couple of meetings; that was all. Then I tried Sidney Lumet, but he didn't like the script, which was no news, since he hadn't liked *Serpico* or *Dog Day Afternoon* at first either. Finally we were in rehearsals with Dan Petrie. Then the money never came, so it went down. If Al had held on, it's just possible that we might have landed another deal. In that sense Oliver is partially right. But how long can an actor remain with a project? He has to get on with the rest of his life."

The cancellation led to a further cooling of Pacino's relationship with Bregman, who decided to pursue his future production ambitions without the benefit of his ex-client and friend. "It was a series of events that neither of us was responsible for," he still claims. "We had both been heavily into the project, and the rug was pulled from under us. It was an unhappy, wounding experience for both of us."

His conversion from manager to producer had been inevitable all along. "I grew tired of playing nursemaid to gifted but insecure actors," he explained. "I'd worked with actors for most of my life, and it wasn't fun anymore. Most of them start off their lives being brutalized by everybody. It's a world of negatives, coupled with an inability to pay your bills or your rent. So actors are very fragile and vulnerable, and dealing with insecure people is hard."

Bregman's career away from Pacino was to have its own share of ups and downs. There were flops with Sean Connery in *The Next Man*, with the British thriller *Venom*, with the Alan Arkin-Marshall Brickman collaboration *Simon* and with John Ritter and Jim Belushi in *Real Men*. There was a good beginning with another ex-client, Alan Alda, in *The Seduction of Joe Tynan*, a smash with *Four Seasons*, flops with *Sweet Liberty* and *A New Life*.

Through all this Bregman remained a producer whose integrity was never in question. "He knows people very, very well," Alan Alda points out, "in the way that a successful salesperson often knows human nature. He knows how people behave, and he can spot the bull. That helps him to be useful to a writer or director. He'll tell you when something doesn't ring true.

"I've had screaming fights with Marty," Alda admits, "but he fights you because he's really trying to make the film better, not because he's just concerned with making a point. Besides, his bark is much worse than his bite. He's actually a soft touch. He has given or loaned money to people I wouldn't give lunch to. He has a total inability to fire someone on a movie. On the other hand, if he feels he's been wronged, he does the legal equivalent of killing you. You have to remember that Marty became a successful manager by taking on people nobody had ever heard of. These people *became* stars, but they were not stars when he began to represent them. He has a very good eye for talent."

Bregman acknowledges his reputation as a strong producer.

"What does that mean?" he asks. "Only that I have opinions and I express them. I guess that makes me seem like an anomaly. I don't tell the director what angles to use or how to stage a scene, but I believe that making a film is a collaborative effort. The actors have an input; the director has an input; the writers and producers have input."

It was daily exposure to the idiosyncrasies of his ex-clients on the production side that originally convinced Bregman that an opportunity existed for him. "Some of them couldn't produce their own lives," he maintains, "let alone a checkbook. Let alone a *movie*! The studio would give them five million dollars or so, and they'd do it all by phone. They're unprepared. One person *has* to see that straight line to the end. One person has to have that vision and channel all the elements and energies to a very specific conclusion. It all depends on a producer attentive to his project. I am involved in every aspect —concept, preproduction, casting, production, postproduction, right up to planning the ad campaign. Nothing is done without my approval. That's the way I like it."

One thing was for sure; with *Serpico* and *Dog Day Afternoon* behind them, Pacino and Bregman had broken up a tested and winning combination. After a year of not talking to each other, Pacino tried to reinstate *Born on the Fourth of July* on his own. His agent, Stan Kamen, approached Orion to consider putting up the money and starting afresh. It never happened.

Another ten years were to pass before Oliver Stone had the clout and, in Tom Cruise, the star to remount the project. Although Bregman's name did not appear on the credits of this production, he played a major role in its reincarnation.

The cancellation of *Born on the Fourth of July* also coincided with the breakup of Pacino's relationship with Marthe Keller, with whom he had planned to share a Malibu beach house during the shooting. Jill Clayburgh and Keller were clearly the two candidates for an admission Pacino made a few years later: "I've been in love twice. The first time, because of my career, I wouldn't have any of it. I knew it was promising, but there were a lot of things happening in my life and I could not deal with it at the time. The second time I found some other reason."

Soon it was reported that Pacino had taken up instead with thirty-year-old Maureen Springer, the owner of a chic beauty salon in Manhattan. A break from actresses? Almost, not quite. Ms. Springer was said to be "an aspiring actress."

"Acting isn't so tough," Springer blithely informed *People* magazine. "You just have to know the right people."

CHAPTER 17

"MOMMA DOESN'T LEAVE YOU"

ALTHOUGH PACINO MAINTAINS that when he's in love, he's a "one-woman man," more and more women were discovering it was a question of hitting the moment. His failure to sustain personal relationships on an elevated emotional basis can be viewed as both revenge and compensation for the treatment he received as a child. Ever since his mother dispatched him to his grandparents as an infant, Pacino has had a dread of being abandoned. "You can depend on women for certain things," he concedes, "but you cannot invest anybody with that much power; it's not fair to yourself or to the person. It's hard to know that, because you *did* invest in your mother. *Momma doesn't leave you.* I guess I probably have an intense fear of being left."

The one sure way to avoid the condition, he swiftly discovered, was to get out first. Despite this, Pacino for a long time remained a split personality romantically, the cynical realist in him constantly arriving to "rescue" the romantic from the pit-falls of trading emotional links, the stage from which he con-stantly recoiled, the one line he stubbornly refused to cross.

In a *Playboy* interview Pacino agreed there had been times in his life when he had "juggled" several women at the one time, although he disagreed with the terminology as well as the male chauvinistic implication. "If you go with three or four different women," he pointed out, "you don't necessarily jug-gle *them*. They could be juggling *you*, going with three or four different guys! There was a time in my life when being dishon-est with women was the natural way to be. I finally said, 'Hey, I have to stop this silliness.' "

If the reins of emotional involvement had to be drawn up short when the perilous stage of interdependence was reached, Pacino maintained that casual sex, in his guise of a superstar icon, was still off the agenda. When girls approached him, as they still did, with offers of no-strings sex, he claimed invari-ably to turn them down: "Somebody was telling me about a woman who said, 'Al Pacino, I would go to bed with him and I'd live with him, I'd do this, this and this.' I said, 'No, not Al Pacino. *No*. The *symbol*. What Al Pacino *represents*.' That atti-tude alienates you. You start pulling away, and you start be-lieving what they call you, a superstar—away from everything else, untouchable, unreachable. Who can live that way? You're living in a psychotic state if you're living that way."

Pacino's continuing dilemma was clear and by now well-trodden earth. He still yearned to be desired for himself, not because of the stardom he had achieved. The question re-mained: Who *was* Al Pacino?

THE REASSEMBLED VERSION of *Godfathers I* and *II* as "a novel for television" was shown on the struggling NBC network in No-vember 1977, spread over four evenings, and with an adver-tised length of nine hours. In practice, this amounted to seven hours and fourteen minutes, excluding commercials.

Since he was busy working on *Apocalypse Now*, Coppola left

the reedit, which incorporated almost an hour of previously unshown footage, mostly from De Niro's segment, entirely to Barry Malkin. The story, now told in chronological order, was no less compelling. And no less ironic, considering Pacino's dominating performance, was his exclusion from Brando's and De Niro's Oscar-winning circle. "Pacino's Michael Corleone may be the most shocking study of deteriorating character in all of American cinema," David Thomson maintained. *"The Godfather* is a masterpiece, and Michael is without doubt its central character, the most resonant metaphor of America. In retrospect, it seems only part of our reluctance to face harsh truths that Brando and De Niro got Oscars as robust, benevolent patriarchs, while Pacino's breathtakingly lucid definition of evil went unrewarded."

There was another reprise of "Al Pacino's Greatest Hits" from an unexpected quarter in the same year, when John Travolta's *Saturday Night Fever* disco dervish, Tony Manero, turned out to be a big Pacino fan. Following Norman (*Serpico*) Wexler's script, Manero had the popular Serpico poster on permanent display in his bedroom and an impressive Sonny Wortzik "Attica! Attica!" impersonation from *Dog Day Afternoon* at the ready.

Pacino ducked when he saw the poster in the movie. "Hey, Al, it's you," his companion, Michael Hadge, said, nudging him.

"That's not Al Pacino," he muttered in reply, "that's Serpico."

Travolta's Manero contradicted him from the screen with his subsequent chant of "Al Pa-chee-no! Al Pa-chee-no!"

Although Pacino could never quite come to terms with Hadge's habit of getting up and walking out if a movie displeased him, he has been known to talk back at the screen while watching movies. In *The Goodbye Girl*, featuring Richard Dreyfuss and Marsha Mason, when Mason's character says, "Nobody knew Al Pacino before *The Godfather*," Hadge looked on in amusement as Pacino yelled back, "You're full of shit, Marsha! You were in a one-act play with me before *The Godfather*!"

It took two film companies, Columbia and Warner Bros., to bring *Bobby Deerfield* to the screen, the risk split between them on the First Artists production. The movie had Pacino reversing the Michael Corleone procedure by starting out in truly awful fashion, self-absorbed, petulant and narcissistic, and reverting to the good ol' boy persona that was his before superstardom had turned his head. Deerfield was a man denying his roots, unable to remember either his father's tap dancing or his own sidesplittingly funny Mae West impersonations that had his family falling about. An excess of adoration, both self and otherwise, had caused his emotions to atrophy. "You're perfect, you know that?" a steady girlfriend informs him early on. He nods briefly, pouts and distractedly replies, "Where's my watch?" When he visits a friend in hospital, his sensitivity is further reflected as he inquires, "How's the pain, Carl? They killin' it for ya?"

Into his life comes Lillian (Keller) with her dazzling good looks, incurable illness and impossible accent. (Or should that be impossible illness and incurable accent?) "You think it's a twick?" she asks as they watch a conjurer during their first meeting. Then she grabs his drink. "May I sip from you?"

Bobby Deerfield produced Pacino's first critical savaging. "Deerfield's character is moody and self-concerned in a way that suffocates the audience's interest," Hal Hinson reported. "Pacino is so enraptured with his own glamorous brooding that our involvement is superfluous, an invasion of privacy." The *Wall Street Journal* complained of "Pacino's stultifying performance," while, according to David Ansen at *Newsweek*, the movie was "not so much about star-crossed lovers as crossed stars."

Gary Arnold saw the movie as "the first landmark embarrassment of Pacino's career. You keep expecting him to murmur, 'Bring me a mirror!'" According to John Alfred Avant,

"People will go to see *Bobby Deerfield* because Al Pacino is the star, and many of them won't believe how bad he is in this movie. . . . Among all this year's movie horrors—*Thieves, Welcome to L.A., Exorcist II: The Heretic, The Deep, A Bridge Too Far*, Fassbinder's *Effi Briest*—*Bobby Deerfield* seems the worst, because the embarrassment one feels for Al Pacino is more memorable than anything in the other movies." (Vincent Canby of the New York *Times* warned that the picture, rated PG, "contains some vulgar language and partial nudity that will be seen by those members of the audience who are not taking a snooze.")

At one point in the film, Keller's Lillian asks Deerfield, "Wouldn't it be iwonic if I began to find you iwwesistible?" It sure would, Marthe, even Pacino's most ardent fans will chorus.

Even Sydney Pollack expressed dissatisfaction and revealed that he had always been unhappy with the ending of the movie. "The thing I was always upset about was, Why does she have to be dying?" he said. "I didn't want to make a film about a girl dying; I wanted it to be about a guy who was resurrected."

Wasn't the time to sort this out *before* production had begun? "We were sort of stuck with that or we couldn't do the picture," Pollack protested. "It was just so locked in. It was in the book and in Alvin Sargent's screenplay, too. I made changes with Alvin, and we did lots of rewriting, but we couldn't seem to make the same story without her dying. I just couldn't come up with anything better."

In the first version Pollack revealed that Deerfield had unplugged Keller from her life-support machine. "It was euthanasia. I was of two minds about that. At first I thought it was a very moving scene, but then I realized it was wrong. I said, wait a minute, this didn't have anything to do with what the picture's about. It's very theatrical, but is he going to get caught? Will somebody walk into the room and find all the tubes and stuff? It was a whole other movie we were starting. So we had to take it out.

"Al and I always agreed that we had another scene to shoot,

but we didn't know what it was. We were racking our brains as I was editing the film. Finally, after I had put it all together, I said, 'I don't want to shoot this mystical scene to find out the end of the picture. I'm going to make some sort of paste-up ending, just for now.' When I put some extra footage of the two of them in a tunnel together with a snapshot superimposed, I said, 'Hey, that's not so bad.' So the makeshift ending was retained."

How about Keller's mysterious undefined illness? "I decided if it isn't implicit in the film, I couldn't get it in by making her say it, so I decided to eliminate scenes dealing with the symptoms of her disease. We made wigs with little bald spots—she was going to be looking at herself in mirrors all the time—but I didn't want things to get that realistic. I wanted it to remain slightly larger than life."

Pollack was asked about the scene, which had early audiences falling about the aisles, where Pacino reaches over to stroke Lillian's head, comes away with a small swatch of hair, then tactfully tries to stick it back on. "What I thought was marvelous about that moment," he replied, "was that it was awful and funny at the same time. I wish I could take credit for that, but I can't—it's in the screenplay. I don't think it gets a *bad* laugh, though. Studio people were coming up to me and saying, 'Sydney, I don't know how you feel about this, but they're laughing when the hair comes out.' I had to keep reassuring them every day that it was OK."

Looking decidedly glum at the unfavorable reviews, not to mention the laughter in the wrong places, Pollack expressed the hope "that people will see how good Al is because it's a performance that doesn't call any attention to itself at all. Al had the guts to be obnoxious for the first hour of the film, to the point where you want to punch him. That's a level of truth that very few actors are willing to give."

Audiences took their cue from the devastating critical reception and shunned *Bobby Deerfield* worldwide. It was a year before Pacino was prepared to talk about its cataclysmic failure, his first professional setback since *The Godfather* made

Pacino with Kitty Winn in *Panic In Needle Park*. *(National Film Archive, London)*

Pacino under the watchful eye of Francis Ford Coppola and Marlon Brando, on the set of *The Godfather*. *(National Film Archive, London)*

Pacino looking apprehensive, as well he might, with scene-stealing co-star Gene Hackman in *Scarecrow*. *(National Film Archive, London)*

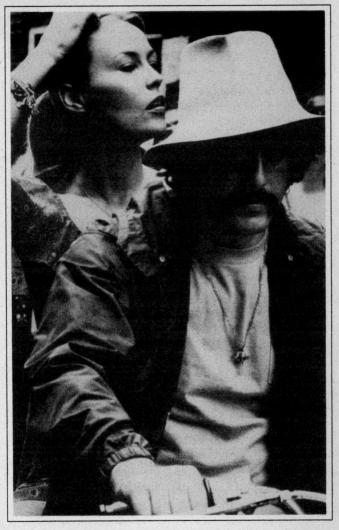

Pacino with Cornelia Sharpe (now Mrs. Marty Bregman) in *Serpico*. *(National Film Archive, London)*

"Come on, Al, cheer up!" Pacino, looking distinctly unhappy, with producer Dino de Laurentiis, on the set of *Serpico*. *(National Film Archive, London)*

Dog Day Afternoon's "Sonny" splashed across the cover of *Gay Scene*.

→

Pacino with buddy John Cazale in *Dog Day Afternoon*. *(National Film Archive, London)*

Director Sydney Pollack conferring with Pacino on the set of *Bobby Deerfield*. *(National Film Archive, London)*

Pacino as Bobby Deerfield. *(National Film Archive, London)*

Pacino with *Bobby Deerfield* co-star and ex-lover Marthe Keller. *(National Film Archive, London)*

Pacino with "guru" Lee Strasberg in *And Justice For All*. *(National Film Archive, London)*

One the set of *And Justice For All* with director Norman Jewison. (National Film Archive, London)

Pacino in a gay disco scene from *Cruising*. *(National Film Archive, London)*

Director and oyster-believer William Friedkin with Pacino, resolving a scene in *Cruising*. *(National Film Archive, London)*

Pacino as a devoted parent in *Author! Author!* *(National Film Archive, London)*

Pacino with co-star and ex-lover Tuesday Weld in *Author! Author!*
(National Film Archive, London)

Pacino with co-star Michelle Pfeiffer in *Scarface*. *(National Film Archive, London)*

Marty Bregman and director Brian De Palma in a huddle on the set of *Scarface*.
(National Film Archive, London)

Marty Bregman. *(courtesy of Jeff Slocomb, Jeff Slocomb Photography, Beverly Hills)*

Enjoying a joke during a break in the weather with director Hugh Hudson on the set of *Revolution*. *(National Film Archive, London)*

Pacino displaying his "medieval clown" brand of humor to Ellen Barkin in *Sea of Love*. *(National Film Archive, London)*

him a household name. Like Pollack before him, he defended the movie as well as his role. "I was after the other side of narcissism," he explained, "that something that happens to a superstar who is idolized. I was after a hint of loneliness, narcissistic detachment, depression, breaking out of that depression, that self-absorbence, and opening up like a flower. In my own life I have not resolved many things; many things I've avoided. *That* is what *Bobby Deerfield* was about. About avoiding, knowing when to duck, when to swerve, when to hide, when to go in, when to roll with punches. That is what I call my way of survival. I've had a lot of selfish incidents in my life. One day I just turned around and said, 'I am a selfish bastard, and I don't have to be.'

"Sometimes characters you play help you work things out in real life," Pacino mused. "It was a move away from anything I'd done before, and I'm very grateful to Sydney for wanting me to do it. Coming at that time in my life, it was very important to me personally. I might have been closer to the character, what he was going through, than any character I've played, that loneliness, that isolation. I'm partial to the movie. It's one of the few I've done that I watch again. It certainly wasn't a career triumph, though."

From a career perspective Pacino had become involved with *Bobby Deerfield* for entirely the wrong reasons. He had been seduced by what the role might provide him, rather than what he might deliver.

CHAPTER 18

"LEARN YOUR LINES, DOLLINK!"

ARLY IN 1977 director Michael Cimino cast John Cazale in a supporting role in *The Deer Hunter*. Meryl Streep, with whom Cazale was living, accepted a part in the movie only so she could be close to him. "They were so happy, it was so apparent, I felt they could do anything," Pacino observed when he visited his buddy and his girl in the tiny West Sixty-ninth Street apartment they shared as "roommate thespians," the legend "Cazale and Streep" on the door recalling great double acts of the past.

After a feeling of lethargy that persisted for several months, Streep persuaded her lover to visit a specialist. The prognosis was shocking and unthinkable: Cazale was dying of incurable bone cancer. Determined somehow or other to "beat the rap," the couple decided to go ahead with *The Deer Hunter*, even though filming was delayed from March to June.

Just before shooting was due to start, routine medical checks carried out for insurance purposes on the entire cast confirmed the diagnosis and set alarm bells ringing at EMI, the movie's backer. Pressure was brought to bear on Cimino to replace Cazale forthwith or to write his character out of the script. When he categorically refused to consider either option, to the point of threatening to walk away from the movie, EMI backed down. The couple's secret remained a secret from most of the cast members.

A remission spell was brief. "John seemed to be limping," one of the cast, Chuck Aspergen, noted. "I thought the heat had got to him." In the end Cazale was so weak he could barely speak his lines. Back in New York, with the movie completed, he registered as an outpatient at Memorial Sloan-Kettering Hospital and began cobalt treatment and chemotherapy. "Meryl was fervent about John," says one close friend. "She took care of him as if there were nobody else on earth. She was always at his side. It was such a statement of loyalty, of commitment. She never betrayed any notion that he would not survive."

His friends and loved ones by his hospital bed, Cazale died at Sloan-Kettering on March 12, 1978. The knowledge that his friend had been terminally ill did nothing to ease the shocking impact of his death on Pacino. Like Streep, he was inconsolable. The actress had exactly three weeks to go before the start of filming on *The Seduction of Joe Tynan*, with Marty Bregman, Jerry Schatzberg and Alan Alda. According to Streep, the movie was made on automatic pilot.

What was the point, Pacino asked himself, all that talent, good humor, wit and perspicacity, snuffed out by a handful of maverick cells? And Cazale's illness was like history repeating itself; only a year earlier Pacino had lost another friend to cancer, the young actor Norman Ornellas, who had appeared with him in *Serpico* as well as onstage.

Pacino had totally identified with the needs and aims Cazale had spelled out: "The process of acting is the process of looking for the person in the character you're playing. That process is very similar to looking for yourself. I sometimes wonder if the inability to find oneself makes one seek this in other people, in characters. I'm closer now, having been an actor for a while, than I've ever been to finding myself." Cazale had scorned recognition for its own sake, wary of the narrow line between fame and infamy; his ultimate goal had been to be "a great actor, pure and simple."

Pacino could see it was a fitting epitaph for both his friends, but one that, tragically, had arrived far too soon.

WHEN NORMAN JEWISON approached Pacino with the role of lawyer Arthur Kirkland in . . . And Justice for All, the director received an unexpected response. "Norman, why don't I get some actors together and read it for you?" Pacino suggested. "Then I'll see how I feel about it." If this was an attempt to cross-fertilize the workshop approach he followed in the theater, the result went on to work in Jewison's favor as all of the assembled cast agreed the project was worthwhile.

Pacino admired the involvement of Kirkland and his crusading character, fighting legal corruption in and out of the courts. He saw Kirkland as a mover, unlike the losers and antiheroes he had played to date, and sensed an originality in the material. According to Oliver Stone, . . . And Justice for All's one-million-dollar salary also represented greener pastures for Pacino and was the real reason behind his abandoning Born on the Fourth of July. Although Stone was mistaken, Pacino would have come out even had he chosen the movie entitled Kramer vs. Kramer instead. When he turned this down, albeit in book form, in favor of . . . And Justice for All, the inexorable Dustin Hoffman moved quickly to fill the breach.

Pacino carried out a considerable amount of research before filming began, working with several lawyers on a variety of cases. Lee Strasberg was signed for the role of Pacino's grandfather, reuniting with his star pupil after their first outing together in Godfather II. To Pacino the erudite Strasberg was God, his pronouncements nothing less than Holy Writ. He loved the story of Strasberg on the beach one day, gazing at the ocean. "Why don't you go in?" someone had asked him. "I love the ocean," Strasberg replied, "but I wouldn't want to get involved."

To Strasberg, Pacino was like a son, the last and finest vindication of his controversial Method interpretation, despite Pacino's never having fully subscribed to Strasberg's most characteristic "sense memory" edict. "Some actors *play* characters," Strasberg said, excusing his star pupil. "Al Pacino *becomes* them. He assumes their identity so completely that he continues to live a role long after a play or movie is over. He's one of the most complex actors I have ever met. But I sometimes worry about him. To be so good at what he does and to be so *immersed* in it has to be a burden."

Although Pacino seemed jocular enough on the set, he refused to talk to the press. "Many people confuse his commitment to work with temperament," Strasberg explained. He saw the movie's change of pace as being good for his friend and protégé. "Al has to begin being concerned with the kind of material he chooses, for his own growth as an actor. This film is good for his sense of humor. Every actor has a tendency to be typed, and Al's done one thing after the next that drives home the same tone. The background differed from *Serpico* to *Dog Day Afternoon* to *Bobby Deerfield*, but audiences recall the same drive, the same magnetism, as in *The Godfather*s. He can't always be himself; he's got to vary."

During filming, Pacino, immersed in his character, responded in typical style when a friend reported he was in trouble with a contract. "Let *me* see that," Pacino offered before he realized what he was saying. It was a throwback to his meeting with the heroin dealer in *Panic in Needle Park* and his attempt at a citizen's arrest during *Serpico*. He laughed as he recalled the incident. "You get the feeling that you *are* able to do these things. It's crazy. I literally took the contract from this guy and began to give a legal opinion. Can you imagine that?"

Even the admiring Strasberg found himself exasperated by his protégé's habit of script improvisation when scenes were due to be filmed. Pacino was against memorizing his lines by rote and a self-confessed slow learner of lines who defined his *personal* method as "becoming the character" and trying to figure out what he would have said in a given situation. Strasberg finally rushed in where angels were scared to tread. "Al," he admonished, *"learn your lines, dollink!"* Several years later Pacino was candid enough to recount the story and admit, as if a great truth had dawned on him: "It was a good piece of advice."

The atmosphere on the Baltimore set of . . . *And Justice for All* was completely different from the chill factor often recorded on *Bobby Deerfield.* Pacino was back working with a director to whom he could totally relate. "The thing I like most about Norman," he claimed, "is his sense of involvement. He's constantly with the movie. He broods about it. Even after it's over, he's with the picture; he cares about it a great deal."

In turn, Jewison was impressed that in Pacino he had found an actor whose commitment matched his own. "For almost eighteen weeks Al Pacino *was* Arthur Kirkland," he declared. "Even at night, when we'd finished shooting, he'd answer to that name. I remember sitting between Pacino and Strasberg at dinner. They were still so much in their roles that I found myself saying, 'Grandpa, pass the salt,' or 'What did you think of the scene today, Arthur?' It was uncanny.

"I think other actors could have played Kirkland," Jewison added, "but I have to say I've never worked with a more committed actor in my life. I don't know that much about Al's personal life, but I think the work *is* his life. He doesn't talk about anything but acting. Yet he really doesn't know that much about film; he's only made seven other movies. That worries him. 'I will be the instrument,' he said to me, 'because I can play all the notes; just lead me.' That's wonderful stuff to hear from an actor, and I haven't heard it since I was in the theater."

Strasberg's wife, Anna, revealed a lighter and little-known side to Pacino: the amateur magician who turned up to entertain her family. "We know when he's going to spring a show on us. He comes into our apartment wearing a huge World

War One overcoat in which he hides his paraphernalia. While he's trying out his tricks, he's all magician, and even if they don't work, we're his friends and we think the world of him, so we act amazed. Actually we *are* amazed. Not so much at his tricks, but at his total absorption into the moment."

The Strasbergs were afforded a better opportunity than most to appreciate the chasm of difference between the private and the public Pacino. As well as his magic tricks, his party pieces included imitations, telling stories, miming, playing the piano, even singing. And he would happily listen for hours to arias sung by Giuseppe di Stefano and Jussi Björling.

PACINO'S UPBEAT VIEW of . . . *And Justice for All* and its prospects continued after the movie was finished. He saw it as an extremely simple picture. "It's about ethics and people," he explained, "about a guy who's trying to do his job and his relationship to the law. To say it's about the legal system sounds boring, but this is not what it is. It's funny and poignant." He saw in the character of Arthur Kirkland a similarity to George C. Scott's role in *The Hospital* or even a less detached Serpico. He admired the involvement of Kirkland and his desire to be part of the system, despite the fact it was driving him nuts.

The character certainly had his hands full in Barry Levinson and Valerie Curtin's original screenplay. At one and the same time he was attempting to acquit a black transvestite and convicted thief (Robert Christian) of robbery, trying to spring a young white (Thomas Waites) imprisoned through an identity mix-up and being coaxed to defend a swinish judge (John Forsythe) arrested on a rape charge. If in the end it boiled down to a rerun of "one man against the system," that in itself was no bad thing since the idea had already proved serviceable on several previous outings.

The basic problem lay in the character of Arthur Kirkland, on whose credibility the success of the movie depended. Kirkland certainly knew which side of his cracked wheat was buttered, as witnessed by his running attendance on his "first client," portrayed as a manic adulterer, speed freak and paternity-suit contender, to the exclusion of his hopelessly incarcerated and presumably much less lucrative clients.

Jewison and his writing team gloss over the latest reason for the white youth's detention—Kirkland's dereliction of duty in having gone over the one-year statute of limitations for presenting new evidence. Then Kirkland ducks out of presenting a corrected version of a botched jail report that would have released the transvestite, choosing instead to accompany a catatonic colleague to hospital. Whom does he blame? His partner, for failing to pass on his scribbled alterations to the appeal judge. Kirkland's despairing "I've had all the incompetence I can take!" seems to beg the question, "Would *you* buy a used defense from this man?"

As this supposedly passionate man of principle describes to his new girlfriend, over a Chinese takeout, the hellish injustice of the statute of limitations episode (he was a lousy three days over the one-year limit, for chrissakes!), the pragmatic woman (Christine Lahti, a fine actress wasted) has the temerity to point out that after all, the law is the law. Horrified at this interruption to his self-serving spiel, Kirkland glares at her for a moment, disbelief plastered all over his features. Is he about to explode in her face? No. Levinson and Curtin decide to wheel out a cheap crack that tells you exactly where Kirkland is at. "Well, if that's your attitude," he quips between mouthfuls of monosodium glutamate, "you'll never get me into bed, dear." The line is fine in itself and is amusingly delivered by Pacino. The problem is that it belongs in another movie.

As conceived, written and portrayed, Kirkland's character is a shambles, but one with which the audience is apparently meant to empathize, despite the fact that his bleeding heart is transparently for himself—forget the clients! Final score: Black transvestite hangs himself in despair; white youth is sodomized in jail, then shot to death. Perhaps Pacino was so desperately looking for a change of pace from the somnolence of Bobby Deerfield that he saw the frenetic Kirkland and the movie's up-all-night-on-bennies pace as the perfect antidote. If so, all it turned out to be was an alternate brand of poison.

David Denby in *New York* magazine was just one of the many critics who hammered their own personal nails into the coffin. "Al Pacino looks sallow and exhausted. Isn't it a bit early for his ascension to Paul Muni's late-career status as the Pasteur-Zola-Last Angry Man of the movies? It's a damn silly thing for an actor to want. Jewison wants us to roar with laughter and then suffer scalding tears of indignation, but the mixture is just plain insensitive. The movie misses out on so many different ways it must set some kind of record."

Vincent Canby in the New York *Times* described the movie as being "in the throes of a nervous breakdown from beginning to end," with "Pacino behaving when the movie opens as if he were at the end of the rope, which leaves him no place to go except crazy with moral indignation."

"Every single problem in the film is inauthentic," Renata Adler claimed in *The New Yorker*. "Every crisis and dilemma it claims to find is false. Pacino has never been so unconvincing." According to the *Village Voice*, "Pacino's performance eventually disintegrates into self-righteous hysteria in a courtroom scene of total renunciation that has to be seen and heard to be believed."

Not everyone was so downbeat about the movie, and certainly not about Pacino's performance. Even while describing . . . *And Justice for All* as "a mess," David Ansen in *Newsweek* saw it as "a vital mess, the most interesting film Jewison has made in years. Much of the credit goes to Pacino, who provides a bedrock of real feeling." Though Arthur Schlesinger, Jr., in the *Saturday Review* saw the movie's "helter-skelter tone" as "swiveling irrationally and usually heading straight for a dead end," he still described it as "a valiant, restless film, quivering with a certain shrill quality. Pacino, moreover, gives a strong, deeply felt, carefully wrought performance."

It speaks volumes for the force of Pacino's portrayal that he received yet another Oscar nomination, his fifth, for his portrayal of Arthur Kirkland. Competition came from Jack Lem-

mon in *The China Syndrome*, Roy Scheider in *All That Jazz*,
Peter Sellers in *Being There*, as well as Dustin Hoffman in
Kramer vs. Kramer. Coppola's faithful Robert Duvall was nominated in the Best Supporting category for his work in *Apocalypse Now*. Pacino lost out to Hoffman for the role he had
turned down. "I refuse to believe that I beat Jack Lemmon,
that I beat Al Pacino, that I beat Peter Sellers, that I beat Roy
Scheider," Hoffman graciously declared as he accepted his
first Oscar award, "and I refuse to believe that Robert Duvall
lost!"

By this time *Kramer vs. Kramer* had gone on to prove one of
the biggest hits of the year, while . . . *And Justice for All* had
barely caused a ripple at box-office tills. The feisty, fiercely
independent Jewison had served Sidney Poitier and Rod Steiger well with *In the Heat of the Night;* his recent *Rollerball* had
served Jimmy Caan less well; . . . *And Justice for All* served
Pacino least of all.

With two flops in a row—although he later claimed . . .
And Justice for All "did OK"—Pacino was clearly missing the
deft touch of Marty Bregman, not to mention Sidney Lumet.
Now he declared that he had "never felt entirely comfortable"
with Bregman in the driving seat. After *Dog Day Afternoon*
their relationship had "changed," before finally disintegrating
in the *Born on the Fourth of July* debacle. The pity of it seemed
to be Pacino's increasingly obvious lack of objective judgment
in choosing roles on his own.

When Pacino formed a production company as a front for
his services, he dubbed the enterprise CHAL Productions—
Charlie Laughton and Al, harking back to the days when their
takeover of the furniture removal market had been imminent.

IN 1979 THE indefatigable Joe Papp brought Pacino together
with Meryl Streep, Christopher Walken and Raul Julia to explore the possibility of a New York Shakespeare Festival staging of *Hamlet*. Pacino agreed, subject to his "workshop" principles being followed. He wanted the actors to read *Hamlet*

together over a five-week period, meeting whenever they could
—shades of the Berliner Ensemble!—and reciting the bard's
text to each other. Only after that would a formal reading in
sequence be attempted, followed by a breather. Before any of
that, however, there had to come a first step: Pacino wanted a
discussion on how Hamlet might have talked to his father *be-*
fore he was a ghost and what his relationship to Ophelia constituted *before* the play's commencement. He had in mind nothing less than a "relationship *Hamlet*, about the family. . . ."

"Anything for art," Papp must have rationalized, or more
pragmatically, "anything for Al," for he gave the go-ahead to
this open-ended agenda despite his previous experience with
The Resistible Rise of Arturo Ui. For several weeks the readings
proceeded satisfactorily, at least as far as Pacino was concerned, the funereal pace suiting him down to the ground.
Then came a major hiccup, as Meryl Streep rehearsed Ophelia's nunnery scene and made the cardinal error, to Pacino, of
standing up too early. She first delivered the line "My lord, I
have remembrances of yours that I have longed to re-deliver,"
before Pacino as Hamlet replied, "I never gave you aught."
Streep then started to rise from the table as she began her next
line, "My honour'd lord—"

Everyone froze as Pacino cut in at this point with an admon-
ishing "MERYL!"

Joe Papp finally broke the silence: "All right, Al, what is it?"

"I think we should still be at the table," Pacino replied. "I
think it's *too soon* to get up. I mean, Meryl calls me 'My honour'd lord,' I'm not *ready* for that yet."

That did it for Papp, who promptly called the whole deal off.
"Oh, those Method actors!" he was heard to sigh.

CHAPTER 19

RICHARD OF THIRD AVENUE

T HE FIRST TIME Pacino had attempted the role of Shakespeare's hunchbacked king Richard III, back in Boston in 1973 with David Wheeler, he treated it as "anything goes." "Things kept coming out of me," he recalled. "I took my hump on and off at will. I put a little stuffing in my back. I played a turkey Richard. I changed my accent—English, Japanese. I did Richard as many different people—Lee Strasberg, George C. Scott, my grandfather."

Six years later much of this remained unchanged, most notably the prospect of a turkey Richard, as Pacino and the company prepared to bring their new *Richard III* off the road and expose the first New York production of the play for thirty years to the glare of Broadway. The reviews along the way would have unnerved ordinary mortals, *Variety* for one describing the actor as "too small for his hump" after Pacino had struggled through weeks of rehearsals during the winter of 1979 in Philadelphia. His preoccupation with the role was such that when he finally left the city, he remarked to the driver that there were people walking around without overcoats. "It's spring, Al," the driver explained, deadpan.

Cast member Max Wright reported Pacino as being in a "paralyzing depression" during the tour, eating a box of Entenmann's chocolate doughnuts a day to try to keep his weight up, stopping smoking—again following Laughton's example—and taking crash-course voice lessons. Coproducer Gerald Schoen observed him walking for several hours after each performance in an effort to wind down. During one rehearsal Wheeler suggested that Pacino consider another shading of his interpretation. The exhausted actor turned to his colleague and friend. "Wait a minute," he told him. "I got the answer! Richard does *this*, right? Richard does *that*? Get *Richard* to play it. You know so much about Richard, maybe *you* should play it! There *is* no Richard! *I'm* Richard!"

Laughton intervened in another scene in which Richard's mother was haranguing him. Pacino, it seemed to Laughton, was *acting* rather than *reacting* to the curses. "Al," he suggested, "if you would just *listen* to what they're saying to you, something will happen."

Looking back on the episode, Pacino agreed with Laughton's analysis: "He knew I wasn't listening, I didn't want to hear those curses at me, coming from my mother and other women. I came that night to the scene, and I just listened. I *heard* them, and my face changed, just from having the faith to listen."

With one week to go before the New York opening, Pacino suddenly snapped out of his depression. His back to the wall, he forced himself into overdrive and began taking personal charge of his destiny and that of his troupe. Two extra directors were called in to supplement the beleaguered David Wheeler's efforts; two actors were fired; then Pacino decided to spread the critics' viewing of the play over four days to improve the odds, as he saw it, and decrease pressure all around. And he ordained that no reviews should be printed until five weeks into the nine-week run. (Pacino himself later highlighted the utter illogicality of the staggered reviews. "You know what's close to a film?" he asked, his spread of critics clearly forgotten. "When you're doing a play and the critics come. One wishes that they would come when you do not know it; then they would be able to see a process. When I know somebody is in the audience, I want to say, 'See how wonderful I am, look how terrific I'm doing here.' And everything goes right out of the window. I blow it. It takes away a certain spontaneity.")

At this stage Pacino might have been well advised to call the whole enterprise off. Instead, he continued working the punishing twelve-hour days he had established almost four months earlier, and for a token two thousand dollars a week, a fraction of what he could have earned elsewhere. The critics' reviews, staggered, late or otherwise, were devastating.

"Attempting *Richard III* has made Al Pacino the toast of Broadway," *People* magazine wisecracked, "burnt toast, that is." Walter Kerr of the New York *Times* sat through the first few scenes admiring Pacino's guts, until matters fell seriously apart: "Give Mr. Pacino credit for a venomously vigorous battle as he puts his dagger through an astonishing number of opponents before he is downed on the field. And give him credit as well for his initial battle with the text. At this stage in his development, he can't win; but you admire him, somewhat surreptitiously, for at least trying to extend his range . . . if Mr. Pacino can say, 'There is no critcher loves me,' there are those about him who don't mind addressing their fellow noblemen as 'Dooks.' We end up," Kerr wrote, "not so much with Richard III as Richard of Third Avenue."

While admitting that Pacino's power to hold and use a stage was formidable, critic Richard Eder added that a strong actor needed a strong director, and only rarely could it be himself.

"Pacino's portrayal of Richard III contains some intelligent and exciting ideas for playing Shakespeare's exuberant villain," he conceded, "and he plays them with a fearsome, absorbing energy. But although he often goes right, he often goes very wrong. What at one moment is riveting, at the next moment, sometimes from excess, sometimes from inappropriateness, becomes ludicrous. . . . What is lacking most of all is direction, and it is always a tragic lack because there is enough strength in the pieces of Mr. Pacino's performance to suggest if it could be drawn together and governed, he could give us one of the great Richards of his generation."

Jack Kroll at *Newsweek* saw Pacino's performance as one that "tries to enlist the audience in an anti-highbrow conspiracy; he stalks about the stage as the malevolent deformed Duke who murders his way to the throne, crumpled beneath his hunchback, flashing the audience looks as if to say, 'Come on, let's cut out all this Shakespeare bull. You and I know this is just good old Godfather stuff, decked out in highfalutin language, so let's have fun.' "

Then there was the problem of Pacino's accent. "You just can't speak 'Now is the winter of our discontent' with 'our' coming out as 'ower,' " Kroll protested. "Not only does it destroy the beat of the verse, it destroys the language itself. You can play Beethoven on a kazoo, but it's still got to be music. It's good that Pacino wants to play Shakespeare, but why shouldn't he want to discipline himself? He's kidding if he thinks he can muscle into Shakespeare like Michael Corleone moving into the big-time rackets."

"My performance was controversial," Pacino had the grace to acknowledge. "It was like a crisis in my life, so it's hard to call the experience an 'I'm glad-or-sad-about-it' one. I *learned* from it. Let's say I'm certainly going to perform *Richard III* again."

He looked back wistfully on what he regarded as the play's success in the Boston church where the concept had achieved continuity and consistency, as well as the "encouraging" reviews that had made him resolve to develop the role further. As far as he was concerned, the problems had begun as soon as the play had been moved from the church to a theater. Despite everyone's best efforts, the conversion had never found its feet.

Pacino recalled Kitty Winn's telling her grandmother how affected she had been by some of the criticism of *Panic in Needle Park*. Her granny had said, "Well, that's awful, you should quit." Winn had decided against taking the step that was always open to an actor. "The thing is in *doing* it," Pacino declared, *"that's* what it's all about. Not in the results of it. After all, what *is* a risk? It's a risk *not* to take risks. Otherwise, you can go stale and repeat yourself. I don't feel like a person who takes risks. Yet there's something within me that must provoke controversy, because I find it wherever I go. Anybody who *cares* about what he does takes risks."

Pacino maintained that in a strange way he felt encouraged, and not purely as a backlash against the savagery of the reviews: "Something challenging, when you get hit hard, when it's not smooth, often illuminates what other people think and alters your own perspective. And that kind of metamorphosis is a positive, cathartic experience. After seventy performances of *Richard*, something started to happen. A scene I thought I would never get or understand, I began to understand. I knew that there was a lot I had to learn. That's why I can't wait to get back on the stage. Also, doing a play like *Richard III* is being involved with words, with where we're from. Four hundred years ago, people were saying and going through these exact same things. You feel that connection, you get that sense of universality, of being a part of things."

Pacino claimed that negative reviews now worried him less than they had in the past: "Sometimes you feel critics are wrong all the time, but I don't take objection to it, because that's the way it goes. They can be wrong, they can be right sometimes. They can be cruel, they can be kind."

But Walter Kerr of the New York *Times* had struck a particularly live nerve. "He said I didn't belong in Shakespeare," Pacino exclaimed. "But Shakespeare is one of the reasons I stayed an actor. Sometimes I spend whole days doing Shakespeare by myself, just for the joy of reading it, saying those words. I do Shakespeare when I'm feeling a certain way. Sometimes I will sit for a day or night, acting out parts. I can go for ten hours straight. Maybe it goes back to the way I worked things out in my subconscious when I was small, when I went home and read out the parts in the movies I'd seen. People are always asking me to do Shakespeare, at home, in colleges, on film locations, in restaurants. It's like playing a piece of music, getting all the notes. It's great therapy. Even after *Richard III* closed, around eight at night I'd find myself walking with a limp. The body doesn't know when a role is over until the mind tells it."

Pacino was zeroing in on the heart of the matter, the basic reason, even beyond therapy, for his involvement in acting: "I have a *need* to do it. My favorite line in *Richard III* is 'Nay, for a need.' *For the need!* The need is *everything*. Appetite—and *need*." And wasn't there a considerable degree of honor in having at least tried? Not to attempt to stretch was surely a betrayal of one's craft. "Sometimes you learn a lot in a role that isn't right for you," Pacino declared. "Sometimes you learn by falling on your face; you learn through the struggle. The experience of being involved with something can be very rewarding, very important to your whole life. It can end up changing the way you look at things. The *engagement*, the *involvement*, is what I like."

His reaction to the fall from grace he was undergoing could have been dismissed as self-justification and hindsight had Pacino not predicted the exact turn of events to Dian Buchman in her interview with him at the beginning of the seventies. "This is *important*," he had stressed back then. "I'm going to have a lot of trouble in my life, and with my career. I've made that decision, because I'm going to *fail*. In order to grow, I've got to take a chance. It's important to me that I do, and it's going to cause trouble, and it's not going to be easy, and I only hope I can take it."

IN STAGING AN adaptation of *Oresteia* with a cast drawn from the Actors Studio, Elia Kazan came up against one problem Pacino had either battled to overcome or discarded as unimportant. "Although the cast were devoted and worked hard," Kazan reported, "they had, almost without exception, poor speech. It was, and still is, parochial, even ethnic, 'off-the-streets,' perfect for *On the Waterfront*. 'If I have the emotion, that is all I need,' they'd been trained by Lee.

"All the people who came out of that group still have to answer the question put to them most often: Why have American actors not succeeded in the classics? Lee would talk about the wonderful Shakespearean scenes he saw in his classes, but what I saw didn't impress me. We never really succeeded in wedding the necessary vocal force, clarity of speech, dexterity of words, and love of the language, to the emotional techniques of the Stanislavski/Strasberg method."

In *SoHo Weekly* Gerald Rabkin took the opposite viewpoint, regarding the decision to avoid the "orotund quasi-British accents that often pass for American classical speech" as a wise one. "Pacino's Richard III is very much an *American* Shakespeare," he pointed out, "and the actors are not blocked by the self-consciousness of their diction."

Another aspect of the critical reaction to Pacino's Shakespearean debut on Broadway may provide a further answer to Kazan's poser. It was hard enough for critics to swallow that indigenous American stage actors, thousands of miles removed from Stratford and the Old Vic, can and often do succeed in classics. How much harder, therefore, was the idea of a Hollywood superstar slumming on Broadway and aspiring to the same heights? English critic John Peters maintained that the problem for all Hollywood actors was that of being seen to patronize the theater, their work viewed as mere exhibitionism, the "star looks down" syndrome.

To this day Charlie Laughton defends Pacino's interpretation as well as his speech. "Very often," he points out, "the critics expect a certain kind of performance, I call it the Shakespearean Rag. Al didn't do that; he *chose* not to do that. There were so many good things in his performance that got overlooked. Lee Strasberg told me he saw greatness on that stage. I did, too."

Visiting actor Alec McCowen put the setback into a fitting perspective, echoing Pacino's rationale. "Al Pacino is more like English actors," he suggested. "He's not afraid of failing.

An actor in Brando's position is tragic, because he can't afford to fail. That's very bad for a career. It's courageous of Pacino to do what he does in this country, to play Shakespeare on Broadway. But to us it just seems logical. The only way you can grow is in front of a live audience."

CHAPTER 20

CRUISING FOR A BRUISING

Elia Kazan subscribes to the school of thought that all acting is a sexual act. "An actor, as much as an actress," he maintains, "presents himself for desire. 'I'm powerful,' he's saying. 'Look at me, listen to me. I'm important.' He's also saying, 'I'm potent.'" Although the theory has its adherents, Pacino's unwillingness to follow the line through to its logical conclusion on-screen confirms the puritanical streak first indicated in the sixties. "Anybody can do it," he pointed out a decade later. "I don't moralize in it now. Believe me, I think it's fine. I have seen scenes in films that implied sexuality, but the *impending* something I always find more interesting than the act itself. I have rarely seen a scene in a film where the act itself really helped the story. I once said I would do a nude scene if everyone on the set, also everybody in the audience, was nude. Then maybe I would understand."

Pacino shook his head when asked if he would ever portray the act of love on the screen. "No," he replied. "That is something I do privately. If there is a scene, for instance, a dramatic pivotal scene, the pleasure you should have is artistic, but I've not come across anything that has not been gratuitous. I saw one film, and in the middle there were two people fucking, literally, I think. I don't know how they got away with it, but it was rated R, not X, and it was completely unconnected with the story. I am not offended; it's just that it is very, very boring."

So what had Pacino's "presenting himself for desire" achieved, apart from inducing an acute identity crisis? Had it sown doubts that Al Pacino, the humble creature of flesh, blood and bone, could deliver on the level of a fictional Michael Corleone or of Al Pacino, superstar? Had the sexual whirlwind that had sucked him away from Jill Clayburgh blown itself out in an agony of insecurity, even self-disgust?

He still found it flattering that women approached him with offers of bed. "Of course, that doesn't oblige me to do it," he declared. "The fact is women turn me on, girls don't. A woman can be fourteen years old and a girl can be sixty-three. It has nothing to do with age, only with what's inside. When I was a young man, there was a certain celebrity I had a crush on. Some years back I was at a party, and this girl actually approached me and tried to seduce me. I didn't want her to. I couldn't tell her, 'A good part of my young adult life I've had these fantasies of you, and now here you are.' She would probably have said, 'Let's get married,' or something."

He fondly described to *Playboy* one of his last encounters with someone who had seemed to desire him as an unknown. "I was in a swimming pool a couple of years ago and this girl was giving me the eye. I was with some friends and I thought, 'Well, she recognized me,' and that was it. But there was something different about this girl. She *didn't* know who I was. I didn't talk to her or come on to her in any way. I just sat there, but it was a great experience, one that I hadn't had for years. It was delightful."

Pacino's definition of the perfect romance, while still starry-eyed, was now laced with a hint of pragmatism. "Love is very important," he agreed, "but you've got to have a friend first. You want to finally come to a point where you say that the woman you're with is also your friend. There's some connection with trust. That takes time. Love goes through different stages. But it endures. Love endures. Shakespeare said, '. . . even to the edge of doom. If this be error, and upon me proved, I never writ, nor no man ever loved.' You know, it bears it out, even to the edge of doom: 'Love's not Time's fool.' Romantic love can be a lot of crap, though, let me tell you. And it can hurt you. When I think back on some relationships that I really withdrew from, I feel there are certain things I had to resolve that still haven't been resolved."

Pacino held different views on feminism in his private life and in his career. "I used to say I wanted to genuflect to a woman, put her up on a pedestal higher and higher, way up beyond my grasp. Then I'd find another one! But as an actor I haven't felt that way. Women have always had equal importance onstage, and working with them must have altered my sensibility. I've never felt sensitive to the whole issue, because being macho has never been a problem with me. But objectively, sure, I can sympathize with the aims of the movement."

A close friend took it upon himself to encapsulate the oedipal element in Pacino's constant search for the perfect romance. "Al loved his mother dearly, and he's been looking for a substitute ever since, for one special woman who will stay with him always. So far he's had little success in that field."

PERHAPS PACINO'S INVOLVEMENT in *Bobby Deerfield* had represented the emotional equivalent of his alcoholic "bottoming out," and his misguided but still crusading hero of . . . *And Justice for All* had been his first fumbling attempt to clamber out of the pit. His flirtation with Shakespeare's hunchbacked king had been both an attempt to redress the vacuousness of *Deerfield* and a sop to his declared Elizabethan temperament.

Pacino had matured enough not only to understand a saying of Max Beerbohm's, "There is much to be said for failure. It is more interesting than success," but to discern the compensatory appeal in the condition. In place of the panic he had always dreaded with failure, there was an element of peace. The worst had arrived, and he was coping.

Immediately after the run of *Richard III*, Pacino reported for work on *Cruising*, a movie version of ex-New York *Times* editor Gerald Walker's 1970 novel. He was to play an undercover cop, Steve Burns, assigned to investigate a series of grisly murders in New York's gay community. Questions were raised in the course of the screenplay about Burns's own latent homosexuality, together with the psychotic tendencies his growing identification with the killer and the S&M scene seemed to stimulate. At first Maureen Springer was set to make her movie debut opposite Pacino, then her lover. Before production began, however, she became another of his ex-lovers and was replaced—in the movie, that is—by Karen Allen.

After the *Born on the Fourth of July* fizzle, Pacino was finally set for a teaming with William Friedkin, aka Billy the Kid and Hurricane Billy, set to direct the movie from his own script. Pacino's boundless admiration for Friedkin, which may be traced to two of his early movies indicating a predilection for filmed stage plays, was about to be put to the acid test.

The director's adaptation of neither Harold Pinter's *The Birthday Party* nor Mort Crowley's *The Boys in the Band*, however, had been well received, the gay community in particular taking exception to what it regarded as Friedkin's insensitive portrayal of the stereotypes in the latter movie. *"The Boys in the Band* is not about gay life" was Friedkin's individual explanation. "It's about human problems. I hope there *are* happy homosexuals. They just don't happen to be in my film."

His *French Connection*, on the other hand, had been a blockbuster in both critical and commercial terms, gaining both Best Picture and Best Director Oscars, and *The Exorcist* had proved to be a huge box-office hit despite a confused narrative line that aspired to grander issues than the B movie schlock many thought it truly represented.

Perhaps Pacino had even admired the four years Friedkin had slaved away on his next project, a remake of the director's hero Henri-Georges Clouzot's *The Wages of Fear*, spending twenty-one million dollars of both Paramount's and Universal's money in the process. Renamed *Sorcerer* at the last moment by worried studio heads, the resultant mishmash had gone on to lose every cent of its investment. When Friedkin turned to Dino de Laurentiis to find finance independently for *The Brinks Job*, a reconstruction of the 1950 Boston Brinks robbery, the result was another virtually unreleasable movie. Ominously, *Cruising* was also being made without the auspices of a major studio, with Jerry Weintraub, whose project it was, holding the reins for Lorimar Pictures.

Weintraub had bought the rights from *The French Connection*'s producer Philip D'Antoni, who had decided to abandon *Cruising*, and Friedkin with it. "Billy and I felt it would be a great film," said Weintraub during production. "He reread the book and did his research. We saw it as an explosive subject that hadn't been treated before. You can't keep on doing Jesse James and the Dalton Gang. Billy did a tremendous amount of research in the gay community for six months. He went to Badlands, the Mineshaft, the Anvil, the Ramrod, everywhere. A murder at the Anvil last year made both of us say, 'Let's do it!' "

The "research" Weintraub referred to transported Friedkin into the netherworld of leather and sadomasochistic mayhem that formed *Cruising*'s background. To help him, he enlisted the services of a forty-three-year-old former detective, Randy Jurgensen, whose own experiences as an undercover cop had already proved invaluable on *The French Connection*. "I started going to these places without anyone knowing who I was," says Friedkin, "and I felt that it just wasn't interesting enough to show an ordinary gay bar. The sex clubs fascinated me, and I realized that this was a terrific background for my story."

Soon Pacino followed in Friedkin's footsteps. In the company of Jurgensen, and wearing the *de rigueur* black shirt, pants, boots and wristband, he patrolled the seamiest gay dives. In a parodic validation of the *Bobby Deerfield* scene in which Marthe Keller bets the superstar that he can walk down a street without his dark glasses and not be recognized, no one spotted Pacino in these outings.

When he posed the question, "Randy, did you really wear leather? Did you go to the bars and dance with guys?" he was assured that was exactly what happened. In the sixties, when Jurgensen had worked undercover in narcotics, he had been required to look and act like a junkie. Later, assigned to investigate a series of dismemberments and mutilations of homosexuals, he had to look and act gay. The crimes had been traced to two men, one black and one white, who were impersonating police officers and harassing gays. Nicknamed Salt and Pepper, they worked the piers and truck lots where their victims cruised.

Jurgensen had to lose himself in the S&M scene, a world unknown to straights and for that matter to most homosexuals. For the first time, he told Pacino, he had felt completely on his own, nervous and a little scared. In an effort to establish a gay identity for himself, he had obtained the obligatory leather jacket, black boots, tight jeans and studded wristband and rented an apartment in Greenwich Village. He made friends with local gays who helped him assimilate. He had to absorb a whole new code of behavior, making him feel alienated from straight society. Pacino was virtually having the movie's plot spelled out.

Almost from the beginning of filming in Greenwich Village, the *Cruising* unit was picketed by the gay community. Rumors that the movie was "antigay" were particularly inflamed by an article written by the *Village Voice*'s Arthur Bell, a veteran gay rights activist. The protesters' cries of "Hey, hey, ho, ho, the movie *Cruising*'s got to go" came perilously close at times to being featured on the sound track.

Pacino was baffled by the response. "It's the first time I've ever been in this position," he protested. "I'd never want to do anything to harm the gay community, or the Italian-American community, or the police community, or *any* group I happen to represent on-screen. When I read the script, it never occurred to me that the film would be termed antigay. My responsibility to this film is as an actor, to the character I'm playing, not to an issue I'm unqualified to discuss. The way the press focuses on something like this is by throwing my name into it."

When it was put to him that the protests centered on the film's depiction of the sadomasochistic fringes of gay life, rather than the homosexual mainstream, Pacino's frustration overflowed. "That's the *point*!" he snapped. "At first I didn't know these fringes *existed*. I took this role because the character is fascinating, a man who is ambiguous both morally and sexually, who is both an observer and provocateur. It gave me an opportunity to paint a character impressionistically, a character who is something of a blur. I also took the role because Billy Friedkin is one of the best directors working today. It's a film about ambivalence. I thought the script read partly like Pinter, partly like Hitchcock, a whodunit, an adventure story. It never *dawned* on me it would provoke these feelings. I'm coming from a straight point of view, and maybe I'm not sensitive enough in that area. But they *are* sensitive to the situation, and I can't argue with that. The only thing I can say is that it isn't a movie yet."

He claimed he had already conferred with gay leaders and instigated certain script changes to ensure his character would not present a one-sided view of the gay life-style. "I don't like to hurt people, and I won't," he vowed. Still, he found the picketing a considerable distraction. One day, pacing inside his camper parked on Waverly Place, he tried to relax, while waiting for Friedkin to set up a shot, by reading aloud all the parts from Brecht's *Arturo Ui*. The recitation was not only for his own edification and entertainment but for those of his hair-stylist, secretary and makeup man as well. Behind the police barricade erected to keep the gay activists out, he could hear their shouts and whistles. "There they go," he broke off his recitation to say. "They sound like day crickets."

Cruising, it was put to Pacino, was surely his most divisive movie to date. "There is no second to it," he admitted. "I thought *Dog Day Afternoon* was going to be, but nobody bothered us on the set. Nothing else even comes close." Despite everything, he claimed to be pleased with the movie's progress. "There's a power to it, a certain theatricality, no doubt about that. I sensed that when I read it, and I can feel it while we're shooting it. I hope Billy's energy comes off on the screen. It's encouraging to be around him. It's like a temple he is creating and it lifts you."

Pacino's use of the word "temple" hardly seemed appropriate as production continued, with Friedkin pushing the locally recruited gay extras to the limit. Journalist Vito Russo looked around the Cockpit, a subterranean sex club specially constructed in a basement room in the meat-packing district of Greenwich Village. An authentic odor of beer, sweat and the sex drug amyl nitrate permeated the air as a crowd of a hundred men milled around, a few in full-dress leather, most of them shirtless, several wearing only jockstraps.

Russo spotted Pacino, clad in his "uniform," huddled in a dark corner with Friedkin. As a heavy disco beat struck up and cameras began rolling, Pacino made his way through the crowd of gleaming bodies and ordered a drink at the bar. All around him men were dancing, drinking and cruising, some engaging in preliminary sex acts. An empty leather sling hung from the ceiling by four heavy chains. "Cut!" Friedkin yelled.

Even as Pacino was being whisked away to the sidelines, cruising continued for real while the next scene was being set up. "This isn't a film about gay life," Friedkin claimed during the break. "It's a murder mystery with an aspect of the gay world as background. It's no more about gay life than Woody Allen's *Manhattan* was about New Yorkers. The very violence I'm accused of provoking has already been provoked in the streets by the protesters. I'm quite willing to sit down with members of the gay community and have them tell me just how a film like mine is going to provoke more violence against gays. I just don't believe it. And if I did believe it, I wouldn't make this film, I'd stop shooting today. The character in the film who is the killer is not gay. He's a sick person who takes his sickness out on gays. Also, it is not clear that there is only one killer in the film. The Pacino character does not go on the rampage and kill, as has been reported in the press."

Russo, now thoroughly baffled about just what Friedkin's movie *did* constitute, consulted with others on the set, confirming that almost daily script changes were taking place. Actor Richard Cox, originally signed to play the part of the killer, informed Russo he was now one of the victims. When Russo turned up next day to watch Pacino and Paul Sorvino, playing his police captain, enact a scene at Pier 36 beneath the Manhattan Bridge, Sorvino took out a knife and handed it to Pacino. "That's the murder weapon," a crew member whispered to Russo, adding, "Have you heard that Pacino is now the killer? No? Well, it's supposed to be a *big* secret."

When Russo turned up the next day, he had just missed another scene being shot in the Cockpit. He asked an extra if he felt comfortable doing the film. "Not today I don't," came the reply. "I'm not sure why. Maybe it's because of the scene we've just been shooting, the S and M scene with a guy in the leather sling being fist-fucked."

"Yes, but surely that was simulated," said Russo.

"Oh, no, it *wasn't*," the extra insisted. "They had to get that look on the guy's face with the camera, and it was real all right."

Russo spoke to several other extras about the scene. "I feel very grimy about what I've been involved in," said one.

Another told him, "When I watched that scene, I just decided it was too freaky and walked out. I don't want America to think all gays are like that, and if this picture gets released, I'm afraid they will."

When an incredulous Russo decided to query this at the highest level, Jerry Weintraub said, "As far as I know, it's all simulated." Friedkin took a slightly different tack. "I've not asked anyone in the film to perform any acts or do anything they wouldn't do anyway, gladly and proudly. I feel that *Cruising*, in its portrayal of the sex act, will turn a lot of people on."

What *had* Pacino gotten himself into? If *Richard III* was the frying pan, *Cruising* looked all set to light fires under the reputations of everyone involved.

As filming proceeded, both the level of picketing and the virulence of the protests were stepped up. One evening, during a scene being shot at the intersection of Christopher and West streets, the turbulence reached its height, with several hundred protesters thronging the set. Bomb threats were issued; bottles, rocks and cars were hurled at the trucks, cameras and the actors. The attitude of Mayor Ed Koch's motion-picture office was best summed up in its statement: "Anything that brings seven million dollars into our city is all right with us."

Friedkin ignored advice that he should meet with the activists. "He's very, very busy on the production," Weintraub claimed. "Directing a film is very debilitating; he has to keep it moving. *Cruising* is a hundred times more difficult than any other movie. Maybe Francis Coppola had it worse on *Apocalypse Now*. We're in a jungle here, too, and the enemies are all around us. I've got to make a picture, and we're in a war zone. When the movie comes out, I'm sure Billy will do interviews and write the definitive article on the making of this film. Right now he hasn't the time."

A FEW MONTHS later, with the film in the can, Pacino was locked in conflict with Friedkin, Weintraub and Lorimar Pictures. According to columnist Liz Smith, the problem was not so much that Pacino disliked the finished movie, but that he *hated* it. The principals, she claimed, were currently talking only through their lawyers. Partly because of the reams of publicity the controversy had produced, Weintraub confidently predicted a hundred-million-dollar gross for *Cruising*.

The addition of a last-minute panic-stricken preface ("This film is not intended as an indictment of the homosexual world. It is set in one small segment of that world which is not intended to be representative of the whole.") immediately backfired, many regarding it as a tacit admission of guilt. The critics wasted no time with niceties.

"Homosexual activist groups which have been picketing the filming of *Cruising* on the grounds that it would present a distorted view of homosexual life were right," declared Vincent Canby in the New York *Times*. "*Cruising is* a homosexual horror film." It was also, according to New York's *Daily News*, "a depraved, mindless piece of garbage that should never have been made" and, said the *Village Voice*, "hopelessly garbled" and "hardcore homophobic."

Abroad the critical reception was no more favorable than in the United States, raising questions from Richard Roud in Britain's *Guardian* over Friedkin's "unhealthy obsession" with the homosexual theme he had followed after *The Boys in the Band*. Alexander Walker described *Cruising* in London's *Evening Standard* as "a grotesque mess of a movie," while at the Berlin Film Festival it was booed off the screen. Representing those uninterested in the aspect of sexual politics in the controversy, Stephen Farber saw *Cruising* "not as a scandal or as an outrage, but as just another lousy movie."

"There are only three reasons for making a movie," Friedkin once claimed, "to make people laugh, make them cry, or to frighten them." What he had in mind with *Cruising* must remain a mystery.

The gay activists' slogan "This film will kill people" may have turned out to be tragically prophetic. In November 1980 a minister's son parked his car outside the Ramrod bar, the site of much of the filming, unloaded an Israeli submachine gun and fired indiscriminately. Two gay men were slain in a hail of bullets, several more wounded.

It was left to Randy Jurgensen, Pacino's undercover consultant, to act as the movie's sole defender. "People misunderstood *Cruising*," he asserted. "They think Friedkin made it up, but the whole thing was authentic." Jurgensen's "authenticity is all" view was balanced by actor-director Don Scardino, an avowed heterosexual, who played the sole likable gay character in the movie. "I found the murder of my character more morally reprehensible than anything else," he declared, "because I was playing an average guy who happened to be gay.

So what the film ended up saying is that no one is safe. The point of the movie should have been that when you suppress sexuality of any kind, heterosexual or homosexual, it can foster violence. We're not taught to handle growing up gay in this society, so we engender violence against it. *Cruising* had the opportunity to say that, and it didn't."

Another slogan adopted by the activists had carried a pointed message for the lead actor: "Pacino Sucks!" Mercifully the placards and picketing of theaters were short-lived as the movie, largely ignored by the public, disappeared from screens in record time. There was very little of the forecast hundred million dollars for Jerry Weintraub. The 850-strong General Cinema chain even refused to play the movie. With just over eight million dollars in rentals in the till, United Artists, Lorimar's distributors, reported that "as of now, the film is not knocking them dead."

Even the demonstrations he had endured during filming and the virulence of the attacks on the finished movie left Pacino unprepared for the rash of speculation that now sprang up on the reasons for his involvement. Many of his earlier pronouncements were dredged up, ranging from "There are parts around that might unleash a part of me" to "Sometimes characters you play help you work things out in real life" and "By taking on characters that are unlike me, I began to discover these characters in me."

Was his involvement in *Cruising* all down to playing a character who is "ambiguous morally and sexually" and working with a director he had long admired, or were the sexuality and sadomasochism in the movie something he, like Friedkin, had felt compelled to explore? "All of art is a kind of confession, more or less oblique," James Baldwin once declared. "All artists, if they are to survive, are forced, at last, to tell the whole truth, to vomit the anguish up."

With conjecture running the gamut from "Al Pacino is gay" to "Al Pacino is antigay," a close associate entered the fray. "We are talking about an *actor*," he pointed out, "a guy who's played everything from psychotics and cold-blooded killers to drug dealers and junkies, romantic heroes to Richard III! Yes, Al took a wrong turning with *Cruising*. It was a *lousy movie*. End of story."

Charlie Laughton says that *Cruising* "was not the script we signed for. Sure, Al was upset. There were many, many changes made during production." Marty Bregman, it transpired, had already turned down *Cruising* in a previous submission. "Al made the movie while he and I were not in business," he says. "I never liked it. I've never been in business with Jerry Weintraub. He's a great promoter, a great showman. But I don't know that he's a great filmmaker."

Pacino provided a postscript of his own to the *Cruising* furor as well as to the madness of the preceding decade. "If I die," he told an interviewer, "you can make my epitaph, 'He was just beginning to solve some of his problems. In about ten to fifteen years he would have been happy. He had made *such* progress!'"

CHAPTER 21

MAVERICK CHAMELEON

Wᴿɪᴛᴇʀ Nᴀɴᴄʏ Mɪʟʟs discovered a confusing mixture of personalities when she met Pacino in the fall of 1979. She found that the calm, controlled whisper in which he conducted the interview dampened his impact as a personality. For that matter, she detected little else imposing about him for the first hour, apart from his "square jaw and mighty nice smile." Observing his old navy T-shirt, with several gaps at the shoulder seams, the baggy brown trousers and the boots flecked with white tide marks, Mills was put in mind of a penurious college student or perhaps a graduate assistant. His opening admission, "I'm not the most open person in the world," set the tone for what followed.

When Pacino was growing up, the "trials of success" had never seemed to figure. No one had ever talked about the "difficulties" of being a success; it was *great* to be a success! The main problem Pacino was discovering lay in sustaining and consolidating the commodity as well as the enigma of its marriage to everyday social affairs. "Actors are always outsiders," he spelled out. "It's necessary to be able to interpret, and all

189

that gets distorted when people become famous. Our roots were always outside; we're wayward vagabonds, minstrels, outcasts. And that may explain why so many of us want to be accepted into the mainstream of life. But when we are—here's the contradiction!—we sometimes lose our outsider's edge."

The mood of grayish introspection was banished with a flick of a TV switch. Pacino's baseball team, the Angels, were behind 9–5 in the American League play-offs and rallying. "Base hit!" he yelled, leaping up and down on the couch, his morosity instantly converted to wild enthusiasm. "Pitching has become very sophisticated," he told the astonished Mills, jumping up to demonstrate. "The velocity of the pitch," he explained, "is maybe ninety-three to ninety-five miles an hour. . . ."

Gone was the monotonous drone; in its place was a transformed Pacino, laughing conspiratorially, flashing his "killer smile." "Baseball is a beautiful game," he announced, "very classic, very clear. A fine game. You know, I wanted to be a baseball player once. And an actor. And a cowboy."

Following Mills's observation that when he turned the TV on, he had also turned himself on, Pacino replied that he hated being "on" unless it was for a performance. "There's nothing so boring as being 'on,' " he suggested, "nothing so antilife and artificial as being 'on.' " It dawned on Mills that what Pacino was spelling out was his reluctance to talk about himself; as long as the subject was other than Pacino, and one he felt qualified to discuss, conversation could flow.

"I'm basically shy and I usually don't like to talk about things that I don't know much about," he confirmed. "I think I know a little bit about what I've been doing for the past ten years, so I can talk a bit about that." A pause. "But then I take a look at Olivier and Charles Laughton and I say, 'Wow!' I thought I knew something about acting!"

WITH PACINO REPORTEDLY impressed by an Off-Broadway production on the life of Modigliani, ex-real estate financier Keith

Barish bought the film rights to Dennis McIntyre's play for one hundred thousand dollars. Although there was no guarantee Pacino would ever play the role, Barish felt confident he could repeat the star and property pairing he had first achieved with Meryl Streep and *Sophie's Choice*. "Pacino has always wanted to play Modigliani," Barish claimed, "and this purchase gives him an opportunity to work with a writer and bring in a director he likes." His transformation to Hollywood financier, it seemed, was complete. "We won't be filming the play," he blithely admitted. "This covers three days in Modigliani's life when he was staying in Paris and selling his paintings for bread. No, the play will simply be the basis for a movie script."

Pacino was interested enough in the Paris of the romantic period, as well as the subject, to dispatch a friend to Europe to concoct a screenplay. He mentioned Francis Coppola as a possible director, along with Bernardo Bertolucci and Martin Scorsese. Modigliani has yet to emerge from development.

WHEN PACINO IS about to embark on a project, he dreams constantly about his character and the film or play. "Acting is hard work," he declares. "At times it's very energizing and enervating. It's childish. It's also responsible. It's illuminating, enriching, joyful, drab. It's bizarre, diabolical. It's exciting. Eleonora Duse said it's such a horrible word, acting. It makes you feel bad just saying it!" He defines an actor as being an emotional athlete: "The closest I can get to an explanation is it's like breaking into a sweat when you're exercising. You keep running and running, and suddenly you're sweating and it's great."

The opportunity for therapeutic self-examination remains his constant reward. "It's like trying to get at some certain truth, some common denominator, some exchange, some connection, that makes us feel a certain truth in ourselves. The way of acting that you really try to finally learn is how *not* to act. That's where it's at. Acting is *not* acting."

He is at his most effusive and animated when discussing the

craft he knows and loves best, as well as the people behind the scenes who help breathe life into the process: "Great directors can understand staging in a way that can make a scene come alive. Some have a certain way of pacing the scene. Others have a way of setting a kind of ambiance around the set that makes everybody creative around them."

John Huston and Robert Altman ("a guy with vision") were just two directors Pacino wanted to work with in the future. Apart from his own brief experience with directing in the Theater, he appeared to have sublimated any ambitions in that area: "I believe very much that directors are directors and actors are actors. I'd very much like to keep maintaining the independence I have as an actor. You pay me a salary, I come and do the job. The last few pictures I've made have been that kind of thing."

Despite the scars from *Richard III*, Pacino, with three movie disasters in a row behind him, continued to extol the virtues of stage work at the expense of filmmaking. There was simply more to act onstage, he claimed. It was a more demanding craft, filled with new experiences to discover and explore. The play was the source, a symphony orchestrated with words. The stage was challenging, extraordinary, "wild turf." In movies there was forever a sense of being controlled, of holding back, unable to give vent to the desire to improvise freely. Making a movie meant being involved with an impersonal tangle of machines and wires, going back over and over again for the camera. When he performed for a live audience, the audience came back at him; there was continual feedback and interaction. The equation continued to be: movies for dollars and clout; the stage for demands and challenge.

On one point Pacino remained adamant. "I won't act purely for money. I don't think I ever will."

His next project provided further proof of this, together with a reaffirmation of his tenacious commitment to an adopted piece of work. Pacino called theater director Arvin Brown in mid-1979. The two men had known each other for several years and had often talked about cooperating on a project without taking the final step of actually doing something about it. Pacino's suggestion was that Brown consider mounting a revival of David Mamet's *American Buffalo*.

Michael Hadge had first staged the play in his capacity as artistic director of the highly acclaimed Theater at St. Clement's Church, where Pacino's support, both morally and financially, often helped keep the enterprise afloat. In 1975 J. T. Walsh had played the key role of the psychotic Teach, mastermind of the get-rich-quick theft of a rare buffalo nickel coin. Hadge's limited showcase run had received excellent notices. "I'd originally mentioned what a wonderful play it was to Al, but he had no time to pursue it then," he recalls. When *American Buffalo* left St. Clement's, it was staged Off-Broadway by Gregory Mosher with J. T. Walsh and Mike Kellin. A year later *Buffalo* had hit Broadway, this time under Ulu Grosbard's direction and with Robert Duvall as Teach. Frank Rich of the New York Times had described Grosbard's staging as "hissing like a rattlesnake," causing audiences to come away startled, even shaken by Mamet's scatological language. No less disturbing, Rich reported, was the violence that erupted in the second act, with Duvall striking costar John Savage across the head with an iron.

Within months of Pacino's call he and Brown were in rehearsals at New Haven's 484-seat Long Wharf Theater, with Clifton James and Thomas Waites (the jailed white kid from . . . *And Justice for All*) cast in the three-hander opposite Pacino's Teach. There was a distinct possibility of taking the show on the road, although everyone was aware that the 1977 production had played to sparse audiences on Broadway before being bumped after just 133 performances. Far from backing a certainty, Pacino was once more stepping out on the wire.

With the play due to open in New Haven in October 1980 for a five-week run, there was no question of the theater management's being accused of crass commercialism in exploiting Pacino's name. Instead, Long Wharf stuck rigidly to its advertising policy of never mentioning an individual performer's name, no matter how important his marquee value might be. Since the theater played to a guaranteed 80 percent capacity because of its list of subscription patrons, it could be argued it was in a reasonable position to afford this indulgence. If the production did transfer to Broadway, a spokesman confirmed that would be an instant rethink.

American Buffalo represented Pacino's fourth attempt in eighteen months to return to the theater. Apart from the ill-fated *Richard III*, he had worked early in 1979 with director Liviu Ciulei in a series of staged readings, sponsored by Circle in the Square, of Brecht's *In the Jungle of the Cities*. And before beginning work on *Cruising* that summer, he had recruited a group of actors, headed by Ron Liebman, to work with him on *Othello*. The free use of a rehearsal hall at Lincoln Center's Vivian Beaumont Theater had been put at his disposal for several weeks for that project.

American Buffalo was only the second of these attempts to reach the public. This it did in great style, even if the play itself was rapidly taking on all the characteristics of a maverick chameleon. The menacing aspect of Mamet's work had loomed large in the Grosbard-Duvall collaboration, before a subsequent British staging, with Jack Shepherd playing Teach as a flashy East End hoodlum, had pointed up the comic nature of the piece. At New Haven critic Mel Gussow found the play "easily the most amusing *American Buffalo* I have seen. When Mr. Pacino makes his entry on the Long Wharf stage, the play accelerates in a fresh direction. It is not that he is better than Duvall; he is *different*, as different as they were in *The Godfather*. In Pacino's hands his character becomes street-smart, cocksure and self-mocking."

Gussow noted that *Buffalo* was the second modern American play, after *Pavlo Hummel*, that Pacino had revived soon after its original production: "The actor has chosen wisely. In each case he has confirmed a play's position in our dramatic literature, and he has staked out an impressive claim to a challenging contemporary role."

New York producer Elliott Martin saw the play at New

Haven and was convinced that Off-Broadway would provide the perfect ambiance for the initial transfer, although Pacino was given the alternatives of London, Chicago or Spoleto in Italy.

Armed with the glowing reviews from New Haven, *American Buffalo* was set to open in June 1981 at the Downtown Circle in the Square. "Al made the right choice," Martin confirmed as he surveyed the figures for the advance sale, a record for Off-Broadway. "Young people who don't normally come to the theater are lining up for tickets," he declared, attributing the turnout entirely to Pacino, rather than the intrinsic appeal of Mamet's play.

"When I first saw Al do *Buffalo*," Martin added, "I thought the humor had much the same sort of rich texture as the humor of *A Moon for the Misbegotten*, which was obviously a play that had not been fully realized when it was done on Broadway originally. You can't really do a revival unless you are truly bringing something new to it, in terms of the interpretation or concept or how you're presenting it. If you do that, you have not just done a revival; you have contributed something to the life of the play itself; you have made it possible for it to become an ongoing property that can be taken, like *Long Day's Journey into Night*, and done by different artists.

"You have to be really dedicated, like Al is, to take this on. I wouldn't be sitting here at all if he had said, 'Can I have five thousand dollars a week?' or something like that. We'd have said, 'Well, we'll have to wait until you can get the play on Broadway, where it can run for six months.' This way, Off-Broadway, he doesn't commit himself for a long period and doesn't ask for an amount of money that makes it impossible to do. What Al wants out of it is to develop as an artist and to develop this play, which he happens to love."

Returning to the revived *American Buffalo*, critic Frank Rich was another who discerned the flipping of Mamet's verbal coinage, the play's three protagonists now seeming more absurd than vicious. Impressively enough, Rich noted, the basic message remained unchanged, whether funny or horrifying; it was still the tale of men eternally trapped on the bottom rung of the social ladder. Where Duvall had played Teach taut and mean in the 1977 production, Pacino's version, by contrast, was slovenly and abstracted. With his baggy clothes and pasty, ill-shaven face, he was more of a tabby than an alley cat and, according to Rich, "very, very funny, his first fully rewarding performance since *Dog Day Afternoon.*"

Joining the chorus of approval for Pacino was the Associated Press drama critic Jay Sherbult. Pacino, he declared, was "only magnificent as a hollow-eyed, foul-mouthed Teach, his hands alternately jabbing the air or jammed in the pockets of his baggy pants as he paces about the junk shop like a caged tiger."

Critic John Simon was one of the few with distinct reservations, mainly about the play itself, which he dubbed "Bluffalo," going on to describe it as a stew of upside-down Saroyan, thirties gangster movies, Pinter, a dash or two of Beckett and a large dose of scatology and obscenity to lend contemporary relevance. Although he occasionally found the characters funny, he believed it was the funniness of stupidity, to be placed fairly low on the scale of humor.

Although Walter Kerr of the New York *Times* echoed Simon's reservations about the play, "enormously improved in this production over the earlier Broadway version, but it must in the end still do battle with certain limitations," he had no doubts about the quality of the leading player's contribution. Pacino came into the play "like a hand grenade," Kerr raved, hailing his "remarkably complex and illuminating performance."

Playwright David Mamet was naturally delighted with Pacino's enthusiasm for his work. A play that might have languished forgotten had been given a brand-new lease on life. Mamet saw the greatness of the original Broadway production, with Robert Duvall as Teach, as lying in its cold, frightening power. With the current Pacino version he detected a cathartic gentleness. "Both productions," he maintained, "bring out different parts of the play. And in very different ways they both absolutely fulfill it. I couldn't ask for anything better for the play than to have it done with such widely disparate interpretations and yet have both of them remain true to it. What this means to me is that there is something really substantial there if such wonderful but unusual talents as Bobby Duvall and Al Pacino can both find aquality in the play that excites them and allows them to express themselves. When they do this, both are true to the play and yet totally unique. I know Al has a great love for *Buffalo*, and I think he has a great identification with the character. It was something he really, really wanted to do."

American Buffalo reached another new high in Off-Broadway history as the theater increased its top price from twenty dollars to a record twenty-four dollars halfway through the play's run. The hundred-thousand-dollar capitalization had already been recouped as the result of sell-out audiences from the beginning. Including previews, the play ran for a total of four months in New York, with not a single seat unsold.

"There's something about being a *part* of a play where the *experience* of the play is coming through that makes you feel you are doing something sane and purposeful," Pacino declared, luxuriating in his best critical reviews in any medium for years. "Like Hamlet said, 'The play's the thing.' If you can be part of getting that to come through, there's a feeling of completeness; there's a wholeness there. Many actors do much more acting than me, more varied roles. Part of being successful seems to be that you start to do less and less parts. I'm trying to do more now. In a sense doing *Buffalo* is keeping in there."

For reasons best known to himself Ulu Grosbard, director of Robert Duvall's Teach, felt it necessary to sideswipe both Pacino and Dustin Hoffman in a thinly disguised tribute to Duvall. "He [Duvall] is the least career-conscious actor I know," he declared. "Al Pacino and Dustin Hoffman weigh all the career factors before they make a decision. Duvall is all actor; he looks at the part and doesn't worry about what it's going to do to his career. He's the purest actor I know."

What had Pacino and Hoffman, two individuals who can scarcely be accused of chasing obviously commercial subjects, done to deserve this? Perhaps Grosbard's imminent costarring of Duvall with De Niro in *True Confessions* brought about the outburst, or maybe it was the thought of being upstaged by Pacino's new and highly successful version of *American Buffalo*. For whatever reason, his comments appeared irrelevant as well as ill conceived. Duvall needs neither apologists nor invidious comparisons.

Marty Bregman's response was incredulity. "Ulu said that? If he did, that's ridiculous. Is *American Buffalo* a 'career move'? Was *Dog Day Afternoon* a *calculated* career move? Dusty's Lenny? Only with twenty-twenty hindsight."

American Buffalo was no *Richard III*, and Mamet was no Shakespeare; but Pacino was riding a prestigious, certified stage smash. After his conquest of Off-Broadway, there remained the assault on Broadway itself to mount. This the team planned for the 1983 season.

CHAPTER 22

LICKING HIS WOUNDS

PACINO SEES HIMSELF as someone who started in his business by writing and producing comedy sketches. He has always admired comedians—the way their minds work, the way they juxtapose situations to milk laughs, their ability to puncture the tension of life. One of his dearest wishes is to make a comedy, and for a while, back at the beginning of the eighties, a teaming with Diane Keaton was planned. He felt that the combination would have clicked in the same way as it had with Woody Allen, the familiarity between them removing any edge. Unfortunately the project was set aside on the basis of its needing more work.

A major upset, therefore, was the result of a poll conducted by major studios among university students. This indicated that the great moviegoing public—at least on campus—wanted to see Pacino only in serious roles. "So that's what's going to come my way," he grumbled. "It gets back to the old days when you had the studio saying, 'We have to put him only in romantic parts.' So where is the opportunity? Maybe I'm being stubborn, but I refuse to look at myself that way, that I'm a *commodity.* This is such a commercial medium, and I understand and appreciate that you can't ignore the amount of money you're given and do some kind of art film, but it's disturbing to me when I hear they're taking polls. And it's strange, since I haven't done a comedy yet."

Surely the public was entitled to see a full-length version of the sense of humor hitherto glimpsed only in brief snatches on the screen? Still determinedly on the lookout, Pacino again proved that he was capable of sending himself up when the mood was upon him. "I'm tired of being too careful, too protective," he railed. "Actually, look what yes has done to me. I said yes to *Richard III* and to *Cruising.* No wonder I said no for so many years!"

Apart from the chance to play in comedy, the magic ingredient for Pacino in *Author! Author!* was the New York location work involved, as well as the idea of filming a script by Israel Horovitz, the playwright whose *The Indian Wants the Bronx* had helped push Pacino into the big leagues onstage. Although it was hardly the all-out Buster Keaton type of slapstick Pacino really longed to do, the "comedy with a heart" would serve for the moment.

Horovitz had loosely based *Author! Author!* on his own experiences as a divorced father of three children. Pacino was to play Ivan Trevalian, whose wife, Gloria, has just left him stuck with her five kids from four previous marriages. His new play, still with second-act problems, is about to be produced by Alan King and Bob Dishy, both of whom are seeking Dyan Cannon to star. Romantic complications, as they say, ensue. With Gloria being played by Tuesday Weld, the movie represented a reunion of sorts for the couple after their fling in the early seventies. Pacino's remaining on friendly terms with all of his ex-lovers is one of the few constants in his life.

He chose to turn down dramatic roles in Sydney Pollack's *Absence of Malice* and Sidney Lumet's *Prince of the City* in favor of *Author! Author!* He had considerable respect for the producer, Irwin Winkler, who, after the misfire of *The Gang That Couldn't Shoot Straight,* had worked with the De Niro-

Scorsese team on *New York, New York* and *Raging Bull*, among many others in a distinguished career. As for the director, Arthur Hiller, Pacino had admired his work on the George C. Scott-Paddy Chayevesky collaboration *The Hospital*. And the movie was being made for a major studio, in the halcyon days of Sherry Lansing, the purported new boss at 20th Century-Fox ("We're the first to have a woman in charge!").

Despite the personal nature of Horovitz's script, a worrying amount of rewriting, even reconception, became a daily occurrence as filming got under way. Sharp differences of opinion on the treatment soon developed between Pacino and Hiller, a director viewed by many as a hack of all genres, master of none and a surprising choice for Pacino's comedy debut. "Sure, Arthur made *The Hospital*," the argument now ran. "way back in 1973! He *also* made Alan Arkin's *Popi, Love Story* for crissakes, and Warren Beatty's turkey *Promise Her Anything. Silver Streak*? You gotta figure he lucked out with Gene and Richie."

Within a week of the start of shooting, he was dubbed "once-more-and-we're-outa-here" Hiller because of his unfailing habit of following this statement with up to a dozen more takes. When busy Alan King, head of his own film and television company, was asked why he had chosen to get involved in the mayhem that soon developed, he replied, "As a producer I won't hire me as an actor; I'm too expensive, I can't afford me. But when somebody asks me to do a part, I do it. How many roles are there for a middle-aged fat Jew?" He paused, grinned broadly and waved his trademark cigar. "The reason I'm doing this part is all these people are friends of mine and they blackmailed me!"

The retake limit was reached in a scene to be shot in late September 1981 in front of the Plaza Hotel's fountain, where Pacino was to be seen engaged in a lively discussion with Alan King. Shooting was abandoned after the first day, the general consensus being that the scene "played ragged" and needed more polish. Filming was impossible on the second day because of a downpour. The third day it rained again.

By the time the company was reassembled, the Plaza had planted its traditional Christmas tree, a monster of epic proportions, foursquare in the fountain. Similar adornments could be seen outside the nearby General Motors Building and F. A. O. Schwarz's toy store, all of which rendered previously shot autumnal exteriors unusable. Some discussion took place about just giving in to the elements and shooting indoors. Instead, the company decided to reschedule for January 1982 and moved for location work to Gloucester, Massachusetts.

There the close to zero temperatures accurately reflected the relationship between Pacino and Hiller. According to one source, Pacino capped a series of late arrivals by turning up ninety minutes late on the last day of shooting in Gloucester. He was loudly reprimanded by Hiller in front of the assembled cast and technicians. "You've no respect for your fellow actors and crew," the director raged. Pacino stormed off the set, agreeing to return only after listening to Winkler's entreaties.

Pacino frowned when reminded of the incident. "I have to go back there in my mind," he said. "I want to be fair. As I remember it, I didn't know I was supposed to work that day. I remember being ready and wanting to work, but not being told. Let's just say Hiller and I had different tempos. But my struggle was the same as his struggle, to get the movie made."

Back in New York in January at the Plaza, bitter cold caused filming to be abandoned on the first day. The next day, with Pacino and Hiller still incommunicado, a blizzard developed within an hour of the cameras' being set up. "The scene's supposed to take place in September," said Terry Donnolly, the production manager. "Now we've got no fall leaves, and there's snow on the ground. We can't film with this snow, and it's so cold it isn't going to melt. The writer's trying to do a new scene where Al and Alan argue somewhere indoors, in Alan's office maybe. It would have been better in front of the Plaza, but what can you do? It's just one of these things." He gave a long sigh. "Do you have any idea how much it costs when you call in seventy-five extras time after time and have to continually cancel a scene?"

Just then, as if to add to his misery, a young woman rushed up. "Terry, the toilets aren't flushing in Arthur's camper," she said.

"Get another camper," said the distraught Donnolly.

With locations moved to Greenwich Village and Trevalian's elegant brick town house, one production assistant disclosed her recipe for dispensing the crowds of onlookers: "I tell them it's an I Love New York commercial. They move on pretty fast when they hear that." At least on this occasion, much to Pacino's relief, there were no pickets in sight. Instead, there were just a multitude of trucks holding electrical cable, gels, flats, props, sandbags, cameras, sound and light equipment. A nearby table groaned under the weight of coffee, milk, doughnuts and packages of dehydrated cocoa. There were five mobile homes: one for costumes, one for makeup, one for Pacino, one for Dyan Cannon, one for the five kids.

After several hours the unit prepared for a take. Pacino emerged from his trailer, wearing jeans and a corduroy jacket, and disappeared into his ivy-covered house. A few moments later he emerged on the roof and, in character, yelled down to the street, "That is the sickest thing I've ever heard, and I've heard a lot of sick things. I'm a playwright, for God's sake."

This was the cue for one of his kids to reply, "Daddy, don't shoot anybody." Instead, perfectly illustrating a hazard of location shooting, one of the crowd yelled, "Oh, my God, I'm looking right at Al Pacino. I think I'm going to faint!"

AUTHOR! AUTHOR! OPENED to reviews that can best be summarized as "middling to poor." In the New York *Times*, Janet Maslin thought that Pacino handled his role "appealingly and comfortably." The film itself she found mildly amusing, but "a little less animated than it should have been."

"There is nothing sadder than a movie that tries to be adorable and isn't," said Jack Kroll at *Newsweek*. He described Pacino as "a sterling actor—but he could use some funny pills." In Rex Reed's opinion, "Al Pacino hasn't much talent for comedy."

Pauline Kael's theory about Pacino's performance had psychological roots. "If you're in a depressed state," she suggested, "and you're playing a lovable, affectionate fellow, you're likely to develop the sickly slack smile that disfigures Al Pacino in *Author! Author!*"

In defense of the movie, Pacino later claimed that it worked better on television and that he had enjoyed working with the kids. As for the association with Hiller, "Sometimes people who are not really meant to be together get together in this business for a short time. It's very unfortunate for all concerned."

Author! Author! was another disappointing box-office bust, Pacino's fourth in a row, one of a slate of movies that toppled the Lansing regime at Fox. Indeed, if Pacino had not established his credentials so thoroughly in *The Godfathers, Serpico* and *Dog Day Afternoon*, it might have toppled him as well. Regardless of how well his theatrical career was going—and with the acclaim that had greeted *American Buffalo*, his stock in that department had never been higher—there was a desperate need to reestablish his movie career. Instead, he dithered.

Robert Evans offered him the lead in his ill-fated *Cotton Club*, another chance to reunite with Francis Coppola. Liz Taylor wanted him to costar with her on Broadway in a revival of Tennessee Williams's *Sweet Bird of Youth*. He turned them both down and began to spend time at New York's Circle in the Square on a workshop reading of Eugene O'Neill's *The Hairy Ape*.

At the same time he was licking his wounds.

LEE STRASBERG'S DEATH in 1982 came as a considerable blow. The legacy of the man had been passed on through the development of a whole generation of actors, including Montgomery Clift, Marlon Brando, James Dean, Jane Fonda, Patricia

Neal, Paul Newman, Joanne Woodward, Kim Stanley, Rip Torn, Anne Bancroft, Geraldine Page, Dustin Hoffman and Robert De Niro. "Lee told me he wanted to direct only one other thing in his life," says Charlie Laughton, "Al in *Orpheus Descending*. He also wanted Al to do *Richard III* again, but he wouldn't have directed that. He'd already begun preparations in his mind for both productions when he died."

Stella Adler appeared to internalize and externalize at one and the same time in her reaction to her old rival's death. First she asked her class to stand. "A man of the theater died last night," she informed them. One minute's silence was observed before the *grande dame* made her next pronouncement: "It will take ten years before the harm that man has done to the art of acting can be corrected."

As a temporary measure the Actors Studio was taken over by a committee consisting of Elia Kazan, one of its cofounders in 1947, director Arthur Penn, actress Ellen Burstyn and Pacino. When Burstyn and Pacino were separately proposed for the position of artistic director, they both received considerable individual support that threatened for a while to polarize the members. Rather than cause a division, both accepted the post, pledging to keep the studio "a safe place where actors can stretch and grow and take risks they can't take in the commercial world." His widow declared, "Lee would have been very pleased."

It was the calm before the storm. Although many carefully worded press releases were issued in a futile attempt to cover the growing uproar, the studio and the Strasberg estate were soon locked in a litigation tussle over the ownership of a thousand rehearsal tapes made by Lee Strasberg. Did they belong to the studio or to his estate? As far as co-artistic director Burstyn was concerned, the tapes were "teaching tools" essential to the educational process of future aspirants and as such belonged to the studio. Anna Strasberg's contention was that the tapes belonged to her late husband, not the institution that bore his name. She wanted them made available, under her auspices, to "everybody who has an interest in the theater or acting."

Pacino agreed to be called as a witness for Anna Strasberg and sided with her in the subsequent trial, opposing an affidavit signed by Burstyn and the studio's president. While admitting in Manhattan's Surrogate Court that the taping sessions with his late mentor "could get very personal," he denied he had a problem with other actors listening to them. With his help the verdict came down in favor of Strasberg's widow.

Soon afterward Pacino chose to bow out of his duties at the studio, leaving Burstyn as sole artistic director. His farewell press release was terse: "I believe that the turmoil following Lee's death has ended and the situation has been stabilized at the Studio. I make this decision with every warm feeling towards the Studio which is my alma mater and which gave me so much as a young actor."

He gratefully acknowledged his debt to Strasberg: "Lee hasn't been given the credit he deserves. Brando doesn't give him any credit—and the Actors Studio has had such a bad name, which is not representative of what it really did for me. Next to Charlie, it sort of launched me. It really did. That was a remarkable turning point in my life. I'll be grateful to the Actors Studio forever. I'd like to marry that place."

IN 1979 PACINO offered a large olive branch when he acknowledged that without Marty Bregman "I don't know what I would have done. He was just a great influence on my career." The formal contract that had existed between them was described as "expensive, but worth it." It took two more years and a fifty-year-old gangster movie to bring the two back together as star and producer.

Pacino had heard of the original Howard Hawks-Ben Hecht-Paul Muni *Scarface*, widely regarded as the model for all gangster pictures. He was also aware of Bertolt Brecht's interest in the genre and, while he was working on *Arturo Ui*, took the opportunity to study old thirties movies. The one picture he could not track down was the one he most wanted to see: the 1932 *Scarface*.

Driving down Sunset Boulevard one day while on a visit to Los Angeles, he came across a tiny theater playing Hawks's classic. The movie had a huge impact on him. He was struck by its real, positively *grand* feeling and especially by Muni's tremendous performance. When it occurred to him that a remake might be attempted, the logical man to call was Marty Bregman. "Look at *Scarface*," Pacino suggested. "I think there might be a character there for me to play."

"If Al gets excited about something," says Bregman, "*I* get excited. *Scarface* was such an extraordinary movie, considering it was made half a century ago. I realized right away what someone like Al could bring to it. He never had a chance to bring out that steely, streetwise quality except onstage in things like *The Indian Wants the Bronx* and *Does a Tiger Wear a Necktie?*, in both of which he was brilliant. Even in *The Godfather* he was a rich man's son, not a street gangster."

The prospect of a return to the glory days of *Serpico* and *Dog Day Afternoon* was further signaled when Bregman asked director Sidney Lumet to become involved. With Oliver Stone standing by to begin the screenplay, an agreed "approach" had to be ironed out. Pacino's first concept of capturing the thirties flavor of the original was soon ruled out. It was Lumet who came up with the idea of setting the remake in present-day Miami.

The Castro-controlled influx of Marielitos, refugees from the port of Mariel, Cuba, had been allowed into Florida, with President Jimmy Carter's blessing, in the freedom flotilla exodus of 1980. The U.S. authorities had been unaware that Castro had emptied his jails and cleared mental institutions and street corners of thousands of undesirables, a ruse that quickly turned Miami into the festering center of the billion-dollar drug trade. Why not make Tony Montana, one of Castro's least desirables, the Scarface of the eighties, the movie chronicling his blood-stained quest to be king of the cocaine mountain? Pacino and Bregman were instantly taken with the idea. Instead of the twenties, the eighties; for Chicago, read Miami; substitute cocaine for booze; make the Italians Cubans—it all seemed to fit.

After their split, when *Born on the Fourth of July* fell apart, what had made a resumption of Pacino's spiky relationship with Bregman possible? "In some ways now it's less complicated," Pacino took it upon himself to explain. "I'm less the kid now, less the boy. But it always takes two. I have a relationship with Bregman that I don't understand. It's almost *primitive*. On certain levels we have this connection; in other ways we couldn't be further apart. He can get me *very* angry. I don't want to get into 'He did this to *me*,' though, because it implies 'I did this to *him*.' And I'm not completely over these feelings."

Over them enough, it seemed, to look to Bregman to get him back on the cinematic track, and with another screenplay by Oliver Stone, still five years from his dream of bringing *Born on the Fourth of July* to the screen.

CHAPTER 23

"THE WORLD IS YOURS"

SINCE SIDNEY LUMET was preparing to work with Paul New-man at the time on *The Verdict*, Oliver Stone was sent on his own to South America and Miami to research elements of the updated *Scarface*. Frequent dispatches from the front attested to the assiduous, leave-no-substance-unsampled nature of Stone's labors, as well as several hair-raising escapades among the *coqueros*. (Stone later claimed that *Scarface* represented his personal farewell to cocaine.)

When Bregman joined him in Miami, both men were stunned by the dimensions of what they found. They knew that the drug business was huge; despite there being no great industry in Florida, it was by then the second-largest banking area in the world. But when the U.S. attorney told them it was a hundred-billion-dollar-a-year-industry Bregman thought he'd misheard him. "One hundred *million* dollars?" he repeated.

"No," the attorney replied. "One hundred *billion*."

Bregman soon discovered that the cocaine business was much more sinister than the liquor trade ever was. "First, because the money involved is so huge, you have little street gangsters with five million dollars' worth in their freezer, and second, because you're dealing with very substantial South American families who are involved. Remember, cocaine is not a street drug like heroin; it's a middle- and upper-class drug."

Stone not only interviewed federal agents, narcotics investigators and homicide detectives with the Miami Police Department but crossed over to the other side of the law, meeting with the *bandidos* hired to unload contraband from freighters anchored off the Florida Keys, street hustlers who peddled the goods, even drug lords who funded the deals and creamed off the biggest slice of the profits. On the island of Bimini, one of several Caribbean links in the drug chain, he expanded the research already conducted in Colombia, Ecuador and Peru. "I felt my life was on the line," says Stone. "Most of my work, for obvious reasons, was done between midnight and dawn. That's not the safest time to be out alone when you're dealing with people who might decide, on second thoughts, that they had told you too much."

Stone returned both excited and scared by what he had seen and headed for Paris to work on the script. When he contacted Lumet to give him a progress report, he was confused and hurt when the director failed to return his calls. "I couldn't," Lumet explains. "While I'm shooting, I'm like a monk. I'm not in touch with anybody."

On Stone's return Lumet came back into the picture, *The Verdict* being safely in the can. Lumet liked much of what Stone had achieved in sketching Tony Montana's ascent, his usurping of the established mob king Frank Lopez, his inheritance of both his empire and his moll, Elvira. He was turned off, however, as soon as Montana's mother and sister Gina entered the scene. Tony having the hots for Gina was shaky ground, Lumet thought. Bregman and Stone were informed that this element wouldn't work even if it were made overt.

"I don't know how Al felt at this stage," says Lumet. "I never asked him. Apart from the corny elements I objected to, I also wanted to introduce political ramifications, exploring the CIA's involvement in drugs as part of their anti-Communist drive. I didn't want to do it just on a gangster or cop level. As it stood, it was a comic strip. Marty and I argued about it, Marty disagreed with me and I pulled out."

"I walked away from Sidney," Bregman insists. "What he wanted to do was just preposterous. He wanted to make a different film, a political film that showed government involvement in the importation of cocaine. I felt that was a bizarre suggestion. He wanted to rewrite the script and told me it would take six months. I gained the impression he wanted to stall *Scarface* so he could make another movie first. De Palma and I had no intention whatever of making a comic strip. We wanted to give the whole thing a larger-than-life *operatic* quality."

Lumet's replacement, Brian De Palma, was deemed by Pacino "an interesting choice." His track record stretched all the way back to both Jill Clayburgh's and Robert De Niro's debuts in *The Wedding Party* in the sixties, then on to the highs and lows of *Phantom of the Paradise, Obsession, Carrie, The Fury, Blow Out* and *Dressed to Kill.* De Palma had previously written much of his own screenwork, and Bregman thought it would be an attractive proposition for him to work with someone else's material for a change, as well as providing a marriage of style and content.

"*Scarface* is a new way of working for me," De Palma happily confirmed. "Here I've got a very strong script, an actor who knows what he wants and a producer who is in on every detail. This is more like a collaboration."

From the beginning there was tremendous local resistance to *Scarface*'s being shot in Miami, despite meetings Bregman and his associate producer, Lou Stroller, conducted with the authorities. Specifically, Hispanics were said to be concerned that the film represented a blanket indictment of the boat lift refugees, often cited as the prime cause of Miami's rocketing crime rate. "Most of the people we met with are intelligent and articulate" was Stroller's attempt to pour oil on troubled waters. "One of the reasons we chose Miami in the first place was to employ a large number of Cubans. But we won't allow our script to be censored."

Commissioner Demetrio Perez, Jr., had Bregman and his team under siege from the beginning, while Bregman continued valiantly to assure everyone that the unit would be filming in Miami that fall. Then Universal's president, Ned Tanen, entered the arena in the strongest possible terms. "Mr. Bregman is not putting up the money for this feature," he pointed out. "Universal is. And Universal won't make the movie unless I can be assured there will be no problems. The last thing I need is to end up having militants chasing us around the block. I still bear the scars of making other movies on location and such problems I definitely don't need."

On top of Universal's attitude, a Miami *Herald* editorial by Guillermo Martinez sounded the death knell. Martinez objected to a film that was going to "tell the nation and the world that the prototype of the U.S. gangster of the 1980's is a Mariel refugee."

Never one to quit easily or run from a fight, Bregman in the end had to admit defeat. "There was too much at stake to risk being stalled by what Universal perceived as an uncooperative community," he finally conceded.

Pacino had quietly taken up residence in Miami in the early stages of preproduction and had already absorbed what he could of the customs and values of the local community. With the distinctive speech patterns of the Cuban dialect mastered, he continued to speak the patois both during and after rehearsals. Back in California, cinematographer John Alonzo was astonished at his prowess. "The word 'professional' is to me an overused term, but with Al Pacino, you can't overuse it. When I first met him, we hadn't even started production and he was already using his Cuban accent. I spoke to him in Spanish and asked him if it was OK. His response was 'Perfect. The more Spanish I hear, the better I feel.' That to me is a prepared actor."

Pacino limbered up for his role with the help of a physical

education coach as well as an expert in night combat. Instead of internalizing Tony Montana, he chose to open the character up and held lengthy discussions with Bregman, De Palma, Charlie Laughton and dialect coach Robert Easton. Apart from Roberto Duran, who provided a physical model for certain aspects of his character, Pacino found himself inspired by Meryl Streep's work in *Sophie's Choice.* He thought that her way of involving herself in playing someone from another country and another world was particularly fine, committed and courageous.

The unit made the most of the second-choice Los Angeles locations. The refugee internment camp, originally flung together beneath a Miami freeway, was erected between the intersection of the Santa Monica and Harbor freeways, where forty stunt men and six hundred extras were recruited. Miami's bustling Little Havana area was shot in Los Angeles's Little Tokyo, where storefronts and billboards were erected with Spanish signs, together with an ingenious mural of the Miami skyline and a towering, tantalizing neon sign proclaiming The World Is Yours.

Perhaps production designer Ferdinando Scarfiotti's greatest challenge was the construction of the Babylon Club, a bizarre Greco-Roman palace that provided the background for several key scenes. Built on one of Hollywood's largest sound stages, the multilevel complex featured black lacquered tables, a gleaming onyx dance floor, ankle-deep purple carpet, erotic Greek statuary, dancing fountains, pink and blue neon lighting and a dazzling profusion of mirrors that seemed designed to drive John Alonzo crazy.

Shouting matches were reported to be erupting frequently from Universal during *Scarface's* production, the action being equally attributed to Pacino, Stone, Bregman and De Palma. "Because of his stature and the nature of his talent," De Palma later explained, perhaps through gritted teeth, "Pacino has all sorts of ideas about how things should be done. So do I. We worked it out that he was right about some things and so was I. Collectively we were always right." Later he was a little more forthcoming. "A lot of fighting and screaming and jumping up and down *did* go on, but only because you're trying to say, 'This is the way it's supposed to be.' In the end that urge makes you do things you didn't think you were capable of."

For Bregman in particular, De Palma had nothing but praise: "He's forceful, strong-willed, and one of the best producers I've ever worked with. He's very good with casting, and," he pointedly added, "with fielding his way through the egos of certain actors."

Bregman downplays the tales of conflict. "Brian's not a shouter, and at that time Oliver was very passive. When you're working in a confined environment in terms of time and structure, the pressure is enormous, and there's always tension with the work. Making a film is like going to war; that's why most producers tend to stay away. If there were any shouting matches on *Scarface*, it was between Al and myself, and always over a creative matter."

One reason for Stone's "passivity" was Bregman's agreement allowing him on the set daily to watch De Palma at work. Despite the disaster of Stone's first directorial effort, *The Hand*, there was a rumor, clearly unfounded, that he had some damn fool idea of continuing down that road.

In true Method style Pacino remained distant on the set from his movie adversaries, like mobster Lopez (Robert Loggia). Instead, he chose to hang out mainly with Steven Bauer, his partner, Manolo. Bauer was touched by the support he received from Pacino. "I feared rejection until I met Al," he said. "We're both Latin, and with that comes a kind of kindredness." Pacino's relationship with Elvira (Michelle Pfeiffer) was "off and on" depending on the stage of the movie. The same was true with Gina, played by Mary Elizabeth Mastrantonio. (Bauer had tested for Manolo unaware that he was up against Pacino's choice of Jimmy Hayden, a young actor whose bit part in *Cruising* had impressed Pacino but ended up on the cutting-room floor. "Jimmy's a terrific actor," Bregman told him, "but he's wrong for this part." Pacino initially was also dead set against Pfeiffer; so, for that matter, was Universal.

"She's the best," Bregman assured Pacino over the phone after viewing everyone tested. "You want to see for yourself?" There was a pause on the line, then: "Nah. I trust you.")

Production was halted for a week following an incident in which Pacino tripped and fell against an M-14 machine gun. Since hundreds of rounds of ammunition had just been fired, it was still blazing hot and inflicted deep second-degree burns on his left hand as he grabbed it. Pacino was rushed to Sherman Oaks Burn Center in the San Fernando Valley, where he was attended by Dr. Richard Grossman, the distinguished plastic surgeon who had saved Richard Pryor's life back in 1980.

Later, while another scene in a telephone booth was being shot on location at Tudor City Park, Pacino—in character—angrily left the booth after his conversation and slammed the door behind him, catching his finger in the process. After a momentary wince of pain he carried on with the scene. Gee, Al, onlookers thought, isn't that carrying Method acting too far? What they were witnessing was a return to the accident-prone spell Pacino had undergone back in the sixties.

There were fears during another scene that Pacino's striving for realism had been taken too far. After ducking machine-gun fire and diving under a table in the Babylon nightclub, Pacino emerged with "blood" streaming from his nose. It looked at first as if the squibs that had been planted under his armpits had exploded and smashed some glasses, lacerating Pacino's face. With the cast and crew looking on aghast, Pacino licked the "blood" that oozed into his mouth. "This tastes like chocolate," he said as he recognized the sweetened prop mixture. The announcement produced sighs of relief all around.

Two weeks later the unit moved to Montecito in Santa Barbara County, the resort providing two magnificent villas, one to serve as the home of Montana's Bolivian "connection," the other his fortresslike Xanadu, complete with private zoo. When De Palma staged the wedding of Montana and Elvira, he could point to a previous real-life ceremony on the same site, in which Charlie Chaplin and Oona O'Neill had tied the knot.

The crucial wedding sequence had to be postponed when the

California coast was hit by record-breaking storms that wreaked millions of dollars' worth of damage in Santa Barbara County alone. A return to Florida for two weeks of shooting was made despite bomb threats.

"What can I tell you?" Bregman asks acerbically. "It was a damn tough shoot." To cap it all, he and Stone had a monumental falling-out that began with Stone's request to see the "finished" rough cut. Bregman was wary; he thought that he knew how writers' minds worked, and Stone's in particular, and was certain the screenwriter would pick faults with his "baby" no matter what was on the screen. Pacino, who still had looping to do, had seen the cut and said he loved it, and Bregman did not want his impression undermined. Stone's request was refused.

That weekend Bregman received a call from his agent, Marty Baum, who also represented both Stone and De Palma. Bauer, calling from home with Stone and De Palma by his side, begged Bregman to reconsider. "Brian thinks it will be OK," he argued, before putting Stone on the line.

"Listen," Bregman was told, "if there's anything I don't like, I'll only tell you and Brian. Al will never hear about it." On that basis Bregman relented and set up a screening.

Within days Stone had dispatched a fifteen-page memo to Bregman and De Palma, listing in vivid detail what he found wrong with the movie. Next Bregman received a call from Pacino. Could they meet? He had reconsidered his view of the movie and needed to talk it through. When he did, Bregman was incensed to find him verbalizing many of the points in Stone's memo. Although he was able to soothe Pacino's fevered brow, he knew that Stone had violated their agreement. It took years before the rift between them healed.

WITH TWO MONTHS to go before the premiere of *Scarface* in December 1983, *American Buffalo*—its triumphant Off-Broadway revival now the stuff of theatrical legend—was at last set for its Broadway debut at New York's Booth Theater. A warm-up engagement was scheduled at the Kennedy Center for the Performing Arts in Washington. Pacino's cast members for the limited run were J. J. Johnson and James Hayden, who, after *Cruising*, had recently completed a major role opposite Robert De Niro in *Once upon a Time in America*.

After the night's show was over in Washington, Pacino often climbed into his car and drove through the night to New York. Having reached his apartment, he made himself a cup of coffee, then just sat there, wondering what to do with himself next. When the play transferred to Broadway, he drove out to his country home, then turned around almost immediately and headed back to the city. "I just like to move and keep moving," he offers by way of explanation.

If this has partly to do with the "coming-down" process, it also betrays a greater restlessness and melancholia that relate directly to traveling players throughout the ages—Pacino's vagabonds, minstrels and outsiders. For all of them, the concept of a "fixed abode" remained illusory.

A hint of a considerable element of improvisation was given by Elliott Martin prior to the New York opening. "Al continues to explore the play," he said. "He has an entirely different concept from the way he did it Off-Broadway. He's approaching the character differently, and he is dressing differently. This has been a very creative experience. Al is a very imaginative, fertile-minded actor."

Another producer might well have said, "Al, it ain't broke. Why fix it?" Not Martin.

Pacino declined to be specific about any changes he was attempting, while conceding that nothing was ever "set," as it had to be in a finished movie. With him a play would always be in transition, changing as *he* changed. And he maintained that the only way to explore the depths of a piece was by living through it. *American Buffalo* was like a faithful wife: You could let *it* down but it would never let *you* down. He compared his experimentation on Teach with various versions of Shakespearean roles. If every different actor had his own interpretation, why should these individual visions be themselves fixed during the run of a play?

Pacino and his troupe opened on Broadway to tremendous acclaim. Leslie Bennetts had given readers of the New York *Times* ample warning, back in the play's Off-Broadway incarnation, of what they could expect. "In a startling burst of energy," he wrote, "Pacino detonated onto the stage, jittering and skittering and dodging around as if no space were large enough to contain him. Consumed by nervous tics, he twitched and scratched, obsessively hiking up his shoulder and twisting his neck in stiff, jerky, repetitive circles. When he talked his words exploded onto the audience in a hail of spray."

Bennetts's picture of the actor in motion in his own living room at the same time was no less riveting. Pacino was as restless and nervous as in his portrayal of Teach, pacing and fidgeting, avoiding eye contact and contorting his body even when seated so that he could stare out of the window behind him instead of looking at his inquisitor. Bennetts watched, astonished, as Pacino, clearly convinced he *was* Teach, scuttled around the apartment, grabbing food in passing, ripping off a piece of bagel, shelling pistachio nuts at bewildering speed, tossing them into his mouth and noisily rattling the shells in his hand.

His conversation was as erratic as his movements, bursting forth in a torrent of passionate fragments, accompanied by the physical motion that seemed to help him act out much of what he wanted to communicate. Among the intermittent volleys of talk, Pacino defined his criteria for choosing stage material. "I always look at the play as the character," he explained. "If I get the feeling for the way the playwright is talking, even if I'm wrong, even it it's not the way he or she felt, that's what I look for. In movies it's more the character itself, but in theater it's a sense of the play and the language. I like a play to *choose me.* It just sort of stays with me and says, 'Come on, do it. You know you want to do it, so *do it!*' "

A gloomy silence followed this insight, as Pacino's articulation seemed to sputter and stall. The "high" was over. It was as if a curtain had come down.

Just three weeks into *American Buffalo*'s triumphant run, at 6:30 A.M. on Tuesday, November 8, a phone call woke Pacino in his New York apartment. The news was grim. Jimmy Hayden, ironically playing the part of Bobby, the young junkie, opposite Pacino's Teach, had been found dead in his apartment of a drug overdose. The devastated reactions of J. J. Johnson mirrored Pacino's. Johnson at first maintained there was no way he could perform without Hayden that night but in the end yielded to Pacino's advice that they should appear, as a tribute to the young actor. For his part, Pacino knew he had to keep busy to allay the desolation he felt.

In the afternoon Pacino drove up to his country house, forty minutes from the city along the Palisades Parkway, where a small film crew from Universal was waiting to shoot promotional footage for *Scarface*. This was to show him frolicking with his two dogs, playing stickball at an adjacent park, walking with his live-in girlfriend, actress Kathleen Quinlan, and, mainly, talking about the upcoming movie. If this was hardly Pacino's idea of a good time in the first place, it was rendered even less so by the morning's terrible news.

When Arvin Brown joined him, the director's eyes were swollen. As the two men embraced, Brown began sobbing. Pacino would allow no questions from reporters about Hayden. "I loved him, you understand?" he explained. "It's just too soon to talk about it. He was the best young actor I ever saw." Tragically, Hayden had not lived to see his big-screen debut in *Once upon a Time in America*.

Pacino felt frozen by despair that night as he prepared to go onstage. He and J. J. Johnson, together with Hayden's understudy, John Shepard, went on to give superb performances, for which they received an extended standing ovation from the audience. Bows were taken, but on that particular evening none of the actors felt able to force a smile.

"What happened to Jimmy shocked everybody. It affected all of us." Pacino said later, carefully measuring every word. "Everybody. The shock of it was terrible, but we had to go on. It was right, in a sense. I don't know how to explain it exactly. It's like going back and driving a car right after you've had a terrible accident. You *have* to do it. And you have to do it right away.

"I've been around awhile, seen a lot of things," Pacino continued. "But Jimmy—he had that thing, whatever it is, that sort of set him apart. One of the reasons I decided to do this play again was to do it with him and JJ. What happened to Jimmy, what brought him to where he was—we really don't know much about that. I do know his death reached a lot of people. And it did change a bit, a little bit, the way I'm thinking about things. That I couldn't deny."

CHAPTER 24

A KIND OF MATURITY

Pacino bristled when asked about his new love, the dark-eyed Kathleen Quinlan, whose performance as the institutionalized schizophrenic teenager in *I Never Promised You a Rose Garden* had created a sensation back in 1977. "Why do I have to talk about somebody who I do everything with?" he protested. "It's *obvious* how I feel. She's the woman that I'm with all the time. I don't like talking about her. I don't want to make her public by publicizing her. What we have is good. Why spoil it?" He was prepared, however, to talk about Quinlan the actress, and in the most glowing terms. "If you see her in *Rose Garden*, that is the most evident, fabulous piece of acting I've ever seen. A talent like that should be used."

A close acquaintance of Pacino's was more forthcoming. "Al told me he's very much in love with Kathleen," he said. "He is normally very closemouthed about personal things, but they're so much in love that he just blurted it out to me."

For her part, Quinlan had reportedly told a friend, "It's a romance, a big romance. Al is wonderful, so warm and caring. I'm in love." The same friend added, "Kathleen was thrilled when Al took her to meet Anna Strasberg. 'I felt like Al was taking me home to meet his family,' she told me. 'It was great to see how wonderful Al was with Anna's children. I think he'd be a terrific father.' "

What, Pacino was asked, always kept him from taking the next logical step in his relationships with women? "Well, if there were steps I could see," he replied, "I would say I could go on to the next step. At least I can say, for whatever it's worth, that I don't have a divorce situation on my hands. There's a kind of maturity to that."

MARTY BREGMAN'S OUTRAGED response to the original X rating for *Scarface* was typically forthright. "We have been officially designated a *pornographic* film," he said tersely. An appeal was immediately lodged.

Although Brian De Palma claimed to have reedited the movie four times in an attempt to mollify the ratings board, its response was that the movie remained "excessively violent in action and language." De Palma refused to cut the movie further. "Universal will have to fire me and get someone else to reedit," he declared.

Movies given X ratings are prohibited to anyone under the age of seventeen. It is a category that is certainly identified, as Bregman pointed out, with porno movies. Many newspapers and radio and television stations refuse to accept advertising for X-rated movies; several theater groups even have it written into their leases that they will never play an X. "Under no circumstances," Universal's Robert Rehme announced, "will the studio release *Scarface* with an X rating."

With a December 9 opening only weeks away and a huge launch and publicity campaign booked, Bregman was in the latest of the tight corners that had characterized the entire production of the movie. "The board have got us by the throat," he acknowledged, "because of the time factor. We're opening in six weeks in a thousand theaters."

A premiere held in Houston elicited a comment from the

head of a theater chain that seemed to summarize the impasse. "There is no way to change this film to get the lesser R rating without destroying the movie's artistic integrity," he said. "It is a very powerful film with a tour de force performance by Al Pacino. You can certainly argue that because of its violence it should be off limits to those under seventeen, but an X rating stigmatizes a film, paints it with a black brush."

In an attempt to marshal opinion, De Palma asked several movie figures to attend screenings. They included Universal's Ned Tanen, who admitted, "I'm relatively puritanical, which is why Brian wanted me. And I simply don't understand what all the fuss is about. I can't conceive of why anyone should rate the picture X."

According to some press reports, De Palma finally made one cut in the film's bloodiest scene, a pan that showed an arm being severed by a chainsaw. At last *Scarface* was granted an R —together with several hundred column inches of publicity that would have been impossible to buy.

"We never cut one inch," Bregman insists, *"not one frame. We never shot the arm being severed in the first place, so how could we cut it? The fact is, I fought the ratings board and won. Under their rules you are entitled to a final 'trial' before twenty MPAA [Motion Picture Association of America] members. I arrived loaded for bear, producing as witnesses two psychiatrists, the head of the Organized Crime Division in Florida, and several writers, including Jay Cocks from *Time* magazine. The panel voted eighteen to two in our favor. I can be one tough son of a bitch when there's something worth fighting for, something I believe in."

Controversy, whether sought or otherwise, continued to dog the movie's two celebrity previews in New York City and Los Angeles. Author Kurt Vonnegut, together with his wife, photographer Jill Krementz, walked out of the Times Square performance after thirty minutes, muttering, "It's too gory for me." They were closely followed by writer John Irving. Dustin Hoffman stayed but seemed to have difficulty staying awake during the 170-minute movie.

As the audience exited, Cheryl Tiegs called it "The most violent film I've ever seen. It makes you never want to hear the word 'cocaine' again." Actor James Woods approached the movie from a different angle. "Personally," he deadpanned, "I'm all for any movie whose lead character keeps a grenade launcher in his living room."

At the postpremiere bash, held at Sardi's and hosted by Bregman, the movie played to mixed reviews as the celebrities feasted on a buffet of pasta, seafood Newburg, beef bourguignon and a dazzling selection of desserts. "I really liked it," said Cher, "it was a great example of how the American dream can go to shit." Raquel Welch, accompanied by her daughter Tahnee—the two of them looking like sisters—greeted her old friend and collaborator Bregman but chided him: "The violence was just for effect, Marty. A lot of people will enjoy it, but it goes on ad nauseam."

Shortly after midnight Pacino made his entrance to robust applause and a flurry of hugs from friends and well-wishers. He looked sharp in an immaculately tailored herringbone tweed topcoat, over a pinstripe suit, checked shirt and silk tie, and mixed easily with the crowd. When Kathleen Quinlan joined him, the couple stayed for over an hour before the topcoat was donned once more against the rigors of the New York winter.

On the sidewalk outside, Pacino shook hands with costars Steven Bauer and Mary Elizabeth Mastrantonio. "Al Pacino is my favorite actor," Eddie Murphy confessed as he left. "I know all the dialogue from his movies. When I met him inside, I *groveled.*"

Twenty-four hours later the Los Angeles premiere was staged. Bauer was again in attendance, this time accompanied by Tippi Hedren and her daughter Melanie Griffith, to whom he was married at the time. Hedren declared the movie was "too brutal," leaving the unsinkable Joan Collins, a vision in diamanté-studded leather, to have the last word on *Scarface's* language. "I hear there are a hundred eighty-three 'fucks' in the movie." She sighed wistfully. "Why, that's more than most people get in a lifetime!"

IN SHADES OF *Cruising*, *Scarface* began with a disclaimer slapped on before the titles: "*Scarface* is a fictional account of the actions of a small group of ruthless criminals. The characters do not represent the Cuban-American community and it would be erroneous and unfair to suggest that they do. The vast majority of Cuban-Americans have demonstrated a dedication, vitality and enterprise that has [*sic*] enriched the American scene." If this was designed to preclude criticism from spokesmen for the Cuban community, the opposite effect was achieved.

Village Voice columnist Enrique Fernandez pointed to Marty Bregman as the film's true auteur, the one who had conceived, engineered and commandeered the project as a vehicle for Pacino. He had "consciously exchanged depth for flash" when he had switched from Lumet to De Palma. It was possible, Fernandez continued, to imagine what kind of movie Lumet might have made—introspective, culturally dense, political. Bregman, on the other hand, had wanted ZAP, BANG, POW! If not, why had he gone to Oliver Stone? As for Pacino, "He gives a studied, mannered performance that commands the spectator watch and judge. I didn't see Tony Montana. I saw Pacino acting."

Another *Village Voice* scribe, Andrew Sarris, continued the critical assault, judging *Scarface* "much more an event than a movie, and so much more a disaster than an outrage. . . . One wonders if Oliver Stone actually 'wrote' the script, or if Pacino made it up as he went along." To David Denby in the New York *Times*, the movie was "all bluster, macho ritual and mayhem," in the end "a sadly overblown B-movie."

Rex Reed deemed *Scarface* "familiar stuff, noisy and grim, and ultimately rather pointless. When it's over you feel mugged, debased, like you'd eaten a bad clam." He also confirmed the Miami city fathers' worst fears: "It's probably the worst public-relations black eye ever given to the city of

Miami. Painted in garish, peeling pink, like toenail polish, the city looks like a running cesspool."

James Wolcott detected scenes of diabolical humor among the carnage. "Al Pacino's performance helps," he maintained. "His Montana seems to have studied the *Raging Bull* school of etiquette, spouting things like, 'Don't fuck with me, don't you fucking fuck with me, or I'll blow your fucking head off, you fuck.'"

In the Los Angeles *Herald-Examiner* Peter Rainer indicated that, to judge by his superior *American Buffalo* performance, it might be time for Pacino metaphorically to dab some grease-paint onto the celluloid. "In *American Buffalo* Pacino was intensely alive to the possibilities in his role, and I suspect that the presence of a live audience had a lot to do with his high energy level and invention. The audience kept him honest. In *Scarface*, Pacino doesn't have an audience to work off, and that may have dulled his actor's instincts . . . his movie acting needs a transfusion of old-fashioned theatrical generosity."

Pauline Kael's dissection was fully up to her usual standard. "*Scarface*," she wrote, "is a long, druggy spectacle—manic, yet exhausted. The whole feeling of the movie is limp. This may be the only action picture that turns into an allegory of impotence."

The Kael claws were really out for Pacino: "After a while, Pacino is a lump at the center of the movie. His Tony Montana has no bloom to lose and he doesn't suggest much in the way of potential. This is a two-hour-and-forty-nine-minute picture with a star whose imagination seems impaired."

Rick Corliss in *Time* magazine provided a welcome element of balance to Kael's rhetoric. "Pacino creates his freshest characterization in years," he said. "There is poetry to his psychosis that makes Tony a creature of rank awe. And the rhythm of that poetry is Pacino's."

Another isolated pocket of support came from Vincent Canby in the New York *Times*, who perceived in *Scarface* "a revelation, a movie of boldly imagined design."

While the response to Pacino's performance ran a similar

gamut to the picture's reviews, all the way from "brilliant" to "crassly self-indulgent," he remains unapologetic about both the movie and his role in it. "What you see in Tony Montana is what you get," he points out. "I guess that was the idea when we made the picture. It was made with that exaggerated style in mind. Brian De Palma thought of it as an opera in the Brechtian sense, to express the thing that goes with that world —avarice, force and the craziness of the high. I wish, I hope, there's a wit running through *Scarface* and my character. He was always perceived as two-dimensional; that was the *style*. It wasn't about *why* he does *what* he does. He wasn't *meant* to be reflective."

Pressed to say whether he actually *liked* the movie or not, Pacino countered, "I don't feel qualified to answer that. It's really not my place to get into that kind of criticism. I can tell you if I'm happy with what I've done in it or something like that. But I don't know how I could say whether it was a good movie or a bad movie. And it's not just this one I'd say that about. I'd say it about any one of the movies I've been in."

Was he aware from the beginning that it would end up as strong as it did? "Well," Pacino answered slowly, with a grin, "all I can say is that it read pretty rough to me from the first."

So did the majority of critics misjudge *Scarface*? Most assuredly. There are some movies about which it is unwise to rush to judgment, and *Scarface* must be counted an archetypal example. The prerelease publicity surrounding the X certificate and the concentration on the film's graphic use of language and violence damned its prospects in advance.

The majority of U.S. critics trashed Warren Beatty's *Bonnie and Clyde* when it was first shown and were forced to a reappraisal after its triumphant European reception. With *Scarface*, it was the public's refusal to be second-guessed that registered the movie as a major hit. With cable and video, *Scarface* gained even more momentum, outgrossing *Serpico* and *Dog Day Afternoon* combined in all media. The "operatic" approach was vindicated. Bregman's only mistake, it seemed, was in failing to tip the wink by featuring Wagner on the sound track. Audiences worldwide were reminded that Pacino was still very much around and available at their neighborhood theaters. It was, after all, his first hit movie since *Dog Day Afternoon*, almost a decade earlier.

Sure enough, *Scarface* has since become the subject of a considerable degree of critical reappraisal and is regarded by many as a key movie of the eighties. One of Britain's most respected provincial movie critics, Alasdair Marshall, is a leading proponent of this view. "In fifty years' time," he predicts, "when they assess the best fifty movies of the twentieth century, *Scarface* will be on the list."

"It was a brilliant parody of a gangster movie," says Charlie Laughton, "and most people didn't get it. As for Al, in my opinion he gave the greatest performance of his career."

DUSTIN HOFFMAN took to Broadway's boards in the same season as *American Buffalo*, playing his dream role of Willie Loman in Arthur Miller's *Death of a Salesman*. His obsession with the part had begun while working as an assistant stage manager on a production of Miller's *View from the Bridge* and had continued while playing Bernard, the kid next door, opposite Lee J. Cobb's ground-breaking Loman. Since both *Death of a Salesman* and *American Buffalo* were revivals, neither Hoffman nor Pacino was eligible for a Tony, this being awarded only to actors appearing in original plays. Freed of this restriction, one or the other would have been the favorite to take home "Broadway's Oscar."

The two met again in Rizzoli's Fifth Avenue bookstore, while independently browsing. "Which one of you is which?" an autograph hunter yelled as she swooped. "I'm Dustin Hoffman," Pacino told her, deadpan. Hoffman did likewise. "I'm Al Pacino," he said. Their expressions of mock despair gave way to sheepish smiles as they signed their names.

Pacino took *American Buffalo* to London in the fall of 1984, with cast partners J. J. Johnson and Bruce MacVittie. Although they played to capacity crowds and considerable acclaim throughout the Duke of York's season, a few doubts were raised. No one questioned the searing power of Pacino's performance, although it was acknowledged to be firmly in the "over the top" category. "Without Pacino," Steve Grant at *Time Out* maintained, "it's unlikely that any commercial management would have been interested in David Mamet's abrasive, claustrophobic three-hander. The dialogue, though possessing its own harsh music, is a rat-tat-tat of repetition, punctured with homily and obscenity in equal proportions, post-graduate Pinter shifted to the streets of New York. It is Pacino who always holds the stage, bounding on with a stream of four-lettered abuse ('Fuck-in' Ruthie! Fuck-in' Ruthie! Fuck-in' Ruthie!') against a two-timing 'cunt dyke.' Pacino's performance is busy, fussy even, a technical tour de force, but ultimately little more. Maybe he was trying too hard on the first night. Certainly the extrovert style, the continual movements and facial gestures are related to the character, but sometimes it's hard to escape from the feeling that the 'performance' is winning out."

Journalist Chris Peachment was surprised at the absence of the usual clutch of murmuring starlets or sycophantic retinue accompanying Pacino. Instead, he found the star relaxed and comfortable in the presence of two longtime friends, the manager of a repertory theater outside New York and Charlie Laughton. Pacino told Peachment that unlike most actors, he loved doing matinees. "For one thing," he explained, "it happens earlier in the day, so you haven't found time to hit that full pit of despair by the evening. And you haven't had all the day's events heaped up on top of your consciousness and overriding your performance. You feel that there is less pressure on you; you can bring a quality of relaxation to the role."

If expressions like "that full pit of despair" still tended to give the lie to any notion of a man at ease with himself and the world, Pacino's reply to Peachment's next question, innocently asking if he had ever attended the Cannes Film Festival, seemed to serve as confirmation. "It's hard for someone like me," he said, shaking his head. "Everywhere I go, the lights

are in my eyes. That's why I avoid doing all these things, events
and interviews. It's not out of disdain; it's because when I'm
there the event becomes different. It's not an event I can
watch, because I *am* the event. In New York I'm recognized
everywhere I go. If I want to study people, I have to go out in
the back of my station wagon and watch them while I'm being
driven around."

While there was no doubting the genuine practical problems
he described, common to most celebrities, Pacino still appeared to be suffering from lingering traces of *Bobby Deerfield*-
itis, a condition comedian Fred Allen may have had in mind
when coining his definition of a celebrity: "He's a person who
works hard all his life to become known, then wears dark
glasses to avoid being recognized."

Charlie Laughton puts a different interpretation on Pacino's
"full pit of despair," claiming the remark was misunderstood.
"Al was referring to the tremendous fear before he goes onstage which he has in common with most actors. One opera
singer used to say that if he were given the choice of being put
up against a wall and shot or going onstage, he'd really have to
think about it! It's that fear, though, that *makes* a performance.
Most people start feeling it around four in the afternoon, when
they consciously begin to prepare, trying all the while to relax
and deal with those nerves. Very often the better the actor, the
more they feel it."

Pacino was also a man who continued to repay debts. On
September 8, 1984, the final night of Pacino's London run, a
benefit performance of *American Buffalo* was held. All proceeds were donated to defray Julian Beck's hospital bills in
New York, where the Living Theater's founder, Pacino's early
benefactor, lay stricken with cancer.

Pacino continued to play the loner at a small last-night party
thrown at the Duke of York's, attended by a dozen people.
After spending the entire time stuck in a corner talking to a
friend from New York, he shook hands and left, an enormous
bodyguard ushering him through the waiting crowd in St.
Martin's Lane to his limousine.

"Dealing with fame is just too exhausting," he murmured to a journalist. "Everyone seems to want a piece of you. Strangers want to hold you in conversation. Girls come up to you in restaurants and kiss you full on the mouth while your mouth is full of food. You think that sounds good, huh? Well, believe me, the novelty soon wears off!"

CHAPTER 25

"MY NEMESIS, AL PACINO"

T HE CONCEPT OF making a movie based on the American Revolution came to Irwin Winkler in Martin Scorsese's house while the two men were editing *Raging Bull*. Scorsese's collection of toy soldiers caught the producer's attention, the host of tiny redcoats in particular. Why, he wondered, had there been so little attention paid in the American cinema to this key episode in American history?

Soon after, a discussion with his seventeen-year-old son about the American War of Independence revealed, to his embarrassment, how little he knew about it. "I was amazed how few people knew any more about our origins than I did," says Winkler. "Most people believe we celebrate the Fourth of July because that's when we won the war. Not so. July fourth was when the colonists declared their independence. *Then* the war began!" Within days he had called scriptwriter Robert Dillon, whose work on *French Connection II* and *The River* he had admired. "Think about two words," he told him, "American Revolution."

Winkler was unconcerned about the lack of topicality in the

historical theme, being convinced that the conflict had contemporary parallels in the recent Vietnam War. He was fascinated by the way in which the British had kept their supply lines extended across an ocean and shipped in thousands of trained men, weaponry and ammunition. They had fought their battles in accordance with European principles, their thin red lines advancing to the drumbeat, each of the three rows of infantry firing musket volleys in turn.

After their first terrible losses, the American rebels had refused to form into neat rows for the redcoats to mow down. Instead, they learned to use their terrain, hiding in trees Indian style and picking the enemy off, shooting from behind the cover of rocks and attacking after dark, choosing whatever weapons they could muster. The British were shocked at their disregard for the "rules" and traditional "niceties"; what they were witnessing was the true beginning of guerrilla warfare.

As to why the American Revolution had never held great appeal for movie producers, Winkler had several explanations ready. "Maybe people in the past thought there was no market," he told colleagues, "or maybe they were afraid it was too expensive, or nobody thought of it."

He was delighted with the script Dillon produced, which superimposed a personal father and son relationship over the larger canvas. Scottish immigrant fur trader Tom Dobb and his fourteen-year-old son, Ned, freshly arrived in New York City from the Adirondacks, are unwillingly plunged into the conflict when their boat is requisitioned. With Ned pressganged into the army and Dobb enlisted to keep an eye on his son, a dastardly enemy emerges in the shape of British Sergeant Major Peasy.

Winkler was undeterred when Warner Bros. put the development into "turnaround"—up for sale, that is. "No one wanted to make the original *Rocky*," he points out. "The reasons? Fight movies don't work. Women don't go to violent films. Sylvester Stallone—who's he? But I liked *Rocky*'s story and thought its positiveness would work with an audience, and it did." (Having a "put" deal at United Artists, which meant that Winkler could make any subject he wanted, provided it cost less than a million dollars, also helped.)

Never a follow-the-leader producer, Winkler felt that thematically *Rocky* and *Revolution* were similar; both films were about the common man making good against the establishment. "What Hollywood tells you to do is *Return of the Nerds* or *Bachelor Party* or *Police Academy*. If you're going to do films that have some serious import, you're going to be turned down. But I found somebody to do *Raging Bull*, so I guessed I would find somebody to do *Revolution*." After the project had been turned down by every other major studio, he decided the only way to revive its fortunes was to attract a major director.

Hugh Hudson, on the lookout for a new challenge to follow *Chariots of Fire* and *Greystoke: Tarzan, Lord of the Apes*, happened to be working with Dillon on another script and obtained a copy of *Revolution* through his agent.

After the difficulties of both producing and directing *Greystoke*, Hudson was looking to work with a strong, experienced producer and believed he had chanced upon the ideal vehicle. Over a dinner that was arranged with Winkler, Hudson declared that *Revolution* was unlike any other historical epic he had come across. He saw it as a street movie rather than a vast costume drama. It flew against all the dictates of Hollywood dramas in that it had no central love story, no Rhett and Scarlett, no Yuri and Lara, no Louise Bryant and John Reed. In its place Hudson sensed a below-the-belt toughness that made him feel, by the end of the piece, as if he had navigated his way through a popular revolt and arrived at the safe harbor of liberty.

There was no need, he said enthusiastically to Winkler, to recount the exploits of the giants of the day, no need to explain battle plans, no need to graph the course of the war chronologically. The inherent drama of the common man, sucked into the vortex of a conflict over which he had no control, would sweep all before it. Hudson also saw the story as a metaphor. "Every man and woman has a revolution when they reach a certain age," Winkler was informed, "and I see England as being just such a parent figure. It's *everyone's* struggle, *everyone's* problem, to break away. And a revolutionary war is exactly that, an oedipal situation on a collective scale."

Winkler was overwhelmed; at last he had found someone whose enthusiasm matched his own. Although somewhat taken aback at old Etonian Hudson's apparent antiestablishment stance, he felt that this was a man he could trust. "And he seemed to like me!" Winkler recalls with a smile. "I'm an enormous sucker for people who like me."

At Hudson's recommendation he took the project to Goldcrest Films, the British movie company with which the director had a close relationship. There he saw Sandy Lieberson, whom Winkler had first met at William Morris's office a quarter of a century earlier, when the two of them had been message boys at the agency.

"This has the potential to be the best movie script I've ever read," Lieberson told his Goldcrest colleagues, brandishing *Revolution*'s script, "and I want the go-ahead to buy it." Although the board's reaction was far from unanimous, the bait was swallowed. Goldcrest was already involved with two other expensive projects, *Absolute Beginners* and *The Mission*, but had embarked on a determined course of expansion to consolidate its already impressive success story in the eighties. And if a little brinksmanship was involved, wasn't that par for the course in the movie industry?

A first budget was set at ten million dollars "below the line," excluding the cost of the director, the producer and the leading actors. Eight hundred thousand dollars were set aside for an American name actor, with the rest of the cast to be recruited in Britain. When Hudson began to put out feelers for the role of Tom Dobb, he himself had one ideal in mind: Al Pacino.

After weeks of trying to track his quarry down, Hudson finally met Pacino during *American Buffalo*'s London run. Pacino was impressed by Hudson's fire and enthusiasm as well as by the aspect of oedipal rebellion, which carried personal echoes. Even so, he thought that the character of the feisty, apolitical trader lacked definition and turned the role down.

Hudson held discussions with Robert Duvall, then heard that Richard Gere's agents were prepared to talk. When his multimillion-dollar fee was declared out of the question, Gere contacted Hudson personally in New York's Hotel Pierre. "Let's talk acting and leave money out of it," he suggested, clearly desperate to land the role. Sylvester Stallone approached Winkler at a late stage in a belated attempt to secure the lead role. "We could have had a very successful film," Hudson rationalizes, "but on the other hand, Stallone would probably have killed *Revolution* stone dead on every level."

Hudson had earlier fallen out with David Puttnam, who had produced *Chariots of Fire* with him, over his withdrawal of collaboration on *Greystoke*. Now Puttnam, about to produce *The Mission*, was seeking Robert De Niro to star. How much, if at all, this affected Hudson's decision to pursue his own superstar will be denied forever. It may well have been Puttnam who first raised the stakes.

Why had Pacino turned down the role originally? "When your nature is ambivalent to begin with," he explains, "it affects everything you do. Like work. The question becomes, 'What's more appealing: having to work or not having to work?' I'm not a quick yes when it comes to movies. Why do I finally say yes? I get tired of saying no."

It was four months after his first meeting with Hudson before Pacino agreed to star in *Revolution*. And even then, despite the challenge of creating a "silent movie epic" with Hudson, he still insisted on a rewrite to sharpen up his character.

"It was a bit like a love affair," says Hudson. "I finally got him to agree because I insisted I couldn't make the film without him, which is an almost irresistible lure. I needed the common man element, but I also needed a star. Of course, it was a period role, one he'd never played before, and some people said, 'You're mad, his background is Italian.' But he's from the South Bronx, and I wanted someone from the back streets of Glasgow, a street guy, a street *rat*. Al's from a deprived background, ten years ago he hadn't two pennies to rub together, and that quality comes off him still. He's really been through it.

Also, he's a wonderfully comic actor, and there's quite a lot of humor in the film."

Even the bravest hearts at Goldcrest still felt a twinge when they heard of the fee Winkler proposed for Pacino. "It's a seven-figure salary," he told the press, "lower seven than for Sly Stallone or Bob Redford, but still seven." It turned out to be three million dollars, which left the eight-hundred-thou-sand-dollar reserve looking decidedly sick, especially when Donald Sutherland as Peasy was brought into the equation, Hudson and Winkler arguing that a star of Pacino's magnitude required stellar support.

To add the romantic interest that Hudson had originally be-lieved could be dispensed with, Nastassja Kinski was signed for the beefed-up role of Daisy McConnahay, the rebellious, hotheaded daughter of a New York merchant. One member of the Goldcrest board agitatedly pointed out, "Dillon didn't even have a major female character in his first draft, for God's sake!" Another warned, "You can add an extra million on top of their fees for Concorde flights, limousines and Win-nebagos." The argument for going ahead was that a U.S. sale for the movie, with Pacino on board, was virtually guaranteed.

Suddenly the whole project began to burgeon, the support-ing cast studded with names like Joan Plowright, John Wells, Dave King, Richard O'Brien and Steven Berkoff, with pop singer Annie Lennox of the Eurythmics making her dramatic debut as the Liberty Lady.

Now that they were gambling with Goldcrest's money, canny Warner Bros. was delighted to negotiate a negative pickup deal for the United States. In an attempt to justify the relatively peppercorn $5.6 million from the studio—increased from $4.25 million after Pacino had signed—Goldcrest ex-plained that it was getting a far bigger slice of the U.S. box office in return. Everyone was assured that the necessary fi-nance was in place, even with a new budget nudging $15 mil-lion. As well as Warner's $5.6 million, Norway's Viking Film had pledged another $4 million. Goldcrest was exposed "only" for the rest.

Although negative pickup implies a "hands-off" element of "make the film, deliver it and we'll pay up," Warner's still wanted its own input. The problem with *Revolution* from the outset was the differing concepts of the major participants. As far as Warner's was concerned, *Revolution*, above all, had to be a "relationship movie": Dobb and his son braving the conflict together and emerging triumphant; Dobb and McConnahay meeting and falling in love, then being tragically separated before a dramatic reunion.

There was no question in their minds of Daisy's being killed off halfway through, as one draft had it, leaving Dobb wandering about in a lonely, anticlimactic daze over the end credits. While the background of the American Revolution had to be suitably authentic and affecting, Warner's regarded this as strictly secondary.

Not so for Hudson, who was inspired by the notion of re-creating the "silent movie epic" he had discussed with Pacino. "I see the film as having no conventional story," he declared, "no direct narrator where two, three or even four of the characters dominate the story, just the inexorable unfolding of the years. The *rebellion* should be the major character, swinging in wild extremes, both brutal and lyrical. The main characters we do have, Tom, Daisy and Ned, are swept up in the rebellion and *that* is their story. They give up their private stories to the collective." As far as Hudson was concerned, the romantic element was hackneyed, Warner's "happy ending" a cliché.

Warner's and Hudson's differing notions of *Revolution* were never reconciled. As for the hapless Goldcrest, no two members of the management seemed able to agree what day it was, let alone what kind of movie they were making. And despite the claim by Warner's Terry Semel that the company had a clear idea of what it wanted, the script to which it gave its approval, albeit reluctantly, was regarded as far from a masterwork.

"It wasn't very good," Semel has admitted, "but we felt that for the kind of money we were in for, it would be a decent try. And Hugh, being a good director, might pull off some good reviews when it was all over. If the critics jumped on it even in a nice way, for our investment we could earn a profit."

Pacino was involved with Hudson at every stage of the conceptual discussions, as well as on the various rewrites, and seemed fully in sympathy with his director's views. Maybe in the interaction between them an attraction of opposites was at work: Old Etonian meets Bronx dropout.

Lunching one day in New York's Russian Tea Room before production started, Hudson was approached by a broadly grinning Dustin Hoffman. "I hear you're going to be working with my nemesis, Al Pacino," was his cheery greeting. Although Hudson laughed, having heard of the half-joking comparisons often made between the two actors, he was unaware of the semiserious element of competition between them that had its roots almost twenty years earlier on Off-Broadway and Lee Strasberg's Actors Studio.

PREPRODUCTION ON *REVOLUTION* began in November 1984, the timing essential if a February 1985 production start was to be achieved, and a premiere before the end of the year.

Production designer Assheton Gorton, an Oscar winner for his sets on *The French Lieutenant's Woman,* worked feverishly with costume designer and military expert John Mollo to make sure every historical detail on the production was the essence of authenticity. Gorton examined every known picture of Yorktown, as well as scores of others, from romanticized etchings of the Revolution to smudgy photos of the British in the Crimea, anything that illustrated the look of the period as well as the techniques of war that prevailed from the eighteenth to the nineteenth century. London was scoured for costumes; fifteen hundred were obtained in the end, four hundred of them specially made. Two hundred wigs were rented.

Obvious U.S. locations were eschewed at an early stage, Williamsburg being considered too squeaky clean and present-day Valley Forge off limits. Instead—at an estimated saving of three million dollars—the sleepy market town of King's Lynn in Norfolk, England, would substitute for New York's docks, cathedral city Ely in Cambridgeshire would double for Philadelphia, while Dartmoor in Devon would host the Battle of Manhattan.

By the end of January Hudson had begun to argue that the production should be delayed for three months to allow problems with the script to be properly thrashed out. He was informed by the Goldcrest board that this was out of the question. With the stark choice of going ahead or facing unthinkable cancellation, he acquiesced. A "final" revised budget was pitched at twenty million dollars.

On March 18, 1985, the first day of shooting, Donald Sutherland, every inch Sergeant Major Peasy, led his troops of several hundred musket-bearing redcoats in a march through King's Lynn town center, transformed with flags, signs and costumes to look like upper Manhattan in 1776, after the British had vanquished the rebel army. Pacino was just one of scores of ecstatic onlookers who watched entranced, reveling in the accompanying skirl of fifes and drums. It was, he declared, one of the best sets he'd ever worked on.

He was less enthusiastic about his own first scenes, where he felt all but lost in the crowd, and wasted no time in making his feelings known. "You're paying me all this money," he protested to Hudson. "Why am I being used as an *extra*?"

Hudson was advised from several other quarters that he was shooting too few close-ups of his star and failing to establish a strong enough relationship between Tom Dobb and his son. Although he went back and did some reshooting, many thought there was still a lack of intimacy in the results.

In all the arguments between Warner's and Hudson, obscured as they were by an unfinished script, one key point had escaped everyone's attention: *Revolution* had never been conceived as a star vehicle, for Pacino or anyone else.

From the very beginning the English weather played havoc with the unit, torrential rain reducing many of the locations to a muddy shambles. Hudson had wanted foul weather and mud, but strictly controlled by his technical crew; there was no question of conveniently switching off Mother Nature's down-pours.

With the construction crew complaining that their hands were sticking to scaffolding in the sub-zero temperatures, the bitter cold that accompanied the storms soon began to take its toll. Nastassja Kinski seemed ill from the start, although no one was sure if it was physically or emotionally based, since she was rumored to have struck a critical point in her marriage. In all, eighty people sought medical attention, mainly for colds, chills and flu, in the first two weeks. For good measure Donald Sutherland slipped on some hard-packed mud and badly gashed his knee.

Pacino's health held up for a month. Then he was hit by a viral infection, anxiously designated "low-grade pneumonia." Hudson's determination to continue shooting, come hell or high water—understandable, perhaps, in view of the daily costs being absorbed by the enormous cast and crew—did little to help. One minute Pacino was inside his tent, insisting that the heat be turned up to pain level; the next he was back out-side, being soaked to the skin. Hudson was finally forced to abandon shooting for a full week while his star convalesced.

A complete absence of camaraderie between Pacino and the English crew had already been noted. His taciturn reserve, even when he was back on his feet, continued to cause resent-ment. He either moped around on the set, speaking to no one, or disappeared between scenes. A crew member recalls being stunned that Pacino refused to speak or communicate socially with Sutherland, on the basis that they were enemies in the film and Pacino wanted to maintain the appropriate dramatic tension.

Stunned or not, Hugh Hudson's assistant, Meg Clark, down-plays this aspect. "So much of what was said was based on misunderstandings," she maintains. "Donald and Al were per-fectly friendly. Donald *understood*. And for much of the time, when Al wasn't ill, we saw a happy, relatively relaxed actor, content to sit off duty chatting to the cockney drummer boys and pose for snapshots with the mums and dads who turned up to watch filming. Al's intensity is to do with his total involvement in his role. Anyone who doesn't appreciate that is going to misread the guy."

Another aspect over which the intrepid Clark was never in doubt was how to find Pacino. "I used to follow the coffee splashes," she explains with a chuckle. "I've never seen anyone drink as much coffee as he did. A mug seemed to be permanently attached to his lip."

Executive producer Chris Burt has his own explanation for Pacino's "distancing" himself during the shoot: "Al is a very private man, very quiet and withdrawn. When the work's finished, he doesn't hang around and chat. It's not his style. Donald Sutherland is a complete contrast, enormously popular and outgoing with everyone, which perhaps made Al seem even more remote in contrast. But it takes all sorts, although the two had one thing in common: their total, committed professionalism. No one was ever kept waiting, even though Al was unwell for much of the time."

He recalls daily discussions with Pacino. "If you want to be considered one of the greatest actors in your profession, you have to weigh up each film very carefully. Every day you've got scripts coming in and directors phoning you up. You can only choose one or two, so from the moment you think you've chosen the wrong one, you're insecure. In that respect, of course, Al is insecure. With *Revolution* he had made a wrong turn, but he never once questioned why he'd taken the film. He questioned instead his *role* in it, how he was being *used* in it. If there had ever been a finished script, he'd have seen that he didn't have enough set pieces."

Although united in the overall "silent movie" concept, a postbattle scene shot in the cornfields highlighted a significant difference in approach between Pacino and his director on the intensity of his affair with Connahay. Hudson was determined to cool this element and had strayed about as far as it was possible to get from Dillon's original scenario, which had Dobb and Connahay having sex in front of a startled Ned.

Hudson's interpretation was to have Dobb, suffering from

battle fatigue, passively accepting a chaste kiss on the cheek from Daisy. Instead, in take after take, Pacino's hands kept straying perilously close to Kinski's breasts. "Get a load of randy Al," one of the crew chortled.

As Hudson exasperatedly set up the umpteenth take, Pacino leaped to his feet. "You don't *understand* me," he told him. "I'm *Al Pacino*. My public *expects* me to react. How can I just lie there and take it?" For the rest of the day the actor was eventually persuaded to do just that, and with the light about to fade Hudson felt satisfied the scene was in the can.

"Wait," Pacino yelled, jumping up again. "I'm not *satisfied*. I want to do it *again*, do you hear? I want it done *again*."

Hudson stared at his star for a few seconds, rather in the manner of a schoolmaster dealing with an errant but brilliant child. "OK, we'll reassemble tomorrow morning," he finally agreed, while the crew groaned in unison in the background.

"Oh, *for fuck's sake*," a prominent cast member was heard to mutter as he disappeared into his tent.

Support for Pacino's "method" came from an unexpected quarter—Kinski herself, whose breasts had been under attack. "For me, Al is incredible," she declared. "He's not one of those actors who comes on the set and then leaves. It means a lot to him to discuss things, to make a scene good enough. His method is to go slowly, build things up, then step back and come back to it, then do that again until finally it happens by itself, so in the end it just flows."

A representative of the press who witnessed the day's performance and had already been refused an interview with Pacino could hardly wait to report on the disarray. "Al Pacino is at heart a New York street kid who is not happy anywhere else," she wrote. "He is also unbelievably defensive about his reputation. And Hugh Hudson does not know how to cope with him."

Incensed with this kind of reportage, Hudson declared the set off limits to the press. "Hudson's brand of haughtiness is not the natural focal point for a happy unit," the reporter countered. "And maybe Pacino's smart enough to realize he's got nothing interesting to say and doesn't want the rest of the world to know that."

Soon the very sight of Nastassja Kinski seemed to produce an instantly apoplectic reaction from her director, not unrelated to her habitual on-set lateness. The prefilming encomiums of both Winkler and Hudson now rang more than a little hollow. "We wanted someone to give us a spark, a sexiness, a romance," Winkler had said with enthusiasm. "There's a vulnerability about her but also a certain madness, a wildness," Hudson had chorused.

Although Hudson had the madness and wildness he wanted, the same qualities landed him with a dreadful dilemma, trying to squeeze a performance out of Kinski while stifling his anger at being held up for hours at a time. "She's incredibly sexual and perfect in the part," said Hudson, "so I shouldn't complain. She has magic, yet if she goes on this way much longer, she won't get any work, for no one will insure her. Everyone's energy is sapped, and her behavior is highly unprofessional and selfish."

Hudson's main problem was that the illnesses of Pacino and Kinski seemed always to be out of sync for their joint scenes. When Pacino would turn up relatively bright-eyed and bushy-tailed, Kinski would be laid low. When Kinski put in an appearance, Pacino would be hit by another bout of flu.

A female member of the crew painted a sympathetic picture of Kinski's plight. "She was a poor soul. I think she had some internal medical problem; there was internal bleeding. She was crying and weeping all over the place and breaking out in spots. As for Al, his flu never really went away."

Although Pacino was treated in royal style by Goldcrest, lavish homes and an accompanying retinue of bodyguard, personal cook, chauffeur and secretary being provided in both London and Norfolk, he managed to treat both establishments as if he were back home, leaving a trail of half-eaten breakfast hamburgers strewn throughout the bedrooms.

While an entourage of friends and colleagues came and left —dialect ace Bob Easton, who had honed his client's Cuban accent for *Scarface,* and Charlie Laughton—Pacino was basically living alone. His most recent romantic partner, the dark-haired beauty Kathleen Quinlan, was not only notable by her absence throughout the shoot but a name forbidden even to be whispered in Pacino's vicinity.

Another affair had bitten the dust.

CHAPTER 26

GUERRILLA FILMMAKING

A s THE *Revolution* unit moved from King's Lynn to Devon, and with no letup in the dreadful weather, Hudson increasingly seemed to be aiming for a *Battle of Algiers* flavor, all hand-held cameras and grainy black and white. His French cameraman, Bernard Lutic, enthusiastically set about the color desaturation and low-key lighting that would approximate a wide-screen, larger-budget *Algiers* feel, faithful to the spirit of Pontecorvo's masterpiece. "I feel as if I'm in Northern Ireland or the Lebanon," Hudson said approvingly as shooting progressed. "I'm not making movies; I'm making *reality*."

Others were intent on more mundane pursuits that produced their own, distinctly surreal moments as filming progressed. Scene: the Devon cliffs, re-creating the Battle of Yorktown, Virginia, in 1781, the final act of the war. A biting wind swirls around the American troops huddled on the exposed terrain. The cannons roar; smoke blossoms in a graphite cloud; a shower of cork falls on everyone's heads. Suddenly a young soldier whips out his Instamatic. "Got Pacino at last, then, ain't I!" he shouts triumphantly.

Pacino continued to insist on rewrites to point up the personal relationships with both his son and Kinski's worryingly ephemeral Daisy McConnahay. Other scenes, which he felt were overwritten, he chose to convey by gestures. Gradually, as a crisis of confidence developed between Pacino and Hudson, the star began to make frequent calls to Irwin Winkler.

Although he was tied up with Stallone's *Rocky IV*, as well as on preproduction of Bertrand Tavernier's *Round Midnight*, Winkler listened with concern to Pacino's tales of woe. Fanned into flame by the adverse press coverage, a feeling began to develop that while Hudson was secure in dealing with classically trained British actors, he had perhaps bitten off more than he could chew in his first encounter with Method acting.

Ignored were the Sundays the two men spent together every week, playing chess in the morning (not very well, Hudson admits) and rehearsing the rest of the day. The only noticeable difference when Winkler visited were the frequent round trips of several hundred miles his chauffeur made to Harrod's in London to purchase such delicacies as lobsters and onions, all of which were available locally. Fresher, at that.

Between weather delays, illness and rewriting, the schedule and cost of *Revolution* began to spiral out of control. In Devon a devastating series of accidents bedeviled the production. Executive producer Chris Burt was getting up at six one morning when the production manager telephoned. "The crane's on the beach," he was told.

"You mean, it's on the *cliffs*," Burt corrected him, "where we left it last night."

"No, I mean the *beach*," came the reply, *"in pieces."*

The giant Titan crane the unit had been using for panning shots had been left in the mud after filming the previous day, without the chocks in place that would have prevented it from sliding hundreds of feet to the beach below. Since the four-hundred-thousand-dollar monster was the only one of its type in the country, it took several days to locate another that began to serve the purpose—with filming again shut down.

Then there was a catering tent fire, the eighty-foot marquee mysteriously going up in flames one morning. For a while there were murmurings that both accidents were maliciously caused by locals miffed by their wives' and girlfriends' being abducted in large numbers by lascivious film folk.

"It's like a little bit of imperialism," one crew member suggested. "All these well-paid people with gold jewelry and perfect teeth suddenly descend on a town and throw their weight around. They go to the local discos in the evening and steal the girls." While lust undeniably was having a field day, sabotage was discounted. In the end sheer negligence was blamed in the case of the careering crane and a faulty propane gas cylinder proved to be the culprit in the catering tent conflagration.

With *The Mission*'s team of David Puttnam and director Roland Joffe stuck in the jungles of Colombia, Puttnam had no doubt where the blame lay for their cash starvation. "Another group of people had different priorities," he raged at Goldcrest and the *Revolution* team. "I don't believe Hugh or Irwin Winkler were prepared to take on to their shoulders the compromises that Joffe absorbed. *Revolution* is shooting in Devon; *we're* in fucking Cartagena. You can't mess around with our cash flow."

His contention that the overruns on *Revolution* and *Absolute Beginners* were killing Goldcrest ignored his own contribution, *The Mission*'s budget having ballooned way beyond its original fifteen-million-dollar estimate. And Puttnam's team was emulating Irwin Winkler in another respect: local supermarkets were shunned for supplies; every mouthful the unit consumed, down to the most humble sandwich, was specially flown from Britain.

Puttnam was still correct in his assumption that *Revolution* was behind all his problems, but hardly in the way he intended. Although Goldcrest had sold Warner's the *package* of *Revolution* and *The Mission*, *Revolution* was the one it had really wanted. *The Mission* was being made on *Revolution*'s back.

The problem with the movie's Norwegian money, more than ever essential to the beleaguered Goldcrest, was that it had been arranged subject to a portion of the movie's being shot in Norway, doubling for upstate New York. Both Hudson and Pacino fought against the trip but were forced in the end to bow to the inevitable. After the rigors of England, Norway, in fact, proved a thoroughly pleasant experience. It also provided some of the most spectacular footage.

Warner's and Hudson were engaged in two fresh battles as filming drew to a close. One was over the fate of Sutherland's Peasy, the movie's chief villain. The studio was determined that he would be killed off at the end; Hudson was equally determined he would not. "Peasy is *England*," he protested. "He doesn't die. Like England, he just goes away." Although Warner's believed this was dramatically unsatisfactory, it gave in.

The second battle, it informed Hudson, was not negotiable. Despite the fact that Daisy's death had already been filmed, she must be resurrected at the climax and reunited with Tom Dobb. "Or else?" Hudson asked.

"Or else we won't take delivery of the movie," he was crisply informed.

Resigned to the necessity of what he saw as an artistic compromise, Hudson decided to stage the couple's reunion in spectacular style. King's Lynn was stripped once more of TV aerials and scaffolding. A long and difficult tracking shot was planned, to be filmed from Pacino's point of view, fighting his way through boats docked in a canal, past cows, jugglers, acrobats and a wrestling match thronged by twelve hundred extras singing and dancing in the streets, to be finally, miraculously, reunited with Daisy.

Unfortunately, by the time all the ducking and weaving had been rehearsed and was about to be committed to celluloid, Daisy had disappeared, Kinski having caught a plane to Rome without bothering to inform anyone. The scene was completed upon her return two days later. "She cost us about half a million bucks," said Winkler ruefully.

Despite their occasional creative differences, Hudson's support for his star never faltered. "Al matched up to my concept of the film," he declared as filming ended, "and he's added to it in the most extraordinary way. It was a great experience, like making a guerrilla movie; Al calls it guerrilla filmmaking, because so much of it was improvised. We adapted all the time, changing the script, often working all night. As a director it's always important to follow your own instinct, but I listened to Al. I never found him difficult, just demanding at times. Yes, he's intense, single-minded. That's what I wanted, and that's what I got!"

Filming had been scheduled to end in June; instead it stretched through to August, the final cost escalating to twenty-six million dollars.

Hudson remained buoyancy itself at the editing stage, contemptuously dismissing the overrun allegations. His vision of the movie remained unchanged, give or take a reunion or two. He had tried to re-create the era as it might have appeared to one simple, frightened and haunted man caught in the midst of the turmoil of momentous events. The conflict itself remained the star.

Since *The Mission* was still being shot and *Absolute Beginners* was in no way ready, *Revolution* was the only potential cash cow available to Goldcrest. The company resisted pressure from Hudson to allow his team more time to edit the movie and insisted on sticking to the original U.S. opening date of mid-December, barely four months distant. This would start money flowing, Goldcrest argued, as well as qualify the movie for Oscar nominations.

There was no inkling of the disaster to come when the final cut was shown to Warner's Bob Daly and Terry Semel. They embraced Hudson warmly and assured him it was the best thing he'd ever done. Following a disastrous sneak preview, however, Pacino flew to London on two separate occasions to do final overdubs in December, with the release moved up to Christmas Day.

He met Meg Clark again while he was being put up in Chelsea for the sessions. "Meg, you've changed so much!" he told her, smiling broadly. The only change Meg could detect was her shedding of the foul-weather gear that had been her uniform during the shoot. It was Pacino who was transformed, now that he was distanced from the arduous location grind and had recharged his batteries back in his beloved New York.

"You can take the boy out of the Bronx," murmured one technician as the dubbing proceeded, "but you can't take the Bronx out of the boy!" In view of the critical notices Pacino's Scottish/cockney-with-a-dash-of-the-Bronx accent was to receive, it was an auspicious remark.

The vitriolic initial reviews stunned everyone. "There may be a smashing movie on the cutting room floor," said David Ansen of *Newsweek*, "but what's on screen is a shambles."

"This movie is *nuts!*" the *Village Voice* concurred, before describing it as "the most hilariously maladroit historical pageant since *King David*. Authentic-looking muskets, swords, breeches, three-cornered hats and all manner of nifty Georgian bric-a-brac abound, but as soon as Pacino speaks, the cast might as well be wearing lampshades on their heads."

As usual, Pauline Kael was lurking in wait. "*Revolution* is so bad," she wrote, "it puts you in a state of shock." Vincent Canby joined the chorus in the New York *Times*: "Pacino has never been so intense to such little effect. It's like watching someone walking around in a chicken costume. It's sloppily written, edited and dubbed. Pacino's very first speech in the film is spoken as if he were a ventriloquist. At the climax, when Pacino explains, 'In this country, ain't no one ever gonna treat nobody like a dog in the dirt,' some critics literally screamed with laughter. It's England's answer to *Heaven's Gate*."

Bruce Kirkland in the Toronto *Sun* was one of the few who disagreed. "Pacino's performance is so naturalistic, so riveting, that it emerges as an exhilarating ride back from the Hollywood dead for the actor." As for the movie, Kirkland found it "an unexpected treasure."

Warner's desperately scoured the country for more reviews it could quote and managed to locate a verbal notice from Gary Franklin of CBS-TV. On a scale of one to ten he awarded the movie a ten plus. "*Revolution* is a beautifully made and performed historical epic," he informed his viewers. "It's superb, intensely human. As for Pacino's accent, who knows how they talked two hundred years ago?"

After a thirty-six-hour stopover in Los Angeles and still sporting his *Revolution* ponytail, Pacino flew off to Jamaica for his Christmas vacation in Warner's jet. His holiday almost outlasted *Revolution*'s brief run at the box office, withdrawn with less than one million dollars in rentals.

Back at his Devon farmhouse, where Hugh Hudson was eagerly awaiting the call from Warner's with details of the reviews, the phone never rang. It was late on Boxing Day before someone had the decency, as well as the nerve, to contact him.

Hudson was shattered. He had gone for authenticity in every field, ignoring every cinematic expectation, and was paying the price. Pacino's accent on its own might well have been acceptable, but he was surrounded by a supporting cast apparently determined to outdo him—Donald Sutherland's Peasy, together with a whole slew of English officers, their "silly ass" accents more readily associated over the years with comedy rather than historical drama. And the dubbing of the entire movie, from Pacino on down, betrayed the abbreviated postproduction imposed on Hudson.

The movie flopped miserably around the world, save for France, where it played on the Champs Élysées for several months, and Italy. Goldcrest, the "great white hope" of the British film industry, was all but toppled. *Absolute Beginners* was to provide the next tremor, *The Mission* eventually delivering the coup de grace.

Pacino harbors deep regrets about *Revolution*. "Hugh wanted me very much," he reflects. "There was a chance, because of the collaboration, that something good would come out of it, because Hugh saw something in me to play the role."

He denies that the movie was a bad experience. "What would make you think that? Not to my mind it wasn't, I didn't see it as that. I saw it as a movie that, OK, wasn't successful. I mean, I thought it didn't work, and that's the way it was received. But actually, I thought there were some interesting scenes in there."

So did Charlie Laughton, among many others. "The success of a film is very much dependent upon the fashion of the day," he suggests. It was already described as "one of the most imaginative epics of the eighties" when revived in 1990 at London's Film Theater.

Pacino himself talks wistfully about gaining access to Warner's vaults and working with Hugh Hudson on assembling a new version from the raw footage, one that would be closer to their original concept—and, he hoped, redubbed. That must remain a tantalizing possibility for the future. In the meantime, there can be only regret for the movie's fate first time around.

"Of course, I wish it hadn't turned out that way," Pacino concedes. "How could I *not* care?"

CHAPTER 27

RUNNING ON EMPTY

HIS AFFAIR WITH Kathleen Quinlan ended, the only production Pacino was in a mood to stage after *Revolution* was the continuing psychodrama of the ambiguities of success. With his film career firmly anchored in the doldrums, he began to question, more seriously than he ever had before, whether the price tag was worth the sacrifices he saw himself making.

"I've been adjusting to fame for fifteen years," he reasoned in Act I. "I know the ups and downs, right? *Wrong.* I still have ambivalent feelings. At one point in my life there was suddenly this sense that I was going to become a commercially popular and successful actor. It became a given. I don't know even now how right that was for me. Commercial movies are not where you *learn.* Not that I'm complaining, but maybe I've neglected another part of my work life or my personal life. In the old days, when I met somebody, there would be a natural evolution. Two people meet, and there's something there or not. You took the time to find out. Now, people just know you right away. Maybe fame is not an easy thing to understand unless you've experienced it."

For his second act, Pacino chose to introduce the prospect of marriage. "It's possible," he conceded. "I think about it sometimes. It could be an actress, or maybe not. I haven't known many women who weren't actresses, it's the world I travel in. With actresses, the work can pull you apart for unnaturally long periods of time. But if you can afford it, there are ways to get together. It's very attractive to me now to see a love relationship in which you are also friends."

Act III even introduced children. "I think when I want to have a family, I will have one. So far there must be a reason why not, but I'll tell you this—it's very appealing. A good relationship makes you feel whole, I guess. Alone, I don't think you ever feel whole."

Had he just defined his own agenda?

IMMEDIATELY FOLLOWING *Revolution*, Pacino financed and shot his own fifty-minute movie version of Heathcote Williams's *The Local Stigmatic*, the play originally introduced to America in the sixties by Harold Pinter. With David Wheeler again directing, Pacino reprised the role of Graham, a vicious cockney greyhound-track bookie who organizes the beating and brutal scarring of an elderly actor, merely, it seems, as a revenge against his being famous. "Fame is the first *disgrace*," Graham hisses to his partner in crime, "because *God* knows who you are."

Pacino spent several years obsessively editing, reediting and endlessly fussing over *Stigmatic*, expending several hundred thousand dollars in the process. He finally showed it to Stanley Cavell's class at Harvard, then at the Museum of Modern Art. Always he stressed that it was unfinished.

He was well aware that *The Local Stigmatic* was unknown and would probably remain that way to the main movie audience. "I don't think people relate to that kind of work," he said. "Acting is such a visual process that if you're not real visible in it, they assume you're not working." With *Stigmatic*'s exposure limited to just a few dozen viewers, Pacino had hit the button. The movie was bidding fair to become the cine-matic equivalent of Joe Papp's *Arturo Ui*, a project suspended in perpetual development.

The failure of *The Local Stigmatic* onstage seemed to have turned the play into a cause, with Pacino campaigning for its recognition. When it was put to him that his apparent obses-sion with the piece expressed his own desire to be punished for the "disgrace" of fame, Pacino laughingly denied the allega-tion and pointed to his series of nonopening plays, the endless "workshop" process: "I remember reading about how the Lunts would spend three months just working on the props. And I had this whole thing about plays never opening, just always rehearsing and calling the audience to watch rehears-als."

To Pacino the whole idea of "maybe never opening" was Utopia, the impossible ideal whose impracticality he was the first to acknowledge, then promptly to condone. "I dream about it," he admitted, *"no clock!* They say that you must put these restrictions on yourself in order to get the thing done. I don't agree. I think it can be done without that, that you can trust the faculty in yourself that says, 'I'm ready to do it this time, because there's not much more I can do, so I'll reveal it now.'"

A string of impresarios may well have breathed a heartfelt "amen," thankful that with *The Local Stigmatic*, Pacino was at least putting his own cash on the line. One reporter overheard Diane Keaton's reaction to Pacino's latest, latest, *latest* cut in 1988: "I'm glad these flash forwards are gone now," she told him. Then she hesitated and frowned. "But it still needs *some-thing*, don't you think?"

Pacino nodded gravely. "You're right, you're right," he sighed.

IT WAS NOT for lack of offers that Pacino backed away from mainstream moviemaking in the latter part of the eighties, more the realization that there had to be a better way. His movie choices since the mid-seventies read like a veritable catalog of misjudgments, especially when weighed against the subjects he had declined. He was constantly reminded of one of Stella Adler's pronouncements: "Actors are as good as their choices."

The advent of Cannon's go-go boys in his life was at least partly to blame for what came to be seen as Pacino's "clandestine" years. If they were, it was not entirely by choice.

Menahem Golan and Yoram Globus had parlayed Cannon from a twenty-cent-a-share operation in 1979 to a peak of forty-five dollars in 1986. By then the company appeared to have signed up the cream of Hollywood talent. Dustin Hoffman was to star in an adaptation of Elmore Leonard's *La Brava*, to be directed by Hal Ashby, Jerry Schatzberg was set to direct *Street Smart*, Jill Clayburgh headed the cast of director Andrei Konchalovsky's *Shy People*—and Pacino was reportedly signed for two movies, a remake of the 1978 Italian production *Investigation of a Citizen Above Suspicion*, to be written by Paul Schrader and directed by Konchalovsky, and a film version of Mamet's *American Buffalo*. For *Investigation* alone, he was to receive four million dollars.

While all roads seemed to lead to Cannon, there were constant rumors about the company's basic instability. It kept on announcing and producing more and more movies every year, but they were movies that nobody went to see. How long could it continue? One Beverly Hills story told of a rich Arab who asked his sons what they wanted for their birthday. The boy who asked for an airplane got Pan Am. The boy who asked for a boat was given Cunard. For the tiny tot who asked for a cowboy outfit, his father bought him Cannon!

With losses produced by the two projects that did get made. *Street Smart* and *Shy People*, as well as a huge list of other turkeys, the go-go empire gradually began to unravel. Dustin Hoffman was first to defect, citing breach of a clause that gave him personal approval of all uses of his likeness in promoting *La Brava*. Cannon had splashed a picture of Hoffman over a full-page *Hollywood Reporter* advertisement that prematurely welcomed him to the company's family. When Golan darkly hinted that he was considering a lawsuit, the reply from Bertram Fields in the Hoffman camp wryly provided the address of the appropriate courtroom. Without so much as dropping the ball, the Israeli cousins claimed Pacino was willing to take over from Hoffman, provided Francis Coppola directed the movie. Now he was making *three* movies for Cannon already!

Unsurprisingly, *La Brava, Investigation of a Citizen Above Suspicion* and *American Buffalo* were never produced. The sprat used by the wily go-go boys to catch their mackerel had been the comparatively low-cost *American Buffalo*. With the imminent collapse of their overextended house of cards it was no longer possible to contemplate loss leaders, no matter how cheap.

Largely thanks to the flirtation with Cannon, two years passed without a resumption of Pacino's movie career. There was more "workshop theater," notably in a production of *Julius Caesar* for Joe Papp. Pacino's Mark Antony, wrote William B. Collins, was "supercharged, excitingly unpredictable and impassioned," his final oration and reading of Caesar's will "acted with such spontaneity as to obliterate memories of lesser performances. And yes, he *is* better than Brando was in the film version."

He dabbled with other plays, like *Chinese Coffee, Crystal Clear* and Dennis McIntyre's *National Anthem*. Ron Rosenbaum described the latter as "an eye-opening experience" when he caught an "on-book reading" for a small subscription audience in New Haven. Three actors stalked across a minimally furnished stage, scripts in hand, exploring their roles, Pacino as a suburban Detroit fireman seizing on a yuppie couple to act out the psychodrama of his nervous breakdown.

Although Rosenbaum admitted this was not the type of material he normally sought out, he saw Pacino bring a manic edge of black comic electricity to his lines that made the experience compelling. "You could almost see his shrewd actor's intelligence seizing on a comic possibility in the middle of a line," he reported, "and by the time he got to the end flicking it inside out like a glove."

Pacino was vague when asked about the possibility of a full-scale production of the play. Would this be yet another unfinished concerto? "We're *working* on it," he protested. "Maybe we'll try out some changes down the line. But that's the kind of thing I really like to do. You know, we did a thing Off-Off-Broadway last year, kind of a workshop of a piece called *Chinese Coffee*." He beamed. "*Nobody* saw it!"

In the wake of Cannon's demise other movie offers came and went, bringing with them ever-increasing pressure to make the right choices. "I try not to judge my own movies, and I never felt my Hollywood career was over," Pacino later claimed. "I always go back to work. What else can I do? Lee Strasberg once told me, 'Dollink, you have to adjust!' "

By the end of 1987 Diane Keaton was again well established, if that is not a contradiction in terms, as Pacino's on-again, off-again companion. Her own career, like that of so many others in the cast, had taken off after *The Godfather*, for which she had received precisely six thousand dollars. "Pacino was great in *The Godfather*, De Niro was great," she herself acknowledges. "I was background music." Keaton in *Godfather II* was a different proposition entirely, transformed into a commanding presence.

Before *The Godfather* she had appeared in Woody Allen's original stage version of *Play it Again, Sam*, as well as the stage musical *Hair*, and was considered, not without reason, a lightweight. After *The Godfather* Keaton emulated Pacino, both in returning to the stage and in embracing an Israel Horovitz play, *The Primary English Class*. It took her five more years before she consolidated her dramatic powers in *Looking for Mr. Goodbar* as well as copping an Oscar for *Annie Hall*.

For a while she was the lady in both Woody Allen's and Warren Beatty's lives. "Diane is real special," Pacino told an acquaintance, "a true *friend*, which is what I look for. I love her spontaneity and sense of humor."

Dinner for Pacino with Keaton's family, the Halls, early in

1987 had been a singular occasion, almost a nonethnic rerun of a similar episode with Woody Allen's Alvy Singer in *Annie Hall*. "I think it would be wonderful to see myself with one man for the rest of my life," Keaton declared. "I don't know if I can, though."

While filming her role as a single mother in *Baby Boom*, in 1988, Keaton claimed to view marriage as a remote prospect. "There's a good chance I won't ever marry," she declared. "I believe it's a fine idea, but—"

Love, however, was a different matter entirely. "Sure, I'm hopeful," she fenced, giggling. "I mean, I'm not dead yet. I have a lot of hope. When you're younger, it's more infatuation; you just know you want, you need, you have. Now I see it as much more accepting people for what they are and being less needy, feeling less righteous."

She refused to talk about the prospect of having a child of her own, drawing in her breath sharply when the subject arose and shaking her head. "I know I can't have all the things I hoped I could have or thought I should be able to have."

After *Baby Boom* Keaton turned decidedly broody and a little more forthcoming. "I would like to be a parent," she now admitted, "but I'm a little old to be having children. I don't know if it's going to happen in the normal way. That doesn't mean that I'm into surrogate motherhood; on the contrary, count me out. I think the best way to do it would be to adopt a child."

In mid-1988 the Los Angeles *Herald-Examiner* claimed that Keaton, at forty-two, was pregnant. "Low profile though their relationship may be," the story continued, "Pacino is definitely the father."

Soon afterward came word of a miscarriage. Neither Pacino nor Keaton would confirm, or deny, either report.

PACINO'S YEARS AWAY from the spotlight were brought to an end when he was presented with not one but two movie scripts he thought had potential: *Johnny Handsome*, from Paramount and *Sea of Love*, from Universal. He spent two months working with director Harold Becker—of *Taps*, *The Onion Field* and *The Boost*—on *Johnny Handsome*, a drama based on the intriguing question of how corrective plastic surgery might affect a hideously deformed criminal's character. Despite their best efforts, they were unable to elevate the material out of the B movie genre. The first half was fine, Pacino thought, but the "third act" fell away badly. Working with Becker, however, proved a pleasant and rewarding experience.

Pacino forwarded *Sea of Love* to Marty Bregman, who thought that the script was basically incomplete and, as it stood, didn't work. Pacino agreed and informed the studio of his decision.

Six months later Tom Pollock at Universal phoned Bregman and asked him to consider producing *Sea of Love*. Bregman explained that he'd already read it and had decided to pass. At Pollock's request he took another look and outlined to Universal's chief what he felt was missing. He agreed to work with writer Richard Price, "to get it where it should have been."

On reading the revised script, Pacino found himself engrossed in the dilemma of Frank Keller, *Sea of Love*'s burnt-out cop, a lonely, vulnerable cynic trying to cope with a mid-life crisis, with nothing to look forward to except the slow death of early retirement on half pay. Price's original script had been transformed into a nail-biting suspense classic, with Keller falling for the glamorous chief suspect while on the trail of a serial killer whose victims are found in the personal ads columns.

Keller's angst had been left intact. What was added, at Bregman's behest and with Price's gruffly reluctant cooperation, were equal doses of mystery and sex.

Charlie Laughton still detected some problems that remained to be ironed out. "I told Al I thought it was very good, although some of it was what we call film-film, conventional. There was a bit of illogicality in the transitions, Al had to work very hard to make some of them convincing, but it all worked."

Keller's predicament—living alone, drowning his sorrows in booze, yearning for love—had Pacino trawling deep into his own experience of love and liquor. It all came flooding back: the whirlwind that alcohol had created for him back in the seventies, the obsessive, running-on-empty bust that had left him drowning in various infatuations.

"The booze makes you susceptible to that insanity that happens to people when they fall in love," he reflected, while discussing Keller's motivations. "There's a willingness to allow the love in us to come out; it's just a matter of when we're ready to let go and give it away."

Was he talking about Keller or himself? Pacino seemed genuinely taken aback by the question but staged a quick recovery. "Me?" he asked, laughing. "I let it out all the time!"

He hastened to emphasize, just in case any doubts remained, that his days of booze swilling were long past. "I'm not willing to take the chance. I think about it, but then I ask myself, 'What would it give me?'" Again he laughed, then ruefully spelled out the answer. "Peace, relaxation, joy, that's all! My friends finally made me realize that drinking was an addiction. After each show I felt entitled to a reward, but now it's ice cream and Oreo cookies!"

The darkest element that lurked in *Sea of Love* was the implicit suggestion that Keller was actually turned on by the potentially self-destructive relationship with the suspect. The more Pacino soaked in the situation, the more he was hooked.

Like Pacino before him, Richard Price was a graduate of the Bronx school of hard knocks, *The Wanderers* and *The Color of Money* having already amply demonstrated his spare, sardonic style. Price had originally engaged Dustin Hoffman's interest in advance of offering the project to Universal. With Hoffman's name attached, it had taken the studio just six hours to give the green light. When Hoffman defected, Pacino seemed the next logical choice. *Plus ça change . . . .*

CHAPTER 28

BRONX REUNION

A PART FROM THEIR acting skills, Pacino, Hoffman, Nicholson and De Niro all have in common "bankability," that mysterious element which translates into the facility to get a movie produced.

Try hawking that screenplay or book around Hollywood on its own, and see how far you get, even if your name is Richard Price. Then try it again with one of these names firmly committed. That's bankability, and not necessarily in the obvious box-office sense. The finished movie itself has to stand up: think of Pacino in any of his flops; think of Dustin Hoffman in *Alfredo, Alfredo, Who Is Harry Kellerman?, John and Mary, Straw Dogs, Straight Time, Agatha* and *Ishtar*; of Nicholson in *The King of Marvin Gardens, Goin' South, The Passenger, The Fortune, The Missouri Breaks, Heartburn* and *Ironweed*; of De Niro in *1900, The Last Tycoon, New York, New York, True Confessions, The King of Comedy, Once upon a Time in America, Falling in Love, The Mission, We're No Angels, Stanley and Iris.* There are several fine movies in this litany of box-office failures, but still, they failed, stars or no stars.

The stars get movies made; they secure finance because they allow their films to "open." After that all bets are off. The studios have to wait and hope for the miraculous juxtaposition of their key players in a great, or even just highly commercial movie. The miracle of Hoffman in *Midnight Cowboy, Papillon, Lenny, All the President's Men, Marathon Man, Kramer vs. Kramer, Tootsie* and *Rain Man*; of De Niro in *Taxi Driver, The Deer Hunter, Raging Bull* and *GoodFellas*; of Nicholson in *Five Easy Pieces, Carnal Knowledge, Chinatown, One Flew over the Cuckoo's Nest, The Shining, Terms of Endearment* and *The Witches of Eastwick*; of Pacino in *The Godfather I* and *II, Dog Day Afternoon, Serpico* and *Scarface*.

Stars turn down roles for a variety of reasons, mainly the less-than-pressing need to work too often at today's salaries. Then there's the fear of overexposure. It's no good harking back to the big studio days and arguing that this never hurt the Clark Gables, Bette Davises, Spencer Tracys, Katharine Hepburns, Humphrey Bogarts et al., because back then moviegoers saw their latest films, and that was that until they made another. Although stars now make fewer movies, in between you can check out their back catalogs on video or television; *total* exposure from single films is therefore that much greater. The three years Dustin Hoffman took off between *Kramer vs. Kramer* in 1979 and *Tootsie* in 1982, or Pacino's four-year layoff after *Revolution*, would have been unthinkable in the old days. Today they can be seen as smart career moves, whether or not they were intended that way.

That the paths of the handful of Hollywood superstars continually cross is hardly surprising, considering that the pool of serious talent is so small. Pacino's break in *The Godfather* arrived courtesy of Jack Nicholson and Warren Beatty, both of whom declined the opportunity to play Michael Corleone. In turn, this landed Robert De Niro Pacino's role in *The Gang That Couldn't Shoot Straight* and indirectly to his own breakthrough in *Godfather II*.

Dustin Hoffman, for so long the wild card in Pacino's pack, might well have starred in *Dog Day Afternoon*. After Pacino dithered on *Lenny* and decided against *Kramer vs. Kramer*, Hoffman leaped at both. The lead in *Sea of Love* was his for the taking. When Hoffman, Pacino and Nicholson all turned *The Last Tycoon* down, De Niro grabbed the chance.

Sidney Lumet wanted Pacino for *Prince of the City*, which he declined because of its similarity of theme to *Serpico*. After turning down *Sea of Love*, the busy sixty-five-year-old director began his fifth collaboration—after *The Hill*, *The Offense*, *The Anderson Tapes* and *Murder on the Orient Express*—with another superstar, Sean Connery.

As well as Connery, *Family Business* starred Matthew Broderick—and, working with Lumet for the first time, the irrepressible, irrefutable and totally inescapable Dustin Hoffman.

Sydney Pollack was the first choice of both Pacino and Bregman to direct *Sea of Love*. He declined, explaining that he was fully involved in what emerged as the ill-fated Robert Redford vehicle *Havana*. While Sidney Lumet liked elements of the script, he regarded it as basically exploitative. "I felt that the sexual murder story, the 'dirty murder,' had nothing to do with Keller's character," he explains. "The best of melodrama to me is when the case you're working on becomes an expression of your characters, like Paul Newman in *The Verdict*, where the very essence was the revival of a dead person. I didn't see that in *Sea of Love*."

When a second director, who would have been making his debut on the big screen from TV, dropped out only weeks before *Sea of Love* was due to start, Bregman held a powwow with Pacino. A list of available directors included Harold Becker. Although he had made some good movies, he had never hit what Bregman calls a home run. When Pacino confirmed the excellent relationship they had established on *Johnny Handsome*, Bregman decided to take a chance; he knew that half the battle was won if Pacino was in collaboration with a director with whom he felt at ease. And he needed a director who would go with the existing structure. He called

Becker, who eagerly snapped up the opportunity to work with an actor he deeply admired.

When it came to casting, Bregman says that Ellen Barkin was his *only* choice for the role of Helen, the chief suspect. "I knew her work, I'd loved *The Big Easy* and when we met, she knocked me out," he recalls. "If you take each of her individual features, none of them quite work. Put them together, though, and she's an absolutely beautiful woman." As he had with Michelle Pfeiffer, Pacino at first held out against Barkin's casting before falling in with Bregman.

Having already met Pacino at informal play readings, Barkin felt no sense of intimidation and wasted no time in letting everyone know why she had signed for *Sea of Love*: "Pacino. I would have said yes even if I never got a chance to read the script. There are probably a handful of great actors around, and he is one of them."

Bregman had been a fan of John Goodman's since their work together on *Eddie Macon's Run*, a Kirk Douglas movie he produced. To have him play Pacino's partner, he had to persuade a reluctant Universal to accept a stop date on Goodman that permitted him to leave, whether *Sea of Love* was finished on schedule or not, to join what became the hit TV series *Roseanne*.

Filming began in May 1988, with interiors scheduled at Toronto's Kleinburg Studios, nestled in the picturesque Humber River valley, half an hour's drive from downtown Toronto. Bregman would have preferred to shoot the whole movie in New York City, but Universal prevailed, on the basis that Toronto would be more economical. It also happened to own Kleinburg Studios. "It was only cheaper on paper," Bregman maintains, "and in retrospect saved us nothing."

Harold Becker was in his element working with Pacino. In several scenes, which he considered thin and manufactured—and the Screen Writers Guild strike meant that any glitches in the script had to remain glitches—he watched as Pacino rode to the rescue, bestowing character and texture to his role. "He was so close to it I'm sure he didn't realize himself the credibility he was giving Keller," says Becker. "To this day I'm sure Al came on the film in the first place because of the character he was playing rather than the story."

During all of the Toronto shoot Pacino insisted on flying to New York every Sunday to attend the baseball games he regularly organized, playing mostly with neighbors, friends and their kids. Deciding to videotape the game one weekend, as a prelude he filmed Becker in Toronto trying to restrain him as he ran to board the plane. "I think he just wanted to direct me for a change!" says Becker, chuckling heartily.

"It's a nice thing Al does on Sundays with these ball games," says Michael Hadge. "He cooks a buffet meal, and the players come back and eat at his house and watch movies. There's a pool there, and there's power ball and a paddle tennis court. It's a very nice, comfortable country house, not sumptuous; he just wants everyone to relax and enjoy themselves."

Pacino succinctly resolved Ellen Barkin's problem of how to play the suspect "mysteriously," leaving the audience constantly unsure of her innocence or guilt. "Ellen, that's not your job," his advice ran. "That's Harold's job; leave it to him." Barkin, in turn, helped Pacino out in the movie's several steamy scenes, an area in which he remained clearly uncomfortable. Noting that Pacino lacked "a kind of easy, meaningless flirtatiousness," Barkin flashes her trademark crooked grin. "It made me a lot more relaxed that it was difficult for him," she teases.

She still exploded when one reporter innocently asked about the same sex scenes—probably for around the fiftieth time. "Did you ask *Al* about these scenes?" she raged, racing on to answer her own question. "No, I don't think so! Why does everybody ask *me* about the sex scenes. Is this fair?"

A few seconds later she smiled. "I think the movie does have some great sex scenes," she conceded, "because you watch them and it's sex up there, but it's rare that you find something about the character through these scenes. My character is also the one who goes after *him*, and I think there's something about that fact which is terrific. You don't usually see that in movies."

Barkin went on to establish a considerable reputation around the set for her constant kvetching. One item after another was pronounced "not right," from the coffeemaker in her trailer to her hotel room's not being on a high enough floor. She also had complaints on the creative front. "This woman is supposed to be a mystery," she pointed out, clearly mollified by Pacino only to a limited extent, "but you see her apartment and that she has a child. I tried to change that and make sure no one saw anything more about this woman than Keller had when they were out on a date. But I lost that battle."

A "decision" by Harold Becker that barred her from seeing dailies caused additional resentment. "You're denying an actor an important tool," she claims. "I don't know if they think you only care about what you look like. Maybe they think if you see yourself and you're not great, you're going to go home and slit your wrists. It's only *actors* that get barred. They never say the cinematographer can't go to dailies because if he sees a bad lighting setup, he'll go home, flip out and not be able to come to work next morning." (Becker: "Ellen *wasn't* barred. I expressed the thought that I *prefer* she didn't go.")

The bottom line for Barkin, as far as Pacino is concerned, is simple: "There's a lot to be learned from sitting across from Al for sixteen weeks on a set. There were many, many times when I had to ask him for help on this film, and he was right there."

WITH THE MOVE to New York, a typical day's exterior filming at Seventy-seventh Street and West End Avenue found the company being all but ignored by the seen-it-all city denizens. "Hey, look, that's Al Capuccino," one eleven-year-old, clearly brought up on *Scarface*, yelled.

"Aww, I wanna see someone get shot!" said his impatient friend, a sixth grader at the Collegiate School opposite.

"Just another bunch of typical jaded New Yorkers," said the boys' art teacher. "Woody Allen is always filming in this corner. Kojak used to do car chases here all the time. You take it for granted."

Apart from watching *Sea of Love* being filmed, the small crowd that gathered might have felt they were watching a Bronx reunion, had they been in the know. Ellen Barkin had lived on the same block as Pacino when she was six years old, Marty Bregman and Harold Becker both were brought up in the Bronx, and Bronx boy Richard Price had begun his career writing about the borough in his novels.

Presided over by the imperturbable Marty Bregman and his associate Lou Stroller, the crew of ninety, working amid the circus of equipment trucks, vans and apparatus, kept the backup smooth and unobtrusive, hampered as they were occasionally by popping flash cubes and the blare of car radios and police sirens that threatened to play havoc with the sound track.

Jim Keegan, a doorman at 365 West End Avenue, had ample opportunity to observe the fierce concentration Pacino brought to his role. "He's kind of intense," he said. "You don't talk to Mr. Pacino when he's working. I remember in one scene, after six takes Mr. Becker said to him, 'We'll make this a wrap, Al,' and you know, that vein in Mr. Pacino's forehead began pulsing. And he looked right at Mr. Becker and said, 'One more time.' And Mr. Becker said, 'Fine, Al,' and they did it one more time."

Richard Price managed to secure himself a small role in the movie—the author as actor. "In the contract," he explained, "I included the standard blackmail clause, that I would say wonderful things about what they did to my script if I got a part in the movie."

Becker saw countless examples of Pacino's adding to scenes on the hoof. "He never does anything the same way twice. He's *living* the moment when the camera rolls, and it changes from take to take. If there's a scene in a restaurant and the waiter walks past, to Al that waiter is a *real* waiter in a *real* restaurant. And he'll react accordingly. If the waiter spills coffee over him, that's not the end of the scene, as it would be with most actors. Al will react as he would in a real restaurant.

"At the end of the movie, where Al is trying to change Ellen's mind as they walk down a busy New York street, we tried to cover the actors with as many of our own people as we could, but being New York—! So Al is hurrying along, keeping up with Ellen, dodging and weaving his way through the crowd, when *wallop*, this huge New Yorker barges straight into him. And it *is* a wallop—Al literally bounces out of the frame. He looked away for a quick second, grinned, then caught up with Ellen again and kept right on talking. I shot a dozen takes of that scene and just had to use that one. You can see that he's just so focused on winning her back that *nothing* is going to stop him. His great determination, his passion, his humor, his great humanity—it all just *shines* through in that scene. And that's the *guy*!

"You know," Becker continues with a smile, "when several fellow directors heard I was going to be working with Al, they all said, 'Welcome to the nightmare.' None of them, oddly enough, had ever worked with him before, but they'd heard these stories, as we all had. They couldn't have been more wrong. It was an experience I treasure, I'm second to none in my admiration for him."

When the movie wrapped in late September, after a grueling schedule through the hot summer of 1988, Bregman had a feeling that something really special was in the can. Nine months later Becker was still putting the finishing touches to *Sea of Love* in the editing room just six weeks before the scheduled September 1989 opening.

"I'm biting my nails," he admitted. "Sure, the response from the previews we've been getting is terrific, but you never know with a picture until it actually opens. This is like coming out of a tunnel after eighteen months."

The most downbeat participants were the leading actor and

his oldest friend. "Al and I thought *Sea of Love* would be a moderate success," says Charlie Laughton, smiling broadly. "We thought that was the most we could hope for. What do we know?"

CHAPTER 29

INTERNATIONAL TREASURE

THE BUZZ ON Santa Monica Boulevard in January 1989 was almost tangible. What were Warren Beatty and Pacino cooking up at Dan Tana's bistro over several bottles of Pelegrino? The answer emerged: a supporting role in Beatty's production of *Dick Tracy*, with Pacino as Big Boy Caprice, the world's largest dwarf.

Beatty's initial approach was to ask Pacino if he knew anyone who could play Big Boy. Pacino called Beatty later. "What did you really mean?" he asked.

"Well," Beatty replied, "if you mean by what did I really mean what I *think* you mean, yes, I mean that."

"Really!" said Pacino.

"Of course," Beatty parried.

At first he feared that Pacino would be too expensive, then soon rationalized the cost: "Al is one of those centrifugal people that cause good acting around them."

In Pacino's hands the role soon expanded. "Big Boy was not a recurring character in the comic strip, so we had to make it up," he explains. "I've always wanted to know what it would

272

be like to make a kind of mask for the character you're going to play, like the ancients did, and here was an opportunity to do it. I was trying to find the operative idea for the name Big Boy —could he be a man who dresses like a boy, sucks lollipops? Partly it was a visual thing; the character had a deformity. I even had a sketch artist read the piece and draw characters for me. He could have been the Hunchback of Notre Dame."

At last Pacino had the comedic role he'd always longed for. When Beatty asked him, "Al, have you ever said 'Action' while the camera's rolling?" Pacino replied that he never had. "You'll say 'Action' for me in this picture," Beatty assured him. His words piquantly reminded Pacino of one of Brando's bon mots: "Just because someone shouts 'Action,' it doesn't mean you have to *do* anything!"

Far beyond the significance of the role itself lay the implication of a looser, lighter Pacino that was emerging as the eighties came to an end. It was as if someone had said, "Less agonizing, Al, and more work," and Pacino had rushed to obey. The wily Beatty had used his persuasive powers on several others, including Jimmy Caan and his partner in misery from *Ishtar*, Dustin Hoffman.

OVER THE YEARS Marty Bregman never lost touch with Vietnam veteran Ron Kovic, who called the producer frequently, asking if he thought *Born on the Fourth of July* would ever be made. Bregman's reply was yes, he thought so—one day. In 1987 Kovic told Bregman he had an opportunity to sell the rights of his book to European television for a fee of twenty-five thousand dollars. "Hold it," Bregman advised, "I'm having lunch with Tom Pollock at Universal, and I'll discuss it with him. But, Ron, if you sell it for television, it's all over."

Pollock, an ex-entertainment lawyer, had represented Oliver Stone back in the seventies and was familiar with the entire *Born on the Fourth of July* saga—or so he thought. At their meeting Bregman reminded him that Universal owned Stone's "great screenplay," but not Kovic's book, a discrepancy Pollock was unaware of. He asked how much it might cost to buy the rights. "Around twenty-five thousand dollars," Bregman replied. "or certainly you could option it for that for several years. Kovic's about to sell it to TV, but I can get it for you if you want it."

When Bregman returned to his office, Kovic was contacted and informed of Universal's interest. With the rights acquired Pollock announced that he was ready to make the picture— with Stone directing, Tom Cruise starring and Bregman producing. Unfortunately the broken fences between Bregman and Stone, post-*Scarface*, had never been mended. When Stone made it clear he wanted to produce the movie on his own, Bregman dropped out of the project, his "baby" for more than a decade. First, he phoned Kovic to wish him well on the venture. His call was never returned; Bregman's impression was that Kovic had been instructed not to have any further conversations with him.

With the movie completed, Pacino's original "desertion" of the project brought forth another scathing coda from Stone. "Al Pacino's a schmuck," he was reported to have informed Italy's *Il Messaggero*, "and as a matter of fact, his career went into the toilet." Rick Nicita of Creative Artists (CAA) is Pacino's agent; his wife, Paula Wagner, represents Oliver Stone. According to Wagner, Stone denies ever having made the remark. Whether he did or not, Ron Kovic certainly joined the anti-Pacino campaign, maintaining that he had felt an instant rapport with Cruise lacking with Pacino: "I never really felt that Pacino connected with me as much as Cruise or that he understood what we had been through. Cruise *understood*."

Oddly enough, back in the movie's preproduction phase in the seventies Kovic had described Pacino as "more than an actor and a star. He's one of the most articulate, sensitive and human persons I've ever met." How quickly they forget!

In 1989, at a United Press International dinner in Los Angeles at which they both were guests, Stone and Bregman—still not speaking after five years—sat at opposite ends of the room. After the meal Bregman felt a hand squeeze his shoulder and turned to see Stone standing there. "Hello, Marty," he said. The hatchet was buried over dinner a few nights later.

When *Sea of Love* opened in September 1989, there was a new Pacino on display, the passage of time markedly etched on his features, and to excellent effect. Dark circles lay under the huge, hypnotic eyes; now there was a measured, mature crackle to the electricity he generated, recalling European superstars like Jean-Paul Belmondo, Yves Montand, Charles Vanel and Jean Gabin. Even in the movie's darkest scenes an element of self-mockery had been added that was absent before. Yet despite the depth and boundless intensity he gave Frank Keller, there was less emphasis on the theatrical "pale cast of thought" that had permeated other performances.

A scene near the beginning of the movie brilliantly establishes Keller's relationship with the bottle. We see him late at night, refilling his glass and staring deeply and morosely into its amber depths. Everything about the way the scene is lit, directed and cut, together with Pacino's soulful stillness, shows us not just a man drinking alone but an individual at his devotions, cocooned against the glittering black New York night. Later we see him, totally smashed, and dippily phoning his ex-wife at 3:00 A.M. with a solicitous "Did I wake you? Listen, I think I've got appendicitis!"

If by day Keller still comes off as sharp, much of it is clearly reflex action. He responds with light sarcasm to the doorman's reply that he has seen "no one of weight" at the murder scene, while still managing to enlist his help and score points off his ex-wife's new husband. In one extraordinarily dark scene, he stretches out on the victim's bed and lies there, quietly allowing his mind to take him where it will.

Invited to the wedding of his partner's daughter, he is the perpetual loner among the gaiety, the specter at the nuptial feast as a pop group belts out—appropriately enough—"Another One Bites the Dust." Overlaid are the mournful, plaintive strains of the old pop tune "Sea of Love," which the murderer has left playing at the scene of the crime and which signals the birth of Keller's plan to catch the killer.

He injects humor into his comforting of the gift-wrapped girl who turns up to meet the murder victim, suggesting that she might feel better if she removes her balloons. When Helen (Barkin) informs him that he's not her type, he flings back, "Well, I'm hell on wheels once you get to know me, honey." Obsessed with her, he crawls back to beg forgiveness after a series of misunderstandings and confesses, with poignant desperation, "I can't even sleep in my own bed anymore unless you're in it." No wonder Helen, as well as the audience, believes the man.

Sea of Love opened to the best movie reviews Pacino had seen since the mid-seventies. Before getting down to the business in hand, Peter Travers at *People* magazine clearly believed that a little deck clearing was in order. "I can't think of another great actor," he declared, "and Pacino *is* a great actor, who has thrown so many curveballs in his career—*Bobby Deerfield, . . . And Justice for All, Cruising, Author! Author!, Scarface* and *Revolution*. These films, like Pacino's performances in them, aren't forgivable or forgettable. They are *memorably, indefensibly atrocious.* In *Sea of Love,* Pacino's first good movie for fourteen years, he is terrific—vital, charming, funny, tough and touching."

Terrence Rafferty referred to Pacino's "riveting comeback performance"; the *Village Voice* agreed: "Pacino is *amazing.*" As for Rex Reed, *"Sea of Love,"* he rhapsodized, "is the sexiest, most erotic, heart-pounding thriller since *Fatal Attraction, but better.* This movie is so original. Taut, tense, terrific." *Variety* raved: "A superlative performance by Al Pacino."

Peter Rainer was bowled over by the "new" Pacino. Gone were what he had seen as the "zonked, mealy-mouthed performances" in movies like *Bobby Deerfield* and *Cruising,* where he had seemed embalmed. "In *Sea of Love* he's got some of his fire back; a joy of acting comes through. It helps that he's playing opposite two actors, John Goodman and Ellen Barkin, whose styles are complementary. They bring out the scrappy, intuitive side of Pacino. They short-circuit his tendency to de-volve ever inward into the recesses of drear. Few actors are better at being 'streetwise' than Pacino. In *Sea of Love*, he's better than he's been in years."

The solitary critic who chose to swim against the tide was the New York *Times*'s Vincent Canby. His description of *Sea of Love* as "a really quite bad movie, over-produced and over-cast, a leaky radiator from which steam emerges without deliv-ering heat" produced a furious backlash from the Pacino camp, which pointedly, and puzzlingly, referred to "[Canby's] hatred of Al." It was left to a third party to explain this particu-lar mystery, dating back, so it was said, to a "serious disagree-ment" Pacino had had with actor-director David Margolies over the theater workshop production of *Chinese Coffee*—the one *nobody* had seen. Pacino, having prevailed, left a disgrun-tled Margolies relaying his feelings to his close friend Canby; the negative review had therefore been anticipated by the star.

After initially refusing to return calls to clarify his position, Canby finally climbed down from his pedestal, maintaining that he felt "no hatred" for Pacino. "Believe me," he declared, "there was nothing personal in my review." He added that he had reviewed Pacino "good and bad over the years," awarding *Scarface* "one of the few decent reviews it got in New York." Pacino was "a paranoid movie actor who must be very upset."

Box office for *Sea of Love* was brisk from the outset; Pacino's "comeback" was a triumphant smash. As producer of all four of his most successful movies outside *The Godfather* saga, Marty Bregman had yet again demonstrated his expertise at selecting Pacino's material. He had also displayed an astute sense of the talent to cast alongside him. "When Ellen Barkin read with Al in my office, they were magic together," he re-called as he accompanied his star on the movie's promotional tour. "Something happened between them. They *sizzled*. The scene where Ellen takes off her clothes was spontaneous, a moment of passion, two people reacting for each other. That's what made it work."

He listened impassively, if a little restlessly, as Pacino expounded his "no clock" theory for theatrical rehearsals, holding out the example of the late John Cassavetes, who had opened his version of O'Neill's *The Iceman Cometh* virtually in workshop form, albeit to derisory notices. "But the clock is also dictated to you by the audience, who are a precondition," the practical Bregman chipped in. "*That* was Cassavetes's problem. He went *beyond* what the public would accept."

"You say that all the time, Marty!" Pacino countered. "*Sure, The Iceman Cometh* was not a success on Broadway, but later it was redone in the Circle in the Square by José Quintero and was recognized as a classic. There *are* people who would enjoy that kind of thing, you know."

The unbeatable Pacino-Bregman partnership clearly remained intact—firmly based on mutual respect—and still crazy after all those years.

Bregman sees Pacino as one of the great actors of our time. "And he's still a leading man," he points out. "The only one in his age range to have sustained that. Women are turned on by him—his vulnerability, his sexuality, his sensuality.

"He's great to work with and very creative. He knows more about the people in the roles he plays than anybody else. He's very well prepared, a complete professional. You hear these stories that he's difficult. He's not. He questions things within the character; he questions himself; he questions scenes that don't ring true to him. He works from a base of truth within the characters. He's extraordinarily intuitive, but if it doesn't logically work for him, then he can't do it.

"In private Al has a wonderful sense of humor although he's not a practical joker. He's sweet and funny; socially he's great fun. Women love him; men love him; he's a charming guy. He's not competitive with other men. He has a very strong code about that; he wouldn't look at another man's wife or girlfriend. He's truly a gentleman, very Sicilian in his relationships.

"The essence of Al Pacino? He never postures, never uses his power. He's really a gentle, nice man and not at all tough. I'm infinitely tougher than he is. I guess we complement each other, which makes our working relationship that much easier and that much deeper. I know what he would do or wouldn't do; I know him *creatively*, better, I think, than anyone else.

"At one time I wasn't as aggressively involved in his career as I am now, not professionally but as a friend. There are a lot of forces pulling in many directions, and I feel protective and care about what he does. I try to protect him from films that would hurt his career. I'm extremely verbal about that now. He's given joy to millions because of his incredible gift. I really feel he's an international treasure."

Approaching his fiftieth birthday in April 1990, Pacino looked back on his hiatus from movies. "You know, I wish, in some ways, the government forced me to make a movie once a year," he said, at least semiseriously. "There would be a sort of regularity, a kind of consistency in the output so that your movies don't become blown all out of proportion. It turns a simple movie into an epic kind of thing, if you make them every few years. I became my own worst enemy by being over-careful. The ups are too up, the downs are too down, because there's too much riding on them psychologically. I finally realize that it's OK to make commercial films and not to worry about each one being a big hit. My life doesn't *depend* on it."

He acknowledged that at any other point it would have been unthinkable for him to make three movies in a row, yet *Sea of Love*, *Dick Tracy* and *Godfather III*, then almost completed, were each, in their own different ways, tangible evidence of his newfound epiphany.

In particular there can be no underestimating the impact of Frank Keller. "I'm kind of lucky," Pacino concedes, "to go out there and play a character who mirrors what I'm feeling at the time. I'm not saying we're exact duplicates, but his dilemma interested me because he is at a point in his life where he's being asked to retire and the job is all he has. He has no love interest in his life. He has his work. And you know, there's work and there's love. If you lose both, it's a tough time.

"I guess playing the part now, as opposed to playing it ten years ago, I have a closer understanding, a more *tactile* understanding of the character, because of my age and understanding of the situation he's in. He gets the sense that time is running out. He has a one-way ticket, the train is coming out of the tunnel and he sees, in the distance, the big mountain of mortality. And he wants to make his time here count."

It was significant that unlike Pacino's previous characters, Frank Keller bucked the odds, vanquished his demons, quit drinking and landed the girl. Whether life can imitate art only time will tell, but the signs have never been more encouraging. Pacino has discovered that it is possible to forgive oneself, just as surely as one can others. More and more his intensity is overflowing into a renewed lust for life, living and caring. Far from losing any "edge," as he once feared, the phenomenon has actually enriched his art.

Pacino's role in *Dick Tracy* began as a diversion, a favor, a send-up, a lark. And it resulted in "a triumph," according to Vincent Canby, David Edelstein and David Denby. While the miniblockbuster itself received mixed reviews, there was no equivocation about Pacino's Big Boy Caprice. "Just as Jack Nicholson's Joker dominated *Batman*," wrote Kathleen Carroll in New York *Daily News*, "Al Pacino will simply kill you with his gleefully comical performance. He is hysterically funny." Roger Ebert hastened to agree: "The scene stealer is Big Boy Caprice, played by Al Pacino with such grotesque energy that we seem to have stumbled on a criminal from Dickens. He really steals the show. A fabulous performance." According to *Variety*, "Pacino virtually runs away with the show. His manic energy lifts the overall torpor and suggests a comic complexity the film otherwise misses."

David Ansen at *Newsweek* found Pacino "Memorably funny," while Sheila Benson at the Los Angeles *Times* declared, "*Dick Tracy* is Pacino's movie." Jack Garner at the Gannett News Service described "Pacino's turn" as "the real thing, a major comedy role that threatens to walk off with the picture." Gene Shalit of NBC-TV raved, "Pacino lets himself go in a wickedly joyous performance." Joel Siegel of ABC-TV saw the performance as "worthy of an Oscar nomination."

At last Pacino's propensity for comedy had traveled intact to the big screen, the "medieval clown" hitherto discernible only to a few select friends, like Charlie Laughton and Michael Hadge, released like a genie from a bottle. Some thought that Pacino's Richard III had been put to cinematic use, while others detected hints of Groucho Marx, even of Jimmy ("Schnozzle") Durante. Laughton traces Big Boy back to Arturo Ui.

In all this one ghost has been laid to rest. Big Boy Caprice is no more Pacino than Michael Corleone, Sonny Wortzick, Frank Serpico, Bobby Deerfield, Tony Montana or any of the other characters he has played over the years. Only *Pacino* is *Pacino*, his newfound wisdom runs. Pacino the *man*, Pacino the *actor*, the life and career finally reconciled.

CHAPTER 30

BACK TO SICILY

THE IDEA OF developing one more installment of the *Godfather* saga was daunting from the start, for both its director and star. After Francis Coppola's triumphant *The Godfather* and *Godfather II*, together earning twenty-one Oscar nominations and nine Oscars and both winning Best Film Awards, the director's career had run an erratic course. On the brilliant *Apocalypse Now* costs had ballooned from the originally budgeted twelve million to thirty million dollars. Many critics chose to review the movie's cost rather than the movie itself. There was a case for similar treatment on Coppola's wildly indulgent twenty-seven-million-dollar *One from the Heart*, while budget and critical blues again haunted *Cotton Club*. "I was so successful so young and so fast and outspoken," Coppola acknowledged, "I think that at first my enthusiasm was perceived as kinda megalomania."

With his Zoetrope empire in ruins after the failure of *One from the Heart* and a lawsuit triggered that was to rumble on for fully eight years, *Godfather III*—and the fee Paramount offered of $5 million and 15 percent of the gross—had become less of a choice for Coppola than an imperative. "It's not just something I'm doing because I want to make a lot of money," he still insisted. "I really think it could be beautiful."

As far back as 1971, after the original *Godfather*'s success, Pacino had talked about the possibility of sequels. "I'd like to age," he said. "I'd like to go to about sixty-five if I could. And there would be *my* son and the way things are now. It's hard to go from thirty-five to fifty; it doesn't seem that much different from forty. But when you go to sixty or past that, you can do a little more." In any event, *Godfather II* had Michael Corleone frustratingly stuck around fifty, suspending Pacino two-thirds of the distance he had wanted to travel.

Over the years several versions of *Godfather III* had been announced, with and without both Coppola and Pacino. Paramount Chairman Frank Mancuso was determined to snare both. "Francis is funny," says Pacino. "He'll give you little hints about things: 'I don't know, maybe I'm gonna do this,' and I'd think, 'Oh, oh, he's planning something'—and this is a couple of years before anything happens!"

It was during the summer of 1989, aware that Mario Puzo and Coppola had been working on a new script since April, that Pacino gave an inkling of the plans afoot. *"The Godfather* is kind of like *Indiana Jones,"* he suggested. "It has chapters. It has a natural evolution. And people seem to want another one. It's been fifteen years since the last episode, and I believe if Francis Coppola and Mario Puzo think something should be done, then it should be. I wouldn't stop them."

A few weeks later it was confirmed that Pacino was indeed to make his long-delayed age leap with *Godfather III*, with location filming set to commence in Italy at the end of November. His salary matched Coppola's $5 million and percentage, with Diane Keaton, as Michael's ex-wife, Kay, collecting $1.7 million.

Together they visited Coppola at his fifteen-hundred-acre Napa Valley estate in September. During their stay at his gracious timbered mansion, harvested grapes were being crushed on the ground floor of the nearby carriage house, the aroma permeating the two stories above the winery that housed Coppola's extensive library, sound and editing rooms and private screening room. In between idyllic walks in the grounds and gourmet meals supervised by Coppola's wife, Eleanor, script conferences and rehearsals were staged that later spilled over to Zoetrope's Kearny Street studios in San Francisco.

The movie's opening scenes were set in 1979, twenty years after the ending of *Godfather II*, with Michael Corleone now a frail sixty-year-old yearning for spiritual redemption—in his terms, business legitimacy. The era of the Vegas casinos is long gone, their proceeds laundered and either languishing in Vatican bank vaults or converted to real estate. While Michael's daughter, Mary, works full-time for the charitable Vito Corleone Foundation, son Anthony has repudiated his bloody inheritance and ignored his father's wishes to enter the legal profession; instead, he is about to make his debut as an opera singer in the ominously vendetta-themed *Cavalleria Rusticana*. Michael's sister, Connie, now back in the Mafia fold, proposes Vincent Mancini, the illegitimate son of their slain brother Sonny, to succeed him. "Michael has always been a master manipulator," Coppola explained. "By the end of Part Two he had become very self-righteous and distrusted everyone. Now he is a man who wants rehabilitation. Reflecting the mood in America at that time, Michael wants to take stock of himself."

Even as Mary is seduced by hotheaded, chip-off-the-old-block Vincent, Michael faces a host of other distractions. The safe financial harbor of the Vatican emerges as a rats' nest of machinations. There are power threats to contend with from up-and-coming mobster Joey Sasa. And can he really trust old family friend Don Altobello? "We are dealing," Coppola pointed out, "with themes related to power, succession, revenge, redemption—and love."

The death of Coppola's twenty-two-year-old son Gian-Carlo —Gio—in a 1986 boating accident had clearly left its mark on the director and worked its way into the texture of the script. Michael Corleone's search for himself mirrored Coppola's own quest. "Maybe the death of Gio put me more in that mood,"

Coppola admitted, "because I myself don't think about the future so much in the same way I did when I was young. If you work hard or you've got a lotta dreams, you think in terms of winning, that you will realize your dreams. And when you lose a son like that, you realize you're lost. That you *can't* win."

There was good news and bad news on the casting front. Initially Frank Sinatra had expressed interest in playing Don Altobello, until it proved impossible to juggle his schedule around the two months he would be required in Italy; Eli Wallach had taken his place. Sought to reenact the *consigliere* Tom Hagen, Robert Duvall bridled at Paramount's view of his worth relative to Pacino. "I did not think it was fair," he protested, "that they offered the lead actor four and a half to five times as much as they offered me. If they would have offered twice as much, that would have been OK—not *ideal*, but OK." Paramount's response to Duvall's $3.5 million demand was to write Hagen out of the script; a new Corleone adviser, Greg Bautzer style, would be played by George Hamilton. Coppola had wanted Julia Roberts for Mary but had settled on Winona Ryder when Roberts was unavailable. After Robert De Niro, considered briefly for the role of Vincent before Coppola decided he was too old, Andy Garcia was Coppola's first and last choice. Coppola's sister, Talia Shire, was back as Connie. Then there was Joe Mantegna as Joey Sasa, Bridget Fonda as photographer Grace Hamilton and Broadway musical star Franc D'Ambrosio as Anthony Corleone.

Coppola freely acknowledged that many of the elements in his concept were inspired by the real-life Vatican's contribution to the billion-dollar failure of Italy's Banco Ambrosio and the attempt on the Pope's life, as well as Europe's attempts at economic unification. Pacino was particularly struck with one line of dialogue that seemed to sum up Michael's dilemma and the energy he had to muster to solve it: "One's reach should exceed his grasp, or what's a heaven for?" He continued to see Michael as an enigma, someone who was searching. "He's different now," he agreed, "but as different as a person like that would be in order to survive the kinds of things that happened to him. . . . I mean, this is a person who had another destiny —at least he thought he did—who had another way to go, had a desire to do something else and was taken off his course and put on another course. The moment when he made the decision to go in that direction has been the thing he has dealt with his entire life. Talk about being responsible for your actions!" At the same time he conceded, "Hey, there's more of Francis in Michael than me."

A COUPLE OF months before filming on *Godfather III* was due to start, in November 1989, producer Elliott Kastner slapped a $6 million breach-of-contract lawsuit on Pacino. The actor, he claimed, had reneged on an "oral agreement" entered into by his agent, CAA's Rick Nicita, in April 1988, to appear in *Carlito's Way*. The movie was to have costarred Marlon Brando.

Kastner said that he had worked with Pacino until January 1989, selecting writers, director and a physical trainer, and that Pacino had induced him to offer a fee of four hundred thousand dollars to add actor Mandy Patinkin to the cast. In all, a million dollars had been spent in preproduction before Pacino had asked for a postponement of the project, concurrently denying the existence of any agreement. Kastner claimed Pacino's defection would cause his company to forfeit "a unique and extremely valuable opportunity to produce a film starring Marlon Brando."

Within months the suit had been dropped. Although no settlement details were released, one strong hint was dropped: *Carlito's Way*, it was announced, would appear at some future point—as a Martin Bregman production.

THAT PACINO AND his director did not agree on every aspect of his portrayal became clear two months later when the star reported for filming with shoulder-length wavy hair. Two weeks were spent persuading Pacino to shed the locks, Coppola arguing that they made him look too sympathetic and romantic.

"He didn't want to do it," Coppola reported with a shake of the head. "Diane didn't want him to do it." Coppola had no doubt whatever that the short, spiky cut he insisted upon was much more appropriate: "It goes to show you how very often everyone else's opinion, though it may be sound, truly cannot serve you well."

Coppola had his famous Silver Fish, a gleaming, customized motor home, installed at Rome's Cinecittà studios well before the start of shooting on November 27, 1989. Soon it was a familiar sight on the set, Coppola often directing from within, his voice relayed to the set by big brother loudspeakers, while he watched the twin walls of video monitors inside. With the various takes completed, he instantly was able to edit from the comfort of his leather swivel chair. Even as he measured coffee into the espresso machine, his eyes seldom left the screens; in the trailer's Jacuzzi he relaxed to the sound of the musical tapestries his father, Carmine, was weaving for key scenes, exhilarated by his ability to transform the bulk of preproduction, production and postproduction from separate entities into an integrated phase. At the end of each day he sat with Pacino, reviewing the partially edited dailies.

WITH DIANE KEATON about to join him in his villa in Rome for *Godfather III*, Pacino continued to parry the question of marriage. He had lost none of his practiced skill.

"I was almost married a couple of times," he admitted, "and don't know what happened. I've certainly had long-standing relationships that *felt* like marriages. Why didn't I propose? I hate to say this, but marriage is a state of mind, not a contract.

"When I think about the law and marriage, I ask myself, 'How did the cops get in on this?' To me, marriage is tied up with my idea of commitment, which is an emotional feeling. I know what that feeling is, and I don't rule out marriage as an option. It's not too late to have kids. It's what I'm looking forward to. Why not? I'd like to think I'll be a better father for having waited. And my not having children has had nothing to do with my career. I can be a father, a husband and an actor. There are twenty-four hours in a day after all."

Pacino kept to himself the fact that he had already crossed the threshold of fatherhood. Following a brief liaison two years earlier he had found himself presented with a baby daughter. Although he was no longer romantically involved with the mother (a former acting teacher at the Strasberg Institute), the baby, Julie Marie, soon became the apple of Pacino's eye. "He is the absolute epitome of the doting father," one close friend confided. "He adores his little daughter and takes time off to see her at every available opportunity. It's given Al a whole new lease on life."

FROM THE BEGINNING of *Godfather III*'s shooting, Coppola issued new script pages up to three times a day to keep up with Coppola's penchant for rewriting. "With Francis the script is like a newspaper," production designer Dean Tavoularis explained, "a new one every day." Veteran *Godfather* director of photography Gordon Willis declared at one point: "Francis has a very expansive mind, and it has a tendency to balloon sometimes and get a little nuts. But he knows that—and in this kind of movie that kind of mind is very fruitful."

There was considerable confusion when Pacino and dozens of the crew, together with Coppola and his Silver Fish, were denied entry and delayed at the gates of the Vatican prior to shooting a crucial scene. Dark looks were cast in particular at coproducer Gray Frederickson. Clearance had been assumed rather than confirmed, it turned out, leaving Coppola fretting over the reception they might find at the numerous other locations around Rome—the magnificent three-hundred-year-old Santa Maria della Quercia Church in Viterto, the sixteenth-century Villa Farnese at Caprarola.

The arrival of Winona Ryder immediately after Christmas was followed the same evening by a request from her boyfriend, Johnny Depp, that a doctor attend her. A nervous collapse was diagnosed; if she were to start work, the unit doctor declared, there was the risk of a complete breakdown. With another of Coppola's coproducers, Fred Roos, simultaneously chasing Julia Roberts again, then *sex, lies and videotape*'s Laura San Giacomo, Coppola had an idea of his own that was as bold as it was outrageous. The rest of the cast and crew almost had a breakdown themselves when faced with his proposed replacement for Ryder: his eighteen-year-old daughter, Sofia. By the time Roos arrived at Cinecittà to report on his progress Coppola already had Sofia costumed and shooting a scene.

The protests over the casting of his daughter, innocently in Rome to spend two weeks' vacation from college with her parents, rumbled on for several weeks. She had no experience in acting apart from small roles in three of her father's movies, following her debut as the baby in the christening scene in the original *Godfather*. Much as many of the cast and crew liked her personally, how could Coppola imagine she would perform among the heavyweight professionals? "I love Sofia very much," said one member of the production team, "but she has this teeny little voice like a little girl. Francis has fucked the love story."

Both Pacino and Sofia's aunt Tally engaged in "earnest discussions" with Coppola. An attempt by Paramount President Sidney Ganis to persuade Pacino to side with him against the casting backfired when the move reached Coppola's ears. Paramount, he raged, had guaranteed him complete artistic control, which by definition certainly extended to casting whomever he chose. Frank Mancuso organized a dinner with Pacino, Keaton and Garcia to pour oil on troubled waters. If he believed the casting was right, all three told him, they felt reassured. "Francis thought the casting would serve us in the film," said Pacino, "because his vision of the part was that kind of innocence. He knew what he wanted. Casting is what a director does; it's part of his expression. So you have to grant him that." Sofia had a special word of praise for the support she got from Pacino on the set: "[Al] was so funny. He told me,

'When you get the urge to act, lie down and wait for it to pass.' That was the best advice I learned the whole time."

With delays—and the budget—mounting, Coppola was in no mood to tolerate anything further that would exacerbate costs outside of his own actions. Coproducers Frederickson and Roos found themselves peremptorily dispatched back to Los Angeles "to work on the production from there," as one release put it. "I fired certain people," Coppola admitted, "basically those who were not living up to the standard of what it would take to pull this off." In their place veteran line producer toughie Chuck Mulvehill was recruited by Zoetrope and soon made his presence felt. The feeling of tension already on the set was increased by the strict security involved and the demand for total secrecy, the bluff edge Coppola usually maintains even during periods of highest stress markedly absent. "This is a big one; this is like *King Lear*," Pacino said. Dean Tavoularis put it this way: "Francis is on the line with this project. He's got to make it good. It can't *not* be good. It's gotta be good. But there's no law that says it's *going* to be good. And that's the stress factor."

At the end of January Coppola's humor was put to the ultimate test as his lawyers filed for bankruptcy for both himself and Zoetrope Productions, with liabilities totaling a staggering $28.9 million. A $12 million bond was posted to forestall seizure of his assets, including his beloved Napa Valley vineyards and estate. When the dust eventually settled, Coppola was $7 million poorer, his *Godfather III* fee already more than swallowed up.

A LOVERS' QUARREL between Pacino and Keaton, apparently over Pacino's reluctance to commit to a permanent relationship, threatened further to disrupt the already chaotic production. As if Keaton's puffy-eyed appearance on the set in the morning weren't enough, the door between their adjoining dressing rooms was shut tight. Then came news of a great personal sadness, the death of Pacino's grandmother Kate Gerard.

Accompanied by a tearful Keaton, Pacino flew back to New York to attend the funeral. On the couple's return to Rome it appeared, despite a still-tangible strain, that an accommodation had been reached. It was as well, for one of the next scenes to be filmed was the big reconciliation in the Sicilian countryside between Michael and Kay. "Our relationship at times has been complicated," Pacino later admitted.

By the time the unit moved to Palermo in March, *Godfather III* was twenty-three days behind schedule and $6 million over its $44 million budget. *"Dove Al?"* ("Where's Al?") was the question on sightseers' lips as filming took place at the foot of the steps leading to the Villa Malfitano. Pacino himself lightened the mood in a scene in which the family was to drink a toast to the success of Anthony's debut; tonic water with a few drops of tamarind juice had been substituted for champagne. "Try again," Coppola urged after the first take. "You're excited, nervous, worried for him. You want him to get through this."

Pacino raised his glass and smiled at his director. "The only thing I'm worried about," he declared, "is drinking this ginger ale again!"

SEVERAL MONTHS AFTER completing *Godfather III*, Pacino visited Sidney Lumet in New York. For once the director broke his "no personal questions" rule. "How about Diane?" he asked, unaware of their latest split. "She's a terrific girl. Why don't the two of you get married?"

The reaction from Pacino was a throaty laugh. And that was all.

"He goes a long time before he says yes to a project," Lumet muses. *"Any project.* Diane? She's one of the great women!"

Marriage remains one plot development Pacino seems determined to keep to himself.

CHAPTER 31

GOIN' WITH THE GLOW

WHETHER GODFATHER III was the "most eagerly awaited" movie of the year or simply the most hyped depends entirely on how one regards the saturation media coverage. The almost inevitable anticlimax, following months of around-the-clock editing and a cliffhanger Christmas opening after an abandoned Thanksgiving launch, was a generally well-reviewed movie that did good but less than blockbuster business. The latter is less surprising when the figures from the first two movies are checked out. *The Godfather*'s U.S. net rentals amounted to eighty-six million dollars in 1972; *Godfather II*'s 1974 haul was a still impressive but decidedly shrunken thirty-two million dollars. For years Paramount has been covering this up by quoting the aggregate business for both films; maybe in the end it fooled itself. Considering that *Godfather III*'s likely net, at 1991 ticket prices, looks set to peak below thirty-five million dollars, it seems the law of diminishing returns has been well and truly observed. Financially, that is. Certainly not artistically.

With Andrew Sarris of the New York *Observer* describing *Godfather III* as "a majestic summation," *Variety*'s Todd Mc-Carthy thought that the most impressive thing about the movie was the way in which Coppola had fused the commercial elements of melodrama, violence, family saga and politics with his extremely personal concerns. "The film is really about aging," McCarthy asserted, "it's about loss of power, it's about passing the mantle and I think on a most intimate level the film is about guilt. I think Pacino is absolutely magnificent and maybe there is a level at which people are taking this film—and him—for granted."

In view of the advance publicity, there was the anticipated reaction to Sofia Coppola's performance. Even while lauding her "lovely and unusual presence," *The New Yorker*'s Pauline Kael said that "her voice lacks expressiveness." Other critics were considerably more forthright. "Her gosling gracelessness comes close to wrecking the movie," *Time*'s Richard Corliss declared. And said Todd McCarthy: "Unfortunately, she can't act on a level with the other people in the film." Andrew Sarris added fuel to the flames: "Sofia just doesn't hack it as an actress or as someone with screen charisma. She doesn't have it." *Entertainment Weekly* went to great lengths to compare other false career starts actors had endured and survived, notably Anjelica Huston under pop John Huston in *A Walk with Love and Death*. While this may serve Sofia Coppola well in the future, it served *Godfather III* not at all.

Todd McCarthy may have made a valid point about the movie and Pacino's being taken for granted, but Alexander Walker, doyen of English film critics, was having none of it. "Coppola," he wrote in London's *Evening Standard*, "has unassailably secured his place as not just a Hollywood director, but a world one." *Godfather III*, he added, was "a masterpiece." On Sofia Coppola: "The controversial choice comes off even better than papa may have hoped." Walker had a stunning compliment up his sleeve for the movie's lead actor, describing Pacino's "seamless portrait of a man being inwardly devoured by something more fearful than the diabetic stroke that fells him, frighteningly, at a crucial part in the story" as *"one of the finest pieces of acting ever seen in American cinema."* After a second viewing Walker saw no reason to modify his praise. "Pacino is, quite simply, *at his peak,*" he now reported.

To the surprise of many, *Godfather III*'s Oscar nominations, for Best Picture, Director, Supporting Actor, Art Direction, Cinematography, Editing and Original Song excluded Pacino as Best Actor. So much for "one of the finest pieces of acting ever seen in American cinema"—totally overlooked by the academy establishment and begging the question, Is Pacino regarded as too much of an outsider, not one of Hollywood's own, straddling as he does the world of cinema and the theater? Instead, the sixth nomination of his career was for Best Supporting Actor in *Dick Tracy* (Joe Pesci won for *GoodFellas*).

Before *Godfather III* opened, Pacino was asked how he felt about the possibility of surpassing even the triumphs of his early years with the movie. His response best sums up the man's attitude to his craft, as well as awards. "I'm just an actor," he replied. "Doing a great role is an opportunity. It's a gift to be able to play a part that can afford your acting talents to be freed."

CHARLIE LAUGHTON'S FREQUENT bouts of overtiredness back in the mid-seventies were eventually diagnosed as multiple sclerosis. The wayward course of the disease led to a progressive loss of mobility that now sees him confined to a wheelchair. The spirit of the man remains indomitable. He still teaches part-time, as well as advising Pacino (as does Hadge), and finds fulfillment in the achievement of his star pupil and closest friend.

"Al's success has been a gradual awakening for me through the years," he acknowledges, "as I'm sure it has been for him. It's very easy for all of us to veer off with our personal problems. It's difficult enough for anyone to cope with success, but with Al's background and family relationships it was even more so for him. He became more and more isolated for a while. Now I think he's done good work on himself to be able not just to cope with it but to *enjoy* his success. Marty has been very good for him in this respect, very supportive. He's a very strong man and has given Al a sense of direction and security.

"Al has a real affinity with the man in the street, as Michael and Marty will testify. They'll call out to him, 'Al! Hey, Al! How ya doin', Al?' He's happy now; there's more *integration*. Some of the strong points in his character which didn't have a chance to develop before have come through. He's maturing, and the riches he has inside are maturing. He has freedom, courage and a great appetite for people and things. He also has the confidence now to shoulder it all.

"You want to know a wonderful thing? To a great extent he's doing it for me. I truly feel when he has some of these wonderful successes that it's *me*. I don't mean my teaching, for I had nothing to do with his talent. But it's great to see him do what I could never do. I love what he's doing. I live my life vicariously through Al."

MICHAEL HADGE CONFIRMED Pacino's across-the-board appeal. "People approach Al all the time, taxi drivers, people in restaurants, wherever," he said. "One guy we bumped into recently was about seventy years old, very distinguished-looking, beautifully dressed, thousand-dollar suit, briefcase in hand. He walked over and shook Al's hand and said, 'Thank you, Mr. Pacino, thank you for all the years.' He was so dignified, and it really hit me just what Al means to so many people. Throughout his career he's taken incredible risks, incredible chances, never sticking to safe choices as so many do. I know him so well, but he still surprises me. Al's career is Al's life, there's no separating the two. And it's a life that's always been lived on the wire. . . ."

SIDNEY LUMET SENSES that Pacino's career is at the crossroads. "He's a great actor who has already given some great performances, but he needs the roles. Even Marlon couldn't do it alone; he would continually pick parts that weren't worthy of

him. The big question is how courageous Al will get about the
parts he'll play. It's a very tough time in Hollywood right now
because the stakes are so high. The studios are going for safer
and safer ground, and that means the roles are going to be
safer and safer. It'll be fascinating to see how Al copes.''

With pillars of strength like Marty Bregman, Charlie Laughton and Michael Hadge flanking him, there is room for enormous optimism. Pacino already has *Frankie and Johnny* in the
can, reteamed with Michelle Pfeiffer, directed by Garry Marshall. Lined up for the future is the story of twenties gangster
Martin ("Moe") Snyder's love affair with singer Ruth Etting,
with Marty Bregman producing for Universal. First, set to roll
in the fall of 1991 in New York, Pacino heads an ensemble cast
of Alec Baldwin, John Cusack, Jack Lemmon, and Alan Arkin
in David Mamet's adaptation of his Pulitzer Prize-winning
play, *Glengarry Glen Ross*, to be directed by James Foley.

Great as Pacino was before, what we saw on the surface of
his art was rooted deep in his own perceived inadequacies.
Now he is mature enough to acknowledge them as hard, painfully earned strengths. Before, he was bolstered by his insecu-
rities; now the backup comes from his newfound ability not
only to cope but positively to *enjoy* his success. This is a man
who has settled his dues. The best, one feels certain, is yet to
come.

As always, the child has proved father to the man. "I still
have my belief in things," Pacino says today, knocking three
times on the wooden table next to him. "I try to get back to the
kind of belief I had when I was acting out parts for my grandfather in our living room or when I was three and performing
on the rooftop of our building."

Although the parable of the Wallendas remains no less vivid,
it can at last be seen in its proper perspective. "What the hell?"
he asks. "If I fall off the wire, I know now that I'll bounce off
the safety net. I'm out of the tunnel and can see the mountain.
That's why I try to get up and say, 'What about today? What
am I going to do *today?*''

Pacino smiles his killer smile, the dark eyes dancing. "I'm
goin' with the glow," he declares, "not *resisting* anymore."

FILMOGRAPHY

ME, NATALIE (National General, 1969)

DIRECTOR: Fred Coe
SCREENPLAY: A. Martin Zweiback
BASED ON A STORY BY: Stanley Shapiro
PRODUCER: Stanley Shapiro
CINEMATOGRAPHY: Arthur J. Ornitz
EDITORS: Sheila Bakerman and Jack McSweeney
MUSIC: Henry Mancini
RUNNING TIME: 111 minutes
CAST: Patty Duke, James Farentino, Martin Balsam, Elsa Lanchester, Salome Jens, Nancy Marciano, Deborah Winters, Al Pacino as "Tony"

PANIC IN NEEDLE PARK (20th Century-Fox, 1971)

DIRECTOR: Jerry Schatzberg
SCREENPLAY: Joan Didion and John Gregory Dunne
BASED ON A NOVEL BY: James Mills
PRODUCER: Dominick Dunne
CINEMATOGRAPHY: Adam Holender
EDITOR: Evan Lottman

RUNNING TIME: 110 minutes
CAST: Al Pacino as "Bobby," Kitty Winn, Alan Vint, Richard Bright, Kiel Martin, Michael McClanathan

THE GODFATHER (Paramount, 1972)

DIRECTOR: Francis Ford Coppola
SCREENPLAY: Mario Puzo and Francis Ford Coppola
BASED ON THE NOVEL *THE GODFATHER* by Mario Puzo
PRODUCER: Albert S. Ruddy
CINEMATOGRAPHY: Gordon Willis
EDITORS: William Reynolds, Peter Zinner, Marc Laub and Murray Soloman
MUSIC: Nino Rota; additional music by Carmine Coppola
RUNNING TIME: 175 minutes
CAST: Marlon Brando, Al Pacino as "Michael Corleone," James Caan, Richard Castellano, Robert Duvall, Sterling Hayden, John Marley, Richard Conte, Al Lettieri, Diane Keaton, Abe Vigoda, Talia Shire, Gianni Russo, John Cazale, Rudy Bond, Al Martino, Morgana King

Academy Award Nomination for Best Supporting Actor: Al Pacino

SCARECROW (Warner Bros., 1973)

DIRECTOR: Jerry Schatzberg
SCREENPLAY AND STORY: Garry Michael White
PRODUCER: Robert M. Sherman
CINEMATOGRAPHY: Vilmos Zsigmond
EDITOR: Evan Lottman
MUSIC: Fred Myrow
RUNNING TIME: 115 minutes
CAST: Gene Hackman, Al Pacino as "Lion," Dorothy Tristan, Eileen Brennan, Anne Wedgeworth, Richard Lynch, Penny Allen

Best Actor Award, Cannes Film Festival, 1973: Al Pacino

SERPICO (Paramount, 1973)

DIRECTOR: Sidney Lumet
SCREENPLAY: Waldo Salt and Norman Wexler
BASED ON THE NOVEL *SERPICO* BY: Peter Maas
PRODUCER: Martin Bregman
CINEMATOGRAPHY: Arthur J. Ornitz
EDITORS: Dede Allen and Richard Marks
MUSIC: Mikis Theodorikis
RUNNING TIME: 130 minutes
CAST: Al Pacino as "Frank Serpico," John Randolph, Jack Kehoe, Biff McGuire, Barbara Eda-Young, Cornelia Sharpe, Tony Roberts, Norman Ornellas

Academy Award Nomination as Best Actor and Golden Globe award as Best Actor: Al Pacino

GODFATHER II (Paramount, 1974)

DIRECTOR: Francis Ford Coppola
SCREENPLAY: Francis Ford Coppola and Mario Puzo
BASED ON CHARACTERS FROM THE NOVEL *THE GODFATHER* BY Mario Puzo
PRODUCERS: Francis Ford Coppola, Gray Frederickson and Fred Roos
CINEMATOGRAPHY: Gordon Willis
EDITORS: Peter Zinner, Barry Malkin and Richard Marks
MUSIC: Nino Rota (conducted by Carmine Coppola)
RUNNING TIME: 200 minutes
CAST: Al Pacino as "Michael Corleone," Robert Duvall, Diane Keaton, Robert De Niro, John Cazale, Talia Shire, Lee Strasberg, Michael V. Gazzo, G. D. Spradlin, Richard Bright

Academy Award Nomination for Best Actor: Al Pacino

DOG DAY AFTERNOON (Warner Bros., 1975)

DIRECTOR: Sidney Lumet
SCREENPLAY: Frank Pierson
BASED ON A MAGAZINE ARTICLE BY: P. F. Kluge and Thomas Moore

PRODUCERS: Martin Bregman and Martin Elfand
CINEMATOGRAPHY: Victor J. Kemper
EDITOR: Dede Allen
RUNNING TIME: 130 minutes
CAST: Al Pacino as "Sonny Wortzik," John Cazale, Charles Durning, James Broderick, Chris Sarandon, Carol Kane, Judith Malina, Penny Allen

Academy Award Nomination for Best Actor: Al Pacino

BOBBY DEERFIELD (Columbia/Warner Bros., 1977)

DIRECTOR: Sydney Pollack
SCREENPLAY: Alvin Sargent
BASED ON THE NOVEL *HEAVEN HAS NO FAVORITES* by: Erich Maria Remarque
PRODUCER: Sydney Pollack
CINEMATOGRAPHY: Henri Decae and Tony Maylam
EDITOR: Frederic Steinkamp
RUNNING TIME: 123 minutes
CAST: Al Pacino as "Bobby Deerfield," Marthe Keller, Anny Duperey, Walter McGinn, Romolo Valli, Stephan Meldegg

. . . AND JUSTICE FOR ALL (Columbia, 1979)

DIRECTOR: Norman Jewison
SCREENPLAY: Barry Levinson and Valerie Curtin
PRODUCERS: Norman Jewison and Patrick Palmer
CINEMATOGRAPHY: Victor J. Kemper
EDITOR: John F. Burnett
MUSIC: Dave Grusin
RUNNING TIME: 119 minutes
CAST: Al Pacino as "Arthur Kirkland," Jack Warden, John Forsythe, Lee Strasberg, Jeffrey Tambor, Christine Lahti, Sam Levene, Robert Christian, Thomas Waites, Larry Bryggman, Craig T. Nelson

Academy Award Nomination for Best Actor: Al Pacino

CRUISING (Lorimar, 1980)

DIRECTOR: William Friedkin
SCREENPLAY: William Friedkin
BASED ON THE NOVEL BY: Gerald Walker
PRODUCER: Jerry Weintraub
CINEMATOGRAPHY: James Coutner
EDITOR: Bud Smirk
MUSIC: Jack Nitzsche
RUNNING TIME: 106 minutes
CAST: Al Pacino as "Steve Burns," Paul Sorvino, Karen Allen, Richard Cox, Don Scardino, Joe Spinell, Jay Acovone, Randy Jurgensen

AUTHOR! AUTHOR! (20th Century-Fox, 1982)

DIRECTOR: Arthur Hiller
SCREENPLAY: Israel Horovitz
PRODUCER: Irwin Winkler
CINEMATOGRAPHY: Victor J. Kemper
EDITOR: William Reynolds
MUSIC: Dave Grusin
RUNNING TIME: 109 minutes
CAST: Al Pacino as "Ivan Travalian," Dyan Cannon, Tuesday Weld, Bob Dishy, Bob Elliott, Ray Goulding, Alan King

SCARFACE (Universal, 1983)

DIRECTOR: Brian De Palma
SCREENPLAY: Oliver Stone
BASED ON THE 1932 FILM SCRIPT BY: Ben Hecht
PRODUCERS: Martin Bregman and Peter Saphier
CINEMATOGRAPHY: John A. Alonzo
EDITORS: Jerry Greenberg and David Ray
MUSIC: Giorgio Moroder
RUNNING TIME: 170 minutes
CAST: Al Pacino as "Tony Montana," Steven Bauer, Michelle Pfeif-

fer, Mary Elizabeth Mastrantonio, Robert Loggia, Miriam Colon, F. Murray Abraham, Paul Shenar, Harris Yulin, Angel Salazar

REVOLUTION (Warner Bros., 1985)

DIRECTOR: Hugh Hudson
SCREENPLAY: Robert Dillon
PRODUCER: Irwin Winkler
CINEMATOGRAPHY: Bernard Lutic
EDITOR: Stuart Baird
MUSIC: John Corigliano
RUNNING TIME: 125 minutes
CAST: Al Pacino as "Tom Dobb," Donald Sutherland, Nastassja Kinski, Joan Plowright, Dave King, Steven Berkoff, John Wells, Annie Lennox, Dexter Fletcher, Sid Owen, Richard O'Brien

THE LOCAL STIGMATIC (Al Pacino, 1985–)

A PLAY BY: Heathcote Williams
DIRECTOR: David Wheeler
PRODUCER: Jim Bullett
CINEMATOGRAPHER: Ed Lachman
EDITORS: Jerry Bluedow and Elizabeth Kling
MUSIC: Howard Shore
RUNNING TIME: 50 minutes (approximate)
CAST: Al Pacino as "Graham," Paul Guilfoyle, Joe Maher, Mike Higgins, Brian Mallon

SEA OF LOVE (Universal, 1989)

DIRECTOR: Harold Becker
SCREENPLAY: Richard Price
PRODUCERS: Martin Bregman and Louis A. Stroller
CINEMATOGRAPHY: Ronnie Taylor
EDITOR: David Bretherton
RUNNING TIME: 113 minutes
CAST: Al Pacino as "Frank Keller," Ellen Barkin, John Goodman, Michael Rooker, William Hickey, Richard Jenkins, Paul Calderon, Gene Canfield

DICK TRACY (Buena Vista, 1990)

DIRECTOR: Warren Beatty
SCREENPLAY: Jim Cash and Jack Epps, Jr.
BASED ON THE CHARACTERS CREATED BY: Chester Gould
PRODUCER: Warren Beatty
COPRODUCER: Jon Landau
CINEMATOGRAPHY: Vittorio Storaro
EDITOR: Richard Marks
MUSIC: Danny Elfman
RUNNING TIME: 105 minutes
CAST: Warren Beatty, Charlie Korsmo, Michael Donovan O'Donnell, Jim Wilkey, Al Pacino as "Big Boy Caprice," William Forsythe, Glenne Headly, Madonna, Ed O'Ross, Seymour Cassel, Charles Durning, Mandy Patinkin, Paul Sorvino, Jack Kehoe, R. G. Armstrong, Dustin Hoffman, Kathy Bates, Dick Van Dyke, Henry Silva, James Caan, Michael J. Pollard

Academy Award Nomination for Best Supporting Actor: Al Pacino

GODFATHER III (Paramount, 1990)

DIRECTOR: Francis Ford Coppola
SCREENPLAY: Mario Puzo and Francis Ford Coppola
BASED ON CHARACTERS FROM THE NOVEL *THE GODFATHER* BY: Mario Puzo
PRODUCER: Francis Ford Coppola
COPRODUCERS: Fred Roos, Gray Frederickson and Charles Mulvehill
CINEMATOGRAPHY: Gordon Willis
EDITORS: Barry Malkin, Lisa Fruchtman and Walter Murch
MUSIC: Carmine Coppola; additional music and themes by Nino Rota
RUNNING TIME: 161 minutes
CAST: Al Pacino as "Michael Corleone," Diane Keaton, Talia Shire, Andy Garcia, Eli Wallach, Joe Mantegna, George Hamilton, Bridget Fonda, Sofia Coppola, Raf Vallone, Franc D'Ambrosio, Donal Donnelly, Richard Bright, Helmut Berger, Don Novello, John Savage, Al Martino

FRANKIE AND JOHNNY (Paramount, 1991)

DIRECTOR-PRODUCER: Garry K. Marshall

COPRODUCER: Nick Abdo

BASED ON THE PLAY *FRANKIE AND JOHNNY IN THE CLAIR DE LUNE* BY: Terrence McNally

SCREENPLAY: Terrence McNally

CINEMATOGRAPHY: Dante Spinotti

CAST: Al Pacino, Michelle Pfeiffer, Hector Elizondo, Kate Nelligan, Nathan Lane, Laurie Metcalf, Jane Morris, Tim Hopper

LIST OF PLAYS

1962

THE ADVENTURES OF HIGH JUMP (Children's Theater)

STAGED: Theater East, New York City
DIRECTOR: Julio Garzone
CAST: Al Pacino

JACK AND THE BEANSTALK (Children's Theater)

STAGED: Cafe Bizarre, New York City
DIRECTOR: Matt Clark
CAST: Al Pacino

1963

HELLO, OUT THERE by William Saroyan

STAGED: Café Cino, New York City
DIRECTOR: Charlie Laughton
CAST: Al Pacino, Owen Hollander, Jeanine Hagerty, Jim Bullett

305

1965

THE CREDITORS by August Strindberg

STAGED: The Actors' Gallery, New York City
DIRECTOR: Frank Bachimarso, Charlie Laughton
CAST: Al Pacino, Julie Crushnic

1966

WHY IS A CROOKED LETTER by Fred Vassi

STAGED: Alec Rubin's Theater of Encounter, West Seventy-second Street, New York City
DIRECTOR: Alec Rubin
CAST: Al Pacino

Obie nomination: Al Pacino

THE INDIAN WANTS THE BRONX by Israel Horovitz (a one-act drama)

STAGED: Eugene O'Neill Memorial Theater, Waterford, Connecticut (workshop production)
DIRECTOR: Julio Garzone
CAST: Al Pacino, John Cazale, Matthew Cowles

THE PEACE CREEPS by John Wolfson

STAGED: New Theater Workshop Co., New York City
DIRECTOR: John Stix
CAST: James Earl Jones, Al Pacino

1967

AWAKE AND SING! by Clifford Odets

STAGED: Charles Playhouse, Boston, Massachusetts
DIRECTOR: Michael Murray
CAST: Al Pacino, Will Lee, Lynn Milgrim, John Seitz, Eda Reiss Merin

AMERICA, HURRAH by Jean-Claude Van Itallie

STAGED: Charles Playhouse, Boston, Massachusetts
DIRECTOR: Michael Murray
CAST: Al Pacino, John Seitz, Jill Clayburgh

1968

THE INDIAN WANTS THE BRONX by Israel Horovitz

STAGED: Astor Place Theater, New York City, in a double bill with
Horovitz's *It's Called the Sugar Plum* (subsequently on tour: Spo-
leto Theater Festival, Italy)
DIRECTOR: James Hammerstein
CAST: Al Pacino, John Cazale, Matthew Cowles
OPENED: January 17, 1968; 204 performances

Best Actor Obie: Al Pacino; Best Supporting Actor Obie: John
Cazale; Best New Play Obie: Israel Horovitz

1969

DOES A TIGER WEAR A NECKTIE? by Don Petersen

STAGED: Belasco Theater, New York City
DIRECTOR: Michael Schultz
CAST: Hal Holbrook, David Opatoshu, Al Pacino, Lazaro Perez,
Richard Bright
OPENED: February 25, 1969; 39 performances

Best Dramatic Actor, Supporting Role Tony: Al Pacino

THE LOCAL STIGMATIC by Heathcote Williams

STAGED: Actor's Playhouse, New York City
DIRECTOR: Arthur Storch (previously directed by Ralph Waite as an
Actors' Studio Workshop production)
CAST: Al Pacino, Michael Hadge, Joe Maher, Paul Benedict
OPENED: November 1969; 8 performances

1970

CAMINO REAL by Tennessee Williams

STAGED: Lincoln Center Repertory Theater, New York City
DIRECTOR: Milton Katselas
CAST: Al Pacino, Susan Tyrrell, Jessica Tandy, Jean-Pierre Aumont

RATS by Israel Horovitz

STAGED: Charles Playhouse, Boston, Massachusetts (David Wheeler's Theater Company of Boston)
DIRECTOR: Al Pacino
CAST: Jack Kehoe, Andrew Winner

1972

THE BASIC TRAINING OF PAVLO HUMMEL by David Rabe

STAGED: Charles Theater, Boston, Massachusetts (David Wheeler's Theater Company of Boston)
DIRECTOR: David Wheeler
CAST: Al Pacino, Barry Snider, Jack Kehoe, Lance Henriksen, Richard Lynch, Ron Hunter, Richard Bright

1972–73

RICHARD III by William Shakespeare

STAGED: Loeb Drama Center, Boston, Massachusetts (December 1972) First Presbyterian Church, Boston, Massachusetts (January 1973) (David Wheeler's Theater Company of Boston)
DIRECTOR: David Wheeler
CAST: Al Pacino, Penny Allen, Lance Henriksen, Jan Egleson, Norman Ornellas

1975

THE RESISTIBLE RISE OF ARTURO UI by Bertolt Brecht

STAGED: Charles Playhouse, Boston, Massachusetts (David Wheeler's Theater Company of Boston)

DIRECTOR: David Wheeler

CAST: Al Pacino, John Cazale, Penny Allen, Sully Boyar, Garry Goodrow, Jack Hollander, Jaime Sanchez, Brad Sullivan, Taylor Mead, Paul Benedict

1976

THE LOCAL STIGMATIC by Heathcote Williams

STAGED: Joe Papp's Public Theater, New York City

DIRECTOR: David Wheeler

CAST: Al Pacino, John Cazale, Joe Maher, Jake Dengel

1977

THE BASIC TRAINING OF PAVLO HUMMEL by David Rabe

STAGED: Longacre Theater, New York City (David Wheeler's Theater Company of Boston)

DIRECTOR: David Wheeler

CAST: Al Pacino, Walter Lott, Jack Kehoe, Lance Henriksen, Richard Lynch, Richard Bright, Larry Bryggman, Paul Guilfoyle, Ron Hunter, Brad Sullivan, Rebecca Dark, Tisa Chan

OPENED: April 14 (previews), April 24 (regular performances)

CLOSED: September 3 (117 performances)

Best Dramatic Actor Tony: Al Pacino

1979

HAMLET by William Shakespeare

STAGED: Joe Papp's New York Shakespeare Festival Theater (workshop only)

DIRECTOR: Joe Papp
CAST: Al Pacino, Meryl Streep, Christopher Walken, Raul Julia

THE JUNGLE OF THE CITIES by Bertolt Brecht

STAGED: Circle in the Square, New York City (staged readings only)
DIRECTOR: Liviu Ciulei
CAST: Al Pacino

OTHELLO by William Shakespeare

STAGED: Lincoln Center Vivian Beaumont Theater, New York City
(rehearsals only)
DIRECTOR: Arthur Sherman
CAST: Al Pacino, Ron Liebman

RICHARD III by William Shakespeare

STAGED: Cort Theater, New York City
DIRECTOR: David Wheeler
CAST: Al Pacino, Penny Allen, Lance Henriksen, Max Wright, Paul
Guilfoyle, Larry Bryggman, Paul Benedict, Ron Hunter, Richard
Bright
OPENED: June 10, 1979 (following 25 previews)
CLOSED: July 15, 1979 (33 nonpreview performances)

1980

AMERICAN BUFFALO by David Mamet

STAGED: Long Wharf Theater Company, New Haven, Connecticut
DIRECTOR: Arvin Brown
CAST: Al Pacino, Clifton James, Thomas Waites
OPENED: October 1980; five-week run

1982

AMERICAN BUFFALO by David Mamet

STAGED: Downtown Circle in the Square, New York City
DIRECTOR: Arvin Brown

CAST: Al Pacino, J. J. Johnson, Thomas Waites
OPENED: February 17, 1982 (previews), February 25, 1982 (regular performances)
CLOSED: July 11, 1982

THE HAIRY APE by Eugene O'Neill

STAGED: Circle in the Square, New York City (workshop rehearsals only)
DIRECTOR: Ted Mann
CAST: Al Pacino

1983–84

AMERICAN BUFFALO by David Mamet

STAGED: Kennedy Center for Performing Arts, Washington, D.C., then Booth Theater, New York City
DIRECTOR: Arvin Brown
CAST: Al Pacino, J. J. Johnson, James Hayden (Bruce MacVittie)
OPENED: October 20 (previews), October 27 (regular performances)
CLOSED: February 4, 1984 (102 performances)

1984

AMERICAN BUFFALO by David Mamet

STAGED: Duke of York's Theatre, London
DIRECTOR: Arvin Brown
CAST: Al Pacino, J. J. Johnson, Bruce MacVittie

1986–87

JULIUS CAESAR by William Shakespeare

STAGED: Joe Papp's New York Shakespeare Festival Theater
DIRECTOR: Stuart Vaughan
CAST: Al Pacino, Martin Sheen, Edward Herrmann

1986–87

CRYSTAL CLEAR devised by Phil Young (originally created through improvisation with Anthony Allen, Philomena McDonagh and Diana Barrett)

STAGED: Workshop only, subsequently abandoned
DIRECTOR: Phil Young
CAST: Al Pacino

1988

NATIONAL ANTHEM by Dennis McIntyre

STAGED: On-book reading, New Haven, Connecticut
DIRECTOR: Arvin Brown
CAST: Al Pacino

1989–90

CHINESE COFFEE by Ira Lewis

STAGED: Workshop only
DIRECTOR: Jack Gelber
CAST: Al Pacino, Dominic Chienese

1990–91

SALOME by Oscar Wilde

STAGED: Circle in the Square, New York City (staged readings)
DIRECTOR: Arvin Brown
CAST: Al Pacino, Molly Ringwald

INDEX